INTRODUCTION TO COMPUTER SCIENCE

Motopeda Oluyide

Toronto Academic Press

Introduction to Computer Science

Motopeda Oluyide

Toronto Academic Press
224 Shoreacres Road
Burlington, ON L7L 2H2
Canada
www.tap-books.com
Email: orders@arclereducation.com

ISBN: 978-1-77469-765-8

ABOUT THE AUTHOR

Motopeda Oluyide is a highly experienced business professional with over 17 years of expertise in the oil and gas industry. He currently serves as the Managing Director of East & West African Gas Pipeline Company, where he oversees the strategic direction and growth of the company. Motopeda started his career at British American Tobacco as a Sales Representative and later joined African Petroleum Plc, where he held various roles, including Operations Officer and Sales Manager. He then moved to the oil and gas industry, working as a Business Development Manager at Petrofac and a Project Manager at Saipem. Throughout his career, Motopeda has received several awards and recognition for his contributions to the energy industry, including being named one of the Top 100 Oil and Gas Leaders in Africa by Energy Capital & Power in 2019. Motopeda holds a Bachelor's degree in Chemical Engineering from the University of Lagos and a Master's degree in Business Administration from the Lagos Business School. He is a member of the Nigerian Society of Engineers and the Project Management Institute. Motopeda is passionate about mentoring young professionals and supporting community development initiatives.

Contents

2 Fundamentals of Data Structures and Algorithms 35

3 Operating Systems 67

List of Figures

List of Tables

List of Abbreviations

ADT	Abstract Data Type
AI	Artificial Intelligence
ALU	Arithmetic Logic Unit
APT	Advanced Persistent Threat
CA	Certificate Authority
CAT	Computerized Axial Tomography
CPU	Central Processing Unit
DBA	Database Administrator
DBMS	Database Management System
DCL	Data Control Language
DDL	Data Definition Language
DMA	Direct Memory Access
DML	Data Manipulation Language
DQL	Data Query Language
EEPROM	Electrically Erasable Programmable Read-Only Memory
ENIAC	Electronic Numerical Integrator and Computer
ER	Entity-Relationship
FTP	File Transfer Protocol
GAN	Generative Adversarial Network
GUI	Graphical User Interface
HDD	Hard Disk Drive
I/O	Input/Output
ISO	International Organization for Standardization

ISP	Internet Service Provider
ITU	International Telecommunications Union
LAN	Local Area Network
MALLET	Machine Learning for Language Toolkit
MAN	Metropolitan Area Network
MEG	Magnetoencephalography
MRI	Magnetic Resonance Imaging
NCSA	National Cyber Security Alliance
NP	Nondeterministic Polynomial Time
OCR	Optical Character Recognition
OS	Operating System
OSI	Open Systems Interconnection
PCA	Principal Component Analysis
PDL	Program Development Lifecycle
PET	Positron Emission Tomography
PNN	Perceptron Neural Networks
RAM	Random Access Memory
RDBMS	Relational Database Management System
RIM	Research in Motion
ROM	Read-Only Memory
RTOS	Real-Time Operating Systems
SOFM	Self-Organizing Feature Map
SOM	Self-Organize Map
SQL	Structured Query Language
SSD	Solid-State Drive
SVM	Support Vector Machine
TMN	Telecommunication Management Network
VPN	Virtual Private Network
WAN	Wide Area Network

PREFACE

Computer science is a broad and interdisciplinary field of study that focuses on the fundamental principles and concepts that underlie the design, development, and use of computer systems. It encompasses a wide range of topics, including programming languages, algorithms, data structures, operating systems, computer networks, artificial intelligence, database systems, machine learning, and computer security and ethics. The field of computer science has grown rapidly in recent years and is becoming increasingly important in many areas of modern society, from business and finance to healthcare and entertainment.

Chapter 1 provides an introduction to the fundamentals of computer science, including the history of computing, the components of a computer system, and the basic principles of programming. It covers topics such as the structure of computer systems, software development methodologies, and programming languages. Chapter 2 focuses on algorithms and data structures, examining the fundamental concepts of algorithm design, analysis, and optimization. It covers topics such as sorting and searching algorithms, graph algorithms, and data structures such as arrays, linked lists, and trees.

Chapter 3 delves into operating systems, examining the basic principles of operating system design, including process management, memory management, and file systems. It covers topics such as multitasking, virtual memory, and device drivers. Chapter 4 explores computer networks and telecommunications, examining the fundamental concepts of networking, including network architecture, protocols, and security. It covers topics such as network topologies, network security, and wireless communication.

Chapter 5 focuses on artificial intelligence, examining the basic principles of AI, including machine learning, neural networks, and natural language processing. It covers topics such as computer vision, robotics, and expert systems. Chapter 6 covers database systems, examining the structures and properties of relational databases, as well as the basic principles of database design, normalization, and query optimization. It covers topics such as SQL, NoSQL, and big data.

Chapter 7 delves into machine learning, examining the basic principles of machine learning, including supervised and unsupervised learning, deep learning, and reinforcement learning. It covers topics such as neural networks, decision trees, and support vector machines. Chapter 8 covers computer security and ethics, examining the basic principles of computer security, including cryptography, access control, and security policies. It also covers topics such as privacy, intellectual property, and ethical considerations in the use of technology.

This book is written in an accessible and engaging style, with clear explanations and numerous examples and illustrations to help readers grasp complex concepts. The authors have drawn on their extensive experience in the field of computer science to provide a comprehensive and up-to-date resource for anyone interested in this fascinating subject. Whether you are a student of computer science, a professional in the field, or simply someone with a passion for technology, this book will provide you with the knowledge and skills you need to succeed in the study of computer science. We hope that you find this book informative and enjoyable, and we look forward to taking this exciting journey with you.

—Author

CHAPTER 1

FUNDAMENTALS OF COMPUTER SCIENCE

UNIT INTRODUCTION

Fundamentals of Computer Science refers to the basic principles and concepts underlying computer systems and their applications. It covers a wide range of topics such as computer hardware, software, algorithms, data structures, programming languages, computer networks, and database systems. Computer hardware covers the physical components of a computer system such as the central processing unit (CPU), memory, input/output devices, and storage devices. Understanding the hardware is essential for optimizing the performance of a computer system. Software refers to the programs and applications that run on a computer system (Schwill, 1994). It includes operating systems, system software, and application software. Operating systems are the backbone of a computer system, providing an interface between the hardware and the software. System software includes device drivers, utilities, and programming tools. Application software includes programs used for specific purposes such as word processing, spreadsheets, and gaming.

Algorithms are step-by-step procedures for solving problems, while data structures refer to ways of organizing and storing data efficiently. These concepts are fundamental to computer science and are used in developing programs and applications (Shackelford & LeBlanc, 1997). Programming languages are used to create computer programs, and they are essential in software development. Some popular programming languages include Python, Java, C++, and JavaScript.

Computer networks are used to connect computers and devices, enabling them to communicate and share resources. Network protocols such as TCP/IP and HTTP are used to ensure reliable and efficient communication (Loui, 1995).

Database systems are used to organize and store large amounts of data. Concepts such as database design, data modeling, and database management are essential in creating and maintaining effective database systems.

In summary, Fundamentals of Computer Science covers the basic principles and concepts of computer systems and their applications. It is a broad field that encompasses hardware, software, algorithms, data structures, programming languages, computer networks, and database systems. Understanding these fundamentals is essential for anyone interested in computer science or software development.

Learning Objectives

At the end of this chapter, readers will be able to:

- Understand information representation, including data representation and multimedia.
- Explore the basics of communication and how it relates to computer science.
- Learn about computer hardware, including memory and storage, and logic gates and circuits.
- Examine processor fundamentals, including CPU architecture, assembly language, and bit manipulation.
- Understand system software, including operating systems and language translators.
- Learn about security, privacy, and data integrity, including data validation and verification.
- Explore database concepts, including DBMS, DDL, and DML.
- Understand algorithm design and problem-solving, including computational thinking skills and algorithms.
- Learn about data types and structures, including arrays and ADTs.
- Explore programming basics, including constructs, built-in functions, and structured programming.

Key Terms

- Data Representation
- Multimedia
- Hardware
- Memory and Storage

- Logic Gates and Circuits
- CPU Architecture
- Assembly Language
- Operating System
- Language Translators
- Security, Privacy, and Data Integrity
- Database Management Systems (DBMS)
- Data Definition Language (DDL)
- Data Manipulation Language (DML)
- Algorithms
- Arrays

1.1. INFORMATION REPRESENTATION

Information representation is a fundamental concept in computer science, as it involves the translation of data into a format that can be processed and stored by a computer system. There are various techniques used for information representation, including data representation, multimedia, and file compression (Kosslyn, 1975).

1.1.1. Data Representation

Data representation involves the translation of information into a format that can be processed by a computer system. One of the most common techniques for data representation is binary code. Binary code is a system of representing numbers and letters using a series of 0s and 1s, which can be processed by digital devices. For example, the number 9 can be represented in binary as 1001 (Figure 1.1).

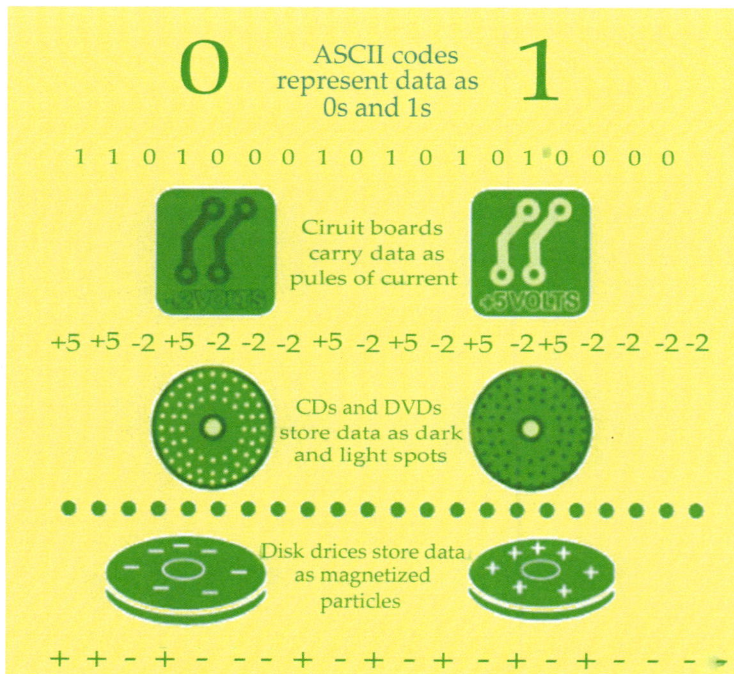

Figure 1.1. Binary Digits data representation in computer science (Source: Java T Point, Creative Commons License).

Another important data representation technique is hexadecimal code. Hexadecimal code is a system of representing numbers and letters using a combination of 0–9 and A-F. Hexadecimal code is commonly used in computer systems for representing colors in graphics and images.

ASCII code is another technique used for data representation. ASCII stands for American Standard Code for Information Interchange, and it is a system of representing letters, numbers, and symbols using a 7-bit binary code. ASCII code is used in many computer systems for representing text and other types of data (Wang, 1990).

In addition to these techniques, data encoding and decoding is also used for data representation. Data encoding involves the process of transforming data into a standardized format, while data decoding involves the process of transforming the standardized data back into its original format.

1.1.2. Multimedia

Multimedia refers to the use of different types of media, such as text, images, audio, and video, in computer applications. Multimedia data can be challenging to represent, due to its size and complexity. There are various types of multimedia, including text, images, audio, video, and animation (Figure 1.2).

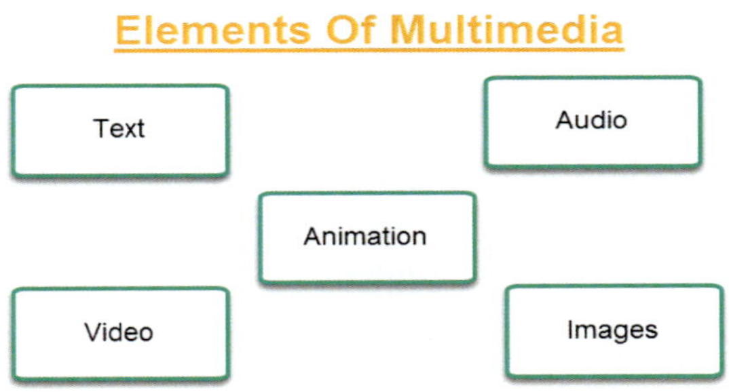

Figure 1.2. Types or elements of the Multimedia (Source: Gupta Tree Point, Creative Commons License).

Text is one of the simplest forms of multimedia, and it can be represented using ASCII code. Images, on the other hand, are more complex and require specialized representation techniques, such as JPEG and PNG formats. Audio data can be represented using various audio formats, such as WAV and MP3, while video data can be represented using various video formats, such as MPEG and AVI (Stemler, 1997).

The challenge with representing multimedia data is that it can take up a significant amount of storage space. For example, a single high-resolution image can take up several megabytes of storage space. To address this challenge, multimedia data can be compressed using various techniques, which we will cover in the next section (Mayer, 2017).

1.1.3. File Compression

File compression is the process of reducing the size of a file, while preserving its content. File compression is essential for reducing the storage space required for multimedia data and other large files. There are two main types of file compression: lossless compression and lossy compression.

Lossless compression involves compressing a file without losing any data. This means that when the file is decompressed, it is exactly the same as the original file. Lossless compression techniques include ZIP and GZIP.

Lossy compression, on the other hand, involves compressing a file by removing some of the data. This means that when the file is decompressed, it is not exactly the same as the original file. Lossy compression techniques include JPEG and MP3.

Overall, file compression is an important technique for reducing the storage space required for large files, particularly multimedia data (Rubin, 1976).

In conclusion, information representation is a fundamental concept in computer science, as it involves the translation of data into a format that can be processed and stored by a computer system. This chapter has covered various techniques used for information representation, including data representation, multimedia, and file compression. By understanding these techniques, computer scientists can efficiently store, process, and communicate different types of data, which is essential in modern computing environments.

TIPS

Keep your hardware dust-free to prevent overheating and maximize its lifespan.

1.2. COMMUNICATION

Communication is the exchange of information between two or more entities. In the context of computer science, communication refers to the exchange of data between computer systems. There are various types of computer networks used for communication, including local area networks (LANs), wide area networks (WANs), and the internet (Leach et al., 2017).

A computer network is a collection of interconnected devices that can exchange data with each other. There are various types of computer networks, including LANs, WANs, and the internet (Figure 1.3).

A LAN is a network that covers a small geographic area, such as a home or office building. LANs are often used for sharing resources, such as printers and files, and for connecting devices, such as computers and smartphones.

A WAN is a network that covers a larger geographic area, such as a city or a country. WANs are often used for connecting LANs in different locations and for providing internet access.

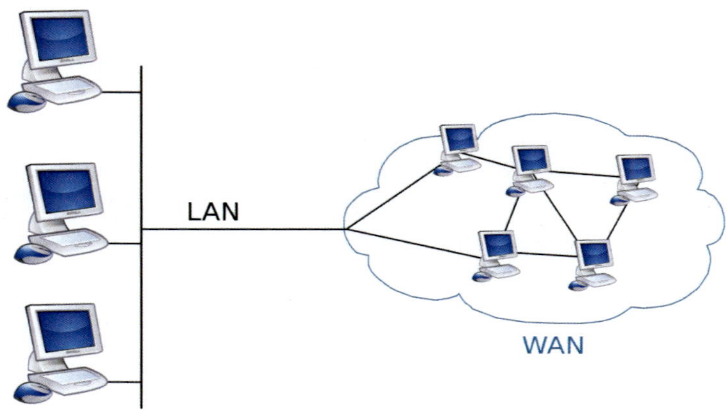

Figure 1.3. Illustration of the LAN and WAN (Gateway Firewall, Creative Commons License).

The internet is a global network of interconnected computer networks. It allows users to access a vast array of resources, such as websites, email, and social media. The internet is based on the TCP/IP protocol, which is a set of rules and standards for communication between computer systems (Aakhus, 2007).

The internet has revolutionized the way people communicate and access information. It has made it possible for people to communicate and collaborate across different geographic locations, and it has provided access to a vast array of information and resources. However, the internet also poses various security and privacy risks.

Cybersecurity threats, such as hacking and malware, can compromise the security of computer networks and the data they contain. Privacy concerns, such as data breaches and online tracking, can compromise the privacy of users' personal information. To address these concerns, various security and privacy measures have been developed, such as firewalls, encryption, and virtual private networks (VPNs).

These measures help to protect computer networks and the data they contain from unauthorized access and use. In conclusion, communication is an essential aspect of computer science, and it involves the exchange of data between computer systems. Networks, including LANs, WANs, and the internet, provide the infrastructure for communication between computer systems. The internet has revolutionized the way people communicate and access information, but it also poses various security and privacy risks. To address these risks, various security and privacy measures have been developed, which help to protect computer networks and the data they contain from unauthorized access and use (McLeod, 2007).

1.3. HARDWARE

Hardware refers to the physical components of a computer system, including the components that process and store data. This section of the chapter covers two essential hardware components: memory and storage, and logic gates and logic circuits.

1.3.1. Memory and Storage

Memory and storage are two critical hardware components that are essential for processing and storing data in a computer system. Memory is a temporary storage location where data and instructions are stored for processing by the CPU. There are various types of memory used in computer systems, including random access memory (RAM) and read-only memory (ROM) (Mottier, 2005).

Figure 1.4. Memory and storage devices in hardware (Source: Daniel Horowitz, Creative Commons License).

RAM is a type of memory that is used for temporary storage of data and instructions that are currently being processed by the

CPU. RAM is volatile, which means that its contents are lost when the computer is turned off. ROM, on the other hand, is a type of memory that is used for permanent storage of data and instructions that are essential for the operation of the computer system. ROM is non-volatile, which means that its contents are not lost when the computer is turned off.

Storage refers to the long-term storage of data on a computer system. There are various types of storage devices used in computer systems, including hard disk drives (HDDs), solid-state drives (SSDs), and optical storage devices. HDDs use spinning disks to store data, while SSDs use flash memory to store data. Optical storage devices, such as CD-ROMs and DVDs, use lasers to read and write data (Erbas-Cakmak et al., 2018) (Figure 1.4).

1.3.2. Logic Gates and Logic Circuits

Logic gates and logic circuits are essential components of digital electronics. Logic gates are basic building blocks that perform logical operations, such as AND, OR, and NOT. There are various types of logic gates, including AND gates, OR gates, NOT gates, NAND gates, and NOR gates (Figure 1.5).

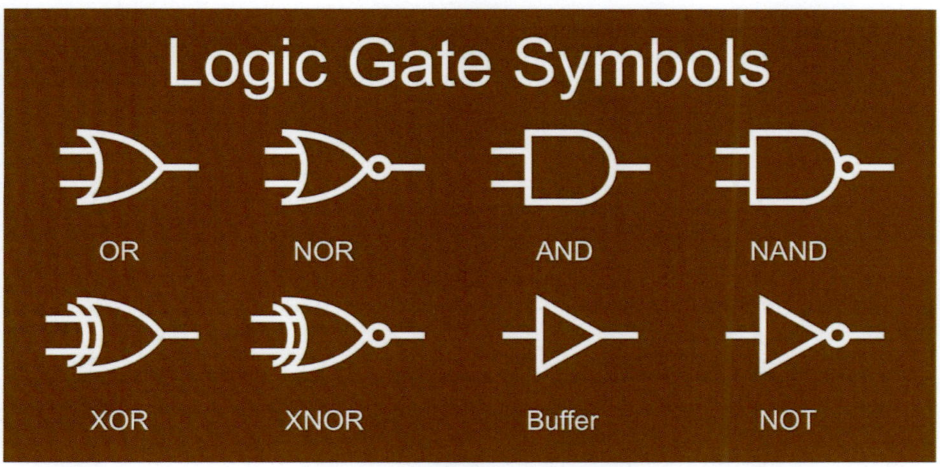

Figure 1.5. Logic gate symbols (Source: TJ Byers, Creative Commons License).

Logic circuits are built using combinations of logic gates to perform complex logical operations. There are various types of logic circuits, including adders, multiplexers, and demultiplexers. Logic circuits are used in computer systems for performing arithmetic operations, logical operations, and memory operations (Zhilyaev & Langdon, 2008). In conclusion, hardware is a critical component of computer systems, and it includes components that process and store data. Memory and storage are two essential hardware components that are used for temporary and long-term storage of data. Logic gates and logic circuits are essential components of digital electronics, and they are used in computer systems for performing complex logical and arithmetic operations. By understanding these hardware components, computer scientists can design and develop more efficient and powerful computer systems.

1.4. PROCESSOR FUNDAMENTALS

The central processing unit (CPU) is the "brain" of a computer system, and it performs the bulk of the data processing operations. This section of the chapter covers three essential aspects of processor fundamentals: CPU architecture, assembly language, and bit manipulation.

1.4.1. Central Processing Unit (CPU) Architecture

The CPU architecture refers to the design and organization of the various components that make up the CPU, including the arithmetic logic unit (ALU), the control unit, and the registers. The ALU performs arithmetic and logical operations on data, while the control unit manages the flow of data within the CPU and between the CPU and other components of the computer system (Thostenson & Chou, 1999) (Figure 1.6).

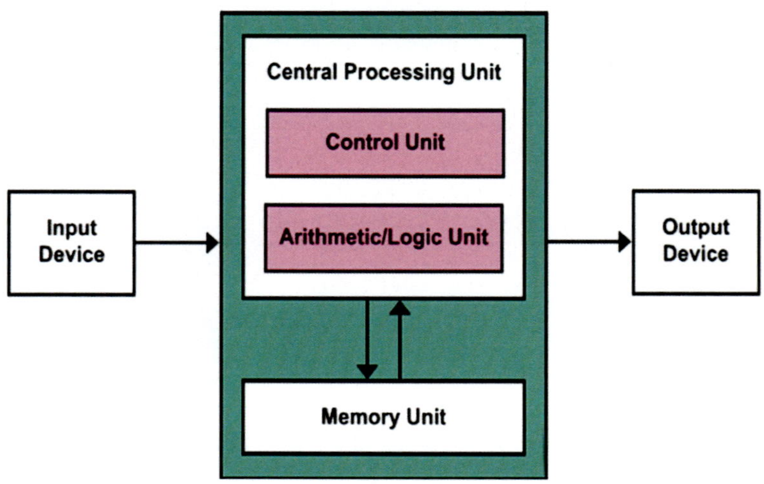

Figure 1.6. Schematic of the CPU architecture (Source: MacKenty, Creative Commons License).

There are various types of CPU architectures, including the von Neumann architecture and the Harvard architecture. The von Neumann architecture is a type of CPU architecture where the same memory and bus system are used for both data and instructions.

The Harvard architecture, on the other hand, uses separate memory and bus systems for data and instructions, which allows for faster data access and processing (Taylor et al., 2003).

1.4.2. Assembly Language

Assembly language is a low-level programming language that is used to write programs that can be executed by the CPU. Assembly language is specific to a particular CPU architecture, and it consists of a set of instructions that the CPU can execute.

Assembly language is considered a low-level language because it provides a direct mapping between the instructions written by the programmer and the machine code executed by the CPU. Assembly language programs are often used for low-level system programming, such as device drivers and operating systems.

Remember

The CPU architecture is the foundation upon which all computational tasks are built, like the scaffolding that supports a towering skyscraper.

1.4.3. Bit Manipulation

Bit manipulation is the process of manipulating individual bits in a binary number to perform logical and arithmetic operations. Bit manipulation is an essential concept in computer science and is used in various areas, including cryptography, compression algorithms, and digital signal processing (PVSSR, 2008).

Bit manipulation operations include bitwise AND, bitwise OR, bitwise XOR, bitwise NOT, bit shifting, and bit masking. Bit manipulation can be used to perform various operations, including counting the number of set bits in a binary number, reversing the bits in a binary number, and checking if a binary number is a power of two.

In conclusion, processor fundamentals are essential for understanding the inner workings of a computer system. The CPU architecture defines the organization and design of the various components that make up the CPU, while assembly language provides a low-level programming language for writing programs that can be executed by the CPU.

Bit manipulation is an essential concept in computer science and is used in various areas, including cryptography and compression algorithms. By understanding these concepts, computer scientists can design and develop more efficient and powerful computer systems (Dey et al., 2012).

1.5. SYSTEM SOFTWARE

System software is a collection of programs that are designed to manage and control the operation of computer hardware. This section of the chapter covers two essential aspects of system software: operating systems and language translators.

1.5.1. Operating System

An operating system (OS) is a software program that manages and controls the hardware resources of a computer system. The OS provides a user interface that allows users to interact with the computer system and the applications installed on it. The OS is responsible for managing the CPU, memory, input/output devices, and storage devices (Figure 1.7)

Figure 1.7. Schematic of different operating systems (Source: Rose Carson, Creative Commons License).

There are various types of operating systems, including Windows, MacOS, Linux, and UNIX. Each operating system has its own set of features and capabilities, and the choice of an operating system depends on the specific requirements of the user or organization (Stonebraker, 1981).

The operating system plays a crucial role in the security and stability of a computer system. The OS provides various security features, such as user authentication, access control, and encryption, to protect the computer system from unauthorized access and use (Tanenbaum & Van Renesse, 1985).

1.5.2. Language Translators

Language translators are programs that translate source code written in a high-level programming language into machine code that can be executed by the CPU. There are various types of language translators, including compilers, interpreters, and assemblers. Compilers are programs that translate source code into object code, which is a form of machine code that can be executed by the CPU. The object code is then linked with other object code and libraries to create an executable program (Vanjani & Aiken, 2020). Interpreters are programs that execute source code directly, without the need for a separate compilation step.

The interpreter reads each line of source code and executes it immediately. Assemblers are programs that translate assembly language code into machine code that can be executed by the CPU. Assembly language is a low-level programming language that is specific to a particular CPU architecture.

In conclusion, system software is an essential component of a computer system, and it includes programs that manage and control the operation of computer hardware. Operating systems provide a user interface and manage the resources of the computer system, while language translators translate source code into machine code that can be executed by the CPU. By understanding these concepts, computer scientists can design and develop more efficient and powerful computer systems (Temple & Edwards, 2002).

Did you Know?

The System Software of a computer, which includes the operating system and device drivers, plays a crucial role in ensuring optimal performance and stability of the machine.

1.6. SECURITY, PRIVACY, AND DATA INTEGRITY

Security, privacy, and data integrity are critical concerns in the design and implementation of computer systems. This section of the chapter covers two essential aspects of security, privacy, and data integrity: first one includes the security, privacy, data integrity, and the second one includes data validation and data verification.

1.6.1. Data Security, Data Privacy, and Data Integrity

Security, privacy, and data integrity are closely related concepts that are essential for protecting computer systems and data from unauthorized access, use, and modification. Security refers to the protection of computer systems and data from threats such as malware, viruses, and hackers. Privacy refers to the protection of personal and sensitive data from unauthorized access and use. Data integrity refers to the accuracy, consistency, and completeness of data (Wang et al., 2019).

There are various techniques and technologies used to ensure security, privacy, and data integrity in computer systems, including encryption, firewalls, access control, and data backup and recovery.

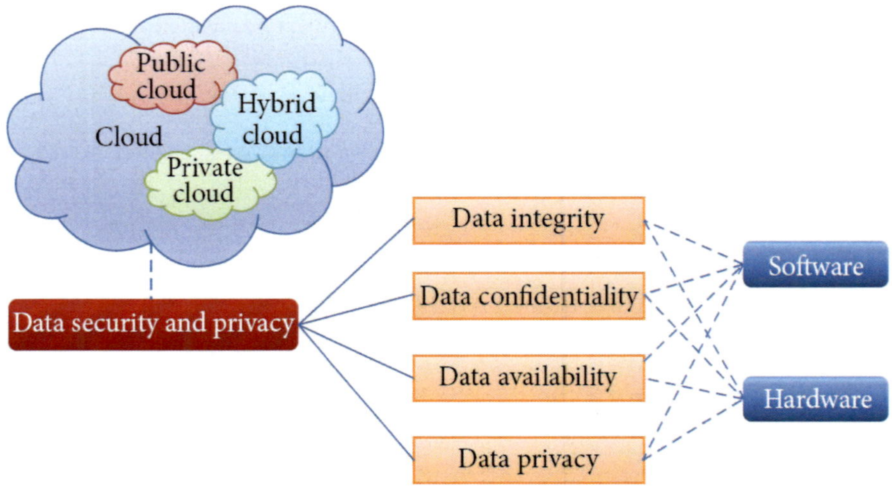

Figure 1.8. Organization of data security and privacy in computer science (Source: Yunchuan Sun et al., Creative Commons License).

1.6.2. Data Validation and Data Verification

Data validation and data verification are essential processes for ensuring the accuracy and completeness of data. Data validation refers to the process of checking whether the data entered into a computer system is valid, while data verification refers to the process of checking whether the data in a computer system is accurate and complete.

Data validation and data verification are critical for preventing errors and inconsistencies in data. They are used in various areas, including data entry, database management, and data analysis.

There are various techniques and technologies used for data validation and data verification, including data cleaning, data profiling, and data quality tools (Hirano et al., 2020).

In conclusion, security, privacy, and data integrity are essential concerns in the design and implementation of computer systems. Data validation and data verification are critical for ensuring the accuracy and completeness of data. By understanding these concepts and using the appropriate techniques and technologies, computer scientists can design and develop computer systems that are secure, private, and reliable.

1.7. ETHICS AND OWNERSHIP

Ethics and ownership are important considerations in the design and implementation of computer systems. This section of the chapter covers three essential aspects of ethics and ownership:

legal, moral, ethical, and cultural implications; copyright issues; and artificial intelligence (AI).

1.7.1. Legal, Moral, Ethical, and Cultural Implications

Computer systems and technology have significant impacts on society, and there are various legal, moral, ethical, and cultural implications associated with their use. The development and use of computer systems can raise ethical issues such as privacy, data protection, and data ownership (Huff & Martin, 1985).

There are also cultural and social implications associated with the development and use of computer systems, including the impact on employment, social inequality, and access to technology. Computer scientists need to be aware of these issues and work to develop computer systems that are socially responsible and ethically sound.

1.7.2. Copyright Issues

Copyright issues are an important consideration in the development and use of computer systems. Copyright laws protect the rights of creators and owners of intellectual property, including software, music, and other digital content.

Computer scientists need to be aware of copyright laws and ensure that their work does not infringe on the rights of others. They also need to be aware of open-source software and other forms of collaborative development, which can provide opportunities for innovation and creativity while respecting the rights of creators and owners of intellectual property.

1.7.3. Artificial Intelligence (AI)

Artificial intelligence (AI) is a rapidly developing field of computer science that involves the development of computer systems that can perform tasks that typically require human intelligence, such as visual perception, speech recognition, and decision-making.

The development of AI raises ethical issues related to the use of technology, including issues of privacy, data protection, and data ownership. AI also raises questions about the impact of automation on employment and social inequality (Vaishya et al., 2020). Computer scientists need to be aware of the ethical and social implications of AI and work to develop AI systems that are socially responsible and ethically sound.

In conclusion, ethics and ownership are important considerations in the design and implementation of computer systems. Computer scientists need to be aware of the legal, moral, ethical, and cultural implications of their work and work to develop computer systems that are socially responsible and ethically sound. Copyright issues and the development of AI also raise important ethical issues that computer scientists need to be aware of and work to address (Makridakis, 2017).

1.8. DATABASES

Databases are collections of data that are organized and stored in a way that allows for efficient retrieval and manipulation of information. This section of the chapter covers three essential aspects of databases: database concepts, database management systems (DBMs), and data definition language (DDL) and data manipulation language (DML) (Figure 1.9).

Figure 1.9. Schematic of the databases (Source: Nexus, Creative Commons License).

1.8.1. Database Concepts

Database concepts refer to the fundamental principles and concepts that underlie the design and implementation of databases. These include the entity-relationship (ER) model, normalization, data modeling, and data indexing. The ER model is a data model that is used to represent the relationships between different entities in a database. Normalization is the process of organizing data in a database to eliminate redundancy and improve data consistency. Data modeling is the process of defining the structure and constraints of data in a database, while data indexing is the process of creating indexes on database tables to improve query performance (Saeed, 2017).

1.8.2. Database Management Systems (DBMS)

A database management system (DBMS) is a software system that is used to manage and manipulate databases. A DBMS provides tools and utilities for creating, modifying, and querying databases, as well as for managing data security and integrity.

There are various types of DBMSs, including relational, object-oriented, and NoSQL DBMSs. Each type of DBMS has its own strengths and weaknesses, and the choice of a DBMS depends on the specific requirements of the user or organization (Zhulin, 2015) (Figure 1.10).

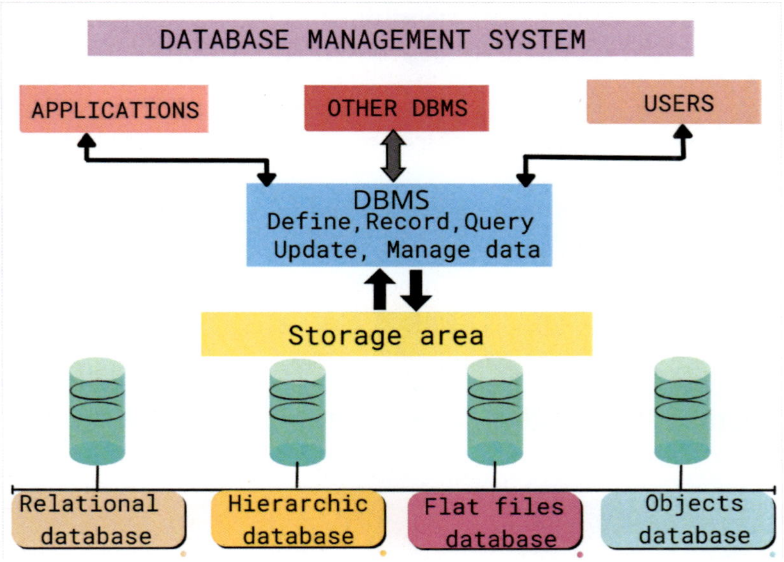

Figure 1.10. Schematic of the database management system (DBMS) (Source: ERP, Creative Commons License).

1.8.3. Data Definition Language (DDL) and Data Manipulation Language (DML)

Data definition language (DDL) and data manipulation language (DML) are two types of programming languages used to create, modify, and manipulate databases.

DDL is used to create and modify the structure of a database, including creating tables, defining indexes, and creating constraints. DML is used to manipulate the data in a database, including inserting, updating, and deleting records.

SQL (Structured Query Language) is a popular programming language used for managing databases. SQL includes both DDL and DML statements, making it a powerful tool for managing and manipulating databases (Özsu & Valduriez, 1996). In conclusion, databases are an essential component of many computer systems, and they are used to store and manage large amounts of data efficiently. Understanding the fundamental principles and concepts of databases, as well as the different types of DBMSs and programming languages used to manage them, is critical for computer scientists working in this field. By applying these concepts and using the appropriate tools and technologies, computer scientists can design and develop efficient and effective database systems.

1.9. ALGORITHM DESIGN AND PROBLEM-SOLVING

Algorithm design and problem-solving are essential skills for computer scientists. This section of the chapter covers two essential aspects of algorithm design and problem-solving: computational thinking skills and algorithms.

1.9.1. Computational Thinking Skills

Computational thinking refers to a problem-solving approach that involves breaking down complex problems into smaller, more manageable components. This involves identifying patterns, creating algorithms, and developing strategies for managing and manipulating data (Durak & Saritepeci, 2018).

Computational thinking skills include abstraction, decomposition, pattern recognition, and algorithmic design. These skills are essential for designing and developing efficient and effective computer systems.

1.9.2. Algorithms

An algorithm is a set of instructions that can be followed to solve a problem or perform a task. Algorithms are used in various computer applications, including search engines, social networks, and online shopping.

Designing efficient algorithms requires an understanding of data structures, programming languages, and computational complexity. Good algorithms are efficient, correct, and easy to understand.

There are various techniques used to design and analyze algorithms, including brute-force algorithms, divide-and-conquer algorithms, and dynamic programming. These techniques can be used to solve various types of problems, including sorting, searching, and graph problems (Fox et al., 1987).

In conclusion, algorithm design and problem-solving are essential skills for computer scientists. Computational thinking skills and algorithm design techniques are used to develop efficient and effective computer systems that can solve complex problems and perform tasks efficiently. Understanding the principles and techniques of algorithm design is critical for computer scientists working in this field. By applying these techniques and developing efficient algorithms, computer scientists can design and develop computer systems that are efficient, effective, and reliable.

1.10. DATA TYPES AND STRUCTURES

Data types and structures refer to the different ways that data can be organized and represented in a computer system. This section of the chapter covers four essential aspects of data types and structures: data types and records, arrays, files, and an introduction to abstract data types (ADTs) (Figure 1.11).

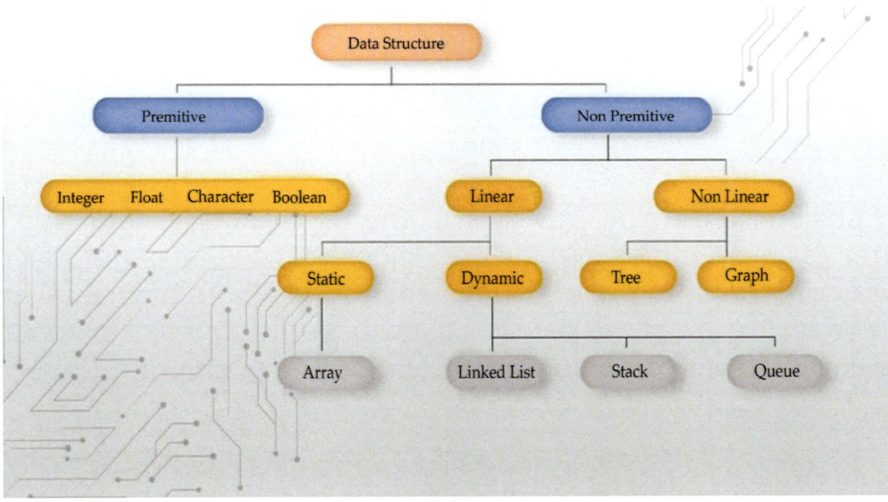

Figure 1.11. Schematic of the data structure (Source: Analytix Labs, Creative Commons License).

1.10.1. Data Types and Records

Data types are the basic building blocks of a programming language. They define the range of values that a variable can take, and the operations that can be performed on those values. Common data types include integers, floats, characters, and Boolean values (Roehrs et al., 2017).

Records are a way of grouping related data together into a single data structure. A record is made up of fields, each of which contains a separate piece of data. Records are commonly used in database systems to store and retrieve information.

1.10.2. Arrays

An array is a data structure that consists of a collection of elements, each of which can be accessed using an index. Arrays can be used to store and manipulate large amounts of data efficiently, and they are commonly used in many computer applications, including numerical analysis and image processing.

1.10.3. Files

Files are a way of storing data permanently on a computer system. They can be used to store text, images, sound, and other types of data. File systems provide a way of organizing and managing files on a computer system, and they provide mechanisms for accessing and manipulating files.

1.10.4. Introduction to Abstract Data Types (ADTs)

An abstract data type (ADT) is a way of defining a data type in terms of its properties and the operations that can be performed on it, rather than in terms of its implementation. ADTs provide a way of abstracting away the details of how a data type is implemented, making it easier to reason about and use in a program (Fürst et al., 2016).

Examples of ADTs include stacks, queues, and trees. These data types provide a way of organizing and manipulating data in a way that is consistent and easy to understand (Figure 1.12).

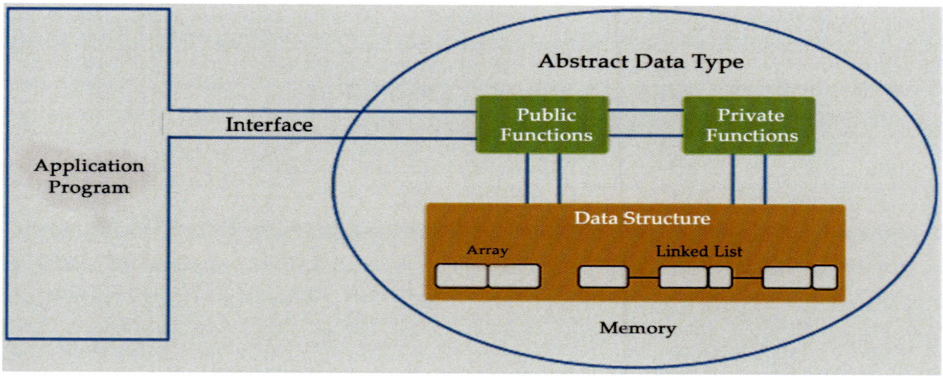

Figure 1.12. Abstract data type in data structure (Source: java t point, Creative Commons License).

In conclusion, understanding data types and structures is essential for computer scientists. Data types provide the building blocks for programming languages, while data structures provide a way of organizing and manipulating data efficiently. By understanding the different types of data types and structures, computer scientists can develop efficient and effective computer systems that can manipulate and process data in a variety of ways.

1.11. PROGRAMMING

Programming is the process of creating computer software using a programming language. This section of the chapter covers four essential aspects of programming: programming basics, constructs, built-in functions, and structured programming.

1.11.1. Programming Basics

Programming basics refer to the fundamental concepts and principles that underlie all programming languages. These include variables, data types, operators, and control structures. Understanding these basics is essential for writing code that is efficient, effective, and easy to read (Ouahbi et al., 2015).

1.11.2. Constructs

Constructs are the building blocks of programming languages. They are used to perform specific tasks, such as controlling program flow, looping over data structures, and manipulating variables. Common constructs include conditional statements, loops, functions, and classes.

1.11.3. Built-in Functions

Built-in functions are predefined functions that are included in programming languages. They provide a way of performing common tasks, such as manipulating strings, performing mathematical operations, and working with data structures. Built-in functions can save time and improve code readability by providing a convenient way to perform common tasks.

1.11.4. Structured Programming

Structured programming is a programming paradigm that emphasizes the use of control structures, such as loops and conditional statements, to organize code. Structured programming makes code more modular, easier to read, and less error-prone (Baker, 1975).

In conclusion, programming is an essential skill for computer scientists. Understanding programming basics, constructs, built-in functions, and structured programming is critical for writing code that is efficient, effective, and easy to maintain. By understanding the principles of programming, computer scientists can develop software that solves complex problems and meets the needs of users.

1.11.5. Software Development

Software development is the process of designing, coding, testing, and maintaining software applications. This section of the chapter covers three essential aspects of software development: the program development lifecycle, program design, and program testing and maintenance.

1.11.6. Program Development Lifecycle

The program development lifecycle (PDL) is a structured approach to software development that consists of several stages: planning, analysis, design, implementation, testing, deployment, and maintenance. The PDL provides a framework for managing software development projects and ensures that software is developed in a consistent, organized, and efficient manner (Hartono & Noda, 1982).

1.11.7. Program Design

Program design is the process of defining the architecture and functionality of a software application. It involves identifying the requirements of the application, creating a design specification, and creating a plan for implementing the design. Good program design is critical for developing software that is efficient, effective, and easy to maintain.

1.11.8. Program Testing and Maintenance

Program testing and maintenance are essential aspects of software development. Testing is the process of evaluating a software application to ensure that it meets the requirements and performs as expected. Maintenance involves making changes to the software application to fix bugs, improve performance, and add new features.

Software testing can be performed using various techniques, including unit testing, integration testing, and system testing. Maintenance can be performed using various strategies, including corrective maintenance, adaptive maintenance, and perfective maintenance. In conclusion, software development is a complex and challenging process that requires careful planning, design, implementation, testing, and maintenance. By understanding the program development lifecycle, program design, and program testing and maintenance, computer scientists can develop software applications that meet the needs of users, are efficient, effective, and easy to maintain.

1.12. COMMUNICATION AND INTERNET TECHNOLOGIES

Communication and internet technologies refer to the systems and protocols used to transmit information over networks, including the internet. This section of the chapter covers two essential aspects of communication and internet technologies: protocols and circuit switching and packet switching.

1.12.1. Protocols

Protocols are sets of rules that govern the exchange of information over a network. They provide a standard way of communicating between devices and ensure that data is transmitted accurately and efficiently. Examples of protocols include TCP/IP, HTTP, and FTP.

1.12.2. Circuit Switching and Packet Switching

Circuit switching and packet switching are two methods used to transmit data over a network. Circuit switching involves the creation of a dedicated communication channel between two devices for the duration of the communication. Packet switching involves the transmission of data in small packets that are sent over the network and reassembled at the receiving end (Hartono, 2020).

Packet switching is more efficient than circuit switching, as it allows multiple devices to share the same network resources. It is the basis for the internet and is used in many other communication systems.

In conclusion, understanding communication and internet technologies is essential for computer scientists. Protocols provide a standard way of communicating between devices and ensure that data is transmitted accurately and efficiently. Circuit switching and packet switching are two methods used to transmit data over a network, with packet switching being more efficient and widely used. By understanding these aspects of communication and internet technologies, computer scientists can develop efficient and effective networked systems that can transmit and receive data in a variety of ways.

1.13. SECURITY

Security is a critical aspect of computer science, particularly with the increasing reliance on digital systems for storing and processing sensitive information. This section of the chapter covers encryption, encryption protocols, and digital certificates, which are essential tools used to secure information.

Encryption is the process of converting plain text into a coded message that can only be read by authorized parties. It involves using an encryption algorithm and a key to scramble the data. Encryption protocols, such as SSL/TLS, are used to secure information transmitted over the internet. They use a combination of encryption and digital certificates to verify the identity of the parties involved and to ensure the confidentiality and integrity of the information (Anderson & Moore, 2009).

Digital certificates are electronic documents that verify the identity of the parties involved in an online transaction. They are issued by a Certificate Authority (CA) and contain information such as the owner's name, public key, and expiration date. Digital certificates are used to authenticate the identity of the parties involved and to ensure the confidentiality and integrity of the information being transmitted.

Encryption, encryption protocols, and digital certificates are critical tools used to secure sensitive information, such as financial transactions and personal data. By using these tools, computer scientists can ensure that information is transmitted securely and that only authorized parties can access it.

In conclusion, understanding security is essential for computer scientists. Encryption, encryption protocols, and digital certificates are essential tools used to secure information transmitted over digital systems. By using these tools, computer scientists can ensure the confidentiality and integrity of sensitive information and protect against unauthorized access and data breaches (Agrawal et al., 2017).

1.14. ARTIFICIAL INTELLIGENCE

Artificial Intelligence (AI) refers to the simulation of human intelligence in machines that can perform tasks that typically require human cognition, such as learning, reasoning, and problem-solving. This section of the chapter covers the basics of AI, including its applications and limitations.

AI is a broad field that encompasses several areas, including machine learning, natural language processing, robotics, and computer vision. AI systems can be trained to perform a variety of tasks, from recognizing speech to analyzing large data sets (Gunning & Aha, 2019).

One of the most promising applications of AI is in the field of healthcare, where AI-powered systems can help doctors diagnose and treat diseases more accurately and efficiently. AI is also used in finance, retail, and other industries to improve customer service, optimize business processes, and automate repetitive tasks (Figure 1.13).

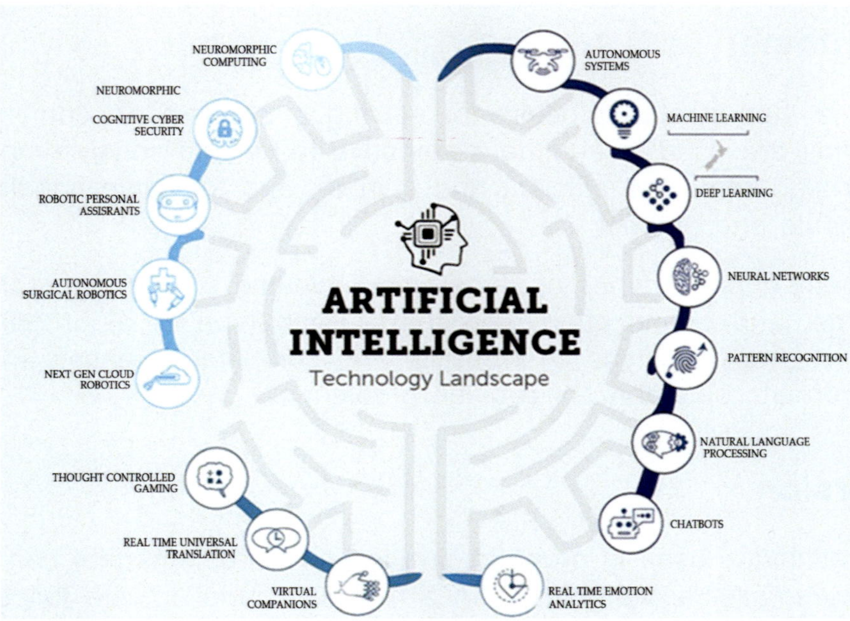

Figure 1.13. Schematic of the Artificial Intelligence Technology Landscape (Source: Nisha Arya Ahmed, Creative Commons License).

Despite its many applications, AI still has several limitations. One of the biggest challenges is creating AI systems that are capable of learning from a variety of data sources and making accurate predictions based on that data. Another challenge is ensuring that AI systems are unbiased and not influenced by factors such as race, gender, or other personal characteristics.

AI systems also require large amounts of data to learn effectively, which can be a challenge in industries where data is scarce or difficult to obtain. Additionally, AI systems are not always transparent, meaning it can be difficult to understand how they make decisions or recommendations (Lu et al., 2018).

In conclusion, AI has enormous potential to revolutionize many industries, from healthcare to finance. However, it is important to understand the limitations and challenges associated with AI, such as biased algorithms and the need for large amounts of data. By developing AI systems that are transparent, unbiased, and capable of learning from a variety of data sources, computer scientists can create more effective and efficient AI systems that benefit society.

1.15. COMPUTATIONAL THINKING AND PROBLEM SOLVING

Computational thinking and problem solving are fundamental skills in computer science. This section of the chapter covers algorithms, recursion, and other key concepts related to problem solving.

1.15.1. Algorithms

An algorithm is a step-by-step process for solving a problem. In computer science, algorithms are used to automate repetitive tasks and solve complex problems. Good algorithms are efficient and reliable, and they can handle a wide range of inputs and outputs.

There are many different types of algorithms, including sorting algorithms, search algorithms, and optimization algorithms. Each type of algorithm is designed to solve a specific type of problem, and computer scientists must choose the appropriate algorithm for a given problem.

1.15.2. Recursion

Recursion is a technique used in programming to solve problems that can be broken down into smaller sub-problems. In a recursive function, the function calls itself with a smaller input until it reaches a base case, where the problem can be solved directly. Recursion is used to solve many problems in computer science, such as searching trees and sorting lists.

1.15.3. Other Key Concepts

Other key concepts related to problem solving include abstraction, decomposition, and pattern recognition. Abstraction involves focusing on the most important aspects of a problem and ignoring irrelevant details. Decomposition involves breaking a problem down into smaller sub-problems. Pattern recognition involves identifying patterns in data or algorithms and using those patterns to solve new problems.

In conclusion, computational thinking and problem solving are essential skills in computer science. Algorithms, recursion, and other key concepts are used to solve complex problems and automate repetitive tasks. By mastering these skills, computer scientists can create more efficient and effective solutions to real-world problems.

1.16. FURTHER PROGRAMMING

Further programming covers advanced topics related to programming in computer science. This section of the chapter covers programming paradigms, file processing, and exception handling.

1.16.1. Programming Paradigms

Programming paradigms are different approaches to programming that are used to solve different types of problems. There are several different programming paradigms, including procedural programming, object-oriented programming, functional programming, and event-driven programming.

Procedural programming is a linear approach to programming that involves breaking down a problem into smaller sub-problems and solving them in a specific order. Object-oriented programming involves using objects to represent real-world entities and defining their properties and behaviors. Functional programming involves using mathematical functions to solve problems. Event-driven programming involves responding to events or user interactions with the program (Van, 2009).

ACTIVITY 1.1.

Imagine you're a computer technician and a client brings in their computer complaining of slow performance. After running diagnostics, you discover that the issue is with their outdated system software, but the client is hesitant to upgrade because they're worried it will disrupt their workflow. How do you explain the importance of keeping their system software up to date and address their concerns?

1.16.2. File Processing and Exception Handling

File processing is an important aspect of programming, as programs often need to read and write data from files. File processing involves opening a file, reading or writing data, and closing the file. Exception handling is the process of dealing with errors or exceptions that may occur during program execution.

Exception handling involves detecting errors, handling them appropriately, and preventing the program from crashing. There are several techniques for handling exceptions, including using try-catch blocks, throwing exceptions, and logging errors.

In conclusion, further programming covers advanced topics related to programming in computer science. Programming paradigms, file processing, and exception handling are important concepts for building robust and efficient programs. By understanding these concepts, computer scientists can create more effective and efficient programs that solve complex problems.

SUMMARY

This chapter Fundamentals of Computer Science covers a wide range of topics related to computer science. It starts with information representation, including data representation and multimedia. The chapter then covers communication and computer hardware, including memory and storage, and logic gates and circuits. Processor fundamentals, such as CPU architecture, assembly language, and bit manipulation are also explored. The chapter also covers system software, including operating systems and language translators, and discusses security, privacy, and data integrity, including data validation and verification. Ethical and ownership issues related to computer science, including copyright and artificial intelligence, are also examined. Database concepts, such as DBMS, DDL, and DML are explored, and algorithm design and problem-solving, including computational thinking skills and algorithms, are discussed. Data types and structures, including arrays and ADTs, are also covered, as well as programming basics, structured programming, and the program development lifecycle. The chapter also covers data representation, including floating-point numbers, file organization, and access, and explores communication and internet technologies, including protocols and packet switching. The purposes of an operating system and translation software are discussed, as well as security and artificial intelligence. The chapter concludes with an exploration of computational thinking and problem-solving, including recursion and algorithms, and programming paradigms, file processing, and exception handling.

REVIEW QUESTIONS

1. What is the role of an operating system in a computer system?
2. What are DBMS, DDL, and DML?
3. What are the different types of data representation used in computer science?
4. What is the importance of security, privacy, and data integrity in computer science?
5. What are the components of computer hardware?
6. What are algorithms and how are they used in programming?
7. What are the different types of programming languages?
8. What is the program development lifecycle and how is it used in software development?

MULTIPLE CHOICE QUESTIONS

1. What does the term "multimedia" refer to in computer science?

a) The process of representing data in binary form
b) The physical components of a computer system
c) The integration of different media types, such as audio and video
d) The process of optimizing computer performance

2. **What is the role of an operating system in a computer system?**
   a) To manage hardware and software resources
   b) To store and organize data
   c) To create and edit multimedia files
   d) To design and develop computer programs
3. **What is a DBMS?**
   a) A programming language used for creating computer programs
   b) A hardware component used for storing data
   c) A system software used for managing databases
   d) A protocol used for communication between computers
4. **What is the purpose of algorithms in computer science?**
   a) To represent data in binary form
   b) To organize and store data efficiently
   c) To solve problems through step-by-step procedures
   d) To manage hardware and software resources
5. **What is the role of language translators in programming?**
   a) To optimize computer performance
   b) To create multimedia files
   c) To translate programming languages into machine language
   d) To manage databases
6. **What is the purpose of logic gates and circuits in computer hardware?**
   a) To manage system resources
   b) To store and organize data
   c) To solve problems through step-by-step procedures
   d) To process logical operations
7. **What are data types and structures used for in programming?**
   a) To represent data in binary form
   b) To manage hardware and software resources
   c) To organize and store data efficiently
   d) To create and edit multimedia files
8. **What is the role of security in computer science?**
   a) To optimize computer performance
   b) To ensure data validation and verification
   c) To manage hardware and software resources
   d) To create and edit multimedia files

Answers to Multiple Choice Questions

1. (c) 2. (a) 3. (c) 4. (c) 5. (c) 6. (d) 7. (c) 8. (b)

REFERENCES

1. Aakhus, M., (2007). Communication as design. *Communication Monographs, 74*(1), 112–117.
2. Agrawal, S., Banerjee, S., & Sharma, S., (2017). Privacy and security of Aadhaar: A computer science perspective. *Economic and Political Weekly, 52*(37), 93–102.
3. Anderson, R., & Moore, T., (2009). Information security: Where computer science, economics and psychology meet. *Philosophical Transactions of the Royal Society A: Mathematical, Physical and Engineering Sciences, 367*(1898), 2717–2727.
4. Artz, D., & Gil, Y., (2007). A survey of trust in computer science and the semantic web. *Journal of Web Semantics, 5*(2), 58–71.
5. Baker, F. T., (1975). Structured programming in a production programming environment. *ACM SIGPLAN Notices, 10*(6), 172–185.
6. Beaubouef, T., & Mason, J., (2005). Why the high attrition rate for computer science students: Some thoughts and observations. *ACM SIGCSE Bulletin, 37*(2), 103–106.
7. Bell, T., Alexander, J., Freeman, I., & Grimley, M., (2009). Computer science unplugged: School students doing real computing without computers. *The New Zealand Journal of Applied Computing and Information Technology, 13*(1), 20–29.
8. Ben-Ari, M., (1998). Constructivism in computer science education. *ACM SIGCSE Bulletin, 30*(1), 257–261.
9. Ben-Ari, M., (2001). Constructivism in computer science education. *Journal of Computers in Mathematics and Science Teaching, 20*(1), 45–73.
10. Carter, L., (2006). Why students with an apparent aptitude for computer science don't choose to major in computer science. *ACM SIGCSE Bulletin, 38*(1), 27–31.
11. Cohoon, J. M., (2001). Toward improving female retention in the computer science major. *Communications of the ACM, 44*(5), 108–114.
12. Cooper, S., Dann, W., & Pausch, R., (2003). Teaching objects-first in introductory computer science. *ACM SIGCSE Bulletin, 35*(1), 191–195.
13. Dey, S., Nath, J., & Nath, A., (2012). An advanced combined symmetric key cryptographic method using bit manipulation, bit reversal, modified Caesar cipher (SD-REE), DJSA method, TTJSA method: SJA-I algorithm. *International Journal of Computer Applications, 46*(20), 46–53.
14. Durak, H. Y., & Saritepeci, M., (2018). Analysis of the relation between computational thinking skills and various variables with the structural equation model. *Computers & Education, 116*, 191–202.

15. Erbas-Cakmak, S., Kolemen, S., Sedgwick, A. C., Gunnlaugsson, T., James, T. D., Yoon, J., & Akkaya, E. U., (2018). Molecular logic gates: The past, present and future. *Chemical Society Reviews, 47*(7), 2228–2248.
16. Fagin, B., & Merkle, L., (2003). Measuring the effectiveness of robots in teaching computer science. *ACM SIGCSE Bulletin, 35*(1), 307–311.
17. Fox, L., Mayers, D. F., Fox, L., & Mayers, D. F., (1987). Algorithms. *Numerical Solution of Ordinary Differential Equations, 1*(1), 198–211.
18. Freedson, P. S., Melanson, E., & Sirard, J., (1998). Calibration of the computer science and applications, inc. accelerometer. *Medicine and Science in Sports and Exercise, 30*(5), 777–781.
19. Fuller, U., Johnson, C. G., Ahoniemi, T., Cukierman, D., Hernán-Losada, I., Jackova, J., & Thompson, E., (2007). Developing a computer science-specific learning taxonomy. *ACM SIGCSE Bulletin, 39*(4), 152–170.
20. Fürst, A., Hoang, T. S., Basin, D., Sato, N., & Miyazaki, K., (2016). Large-scale system development using abstract data types and refinement. *Science of Computer Programming, 131*, 59–75.
21. Gunning, D., & Aha, D., (2019). DARPA's explainable artificial intelligence (XAI) program. *AI Magazine, 40*(2), 44–58.
22. Gusfield, D., (1997). Algorithms on stings, trees, and sequences: Computer science and computational biology. *ACM SIGACT News, 28*(4), 41–60.
23. Hartono, S. B., (2020). Development of a cash flow information system using the SDLC (system development life cycle) method at Madin Al-Junnah. *ISOQUANT: Journal of Economics, Management and Accounting, 4*(1), 1–16.
24. Hirano, T., Motohashi, T., Okumura, K., Takajo, K., Kuroki, T., Ichikawa, D., & Ueno, T., (2020). Data validation and verification using blockchain in a clinical trial for breast cancer: Regulatory sandbox. *Journal of Medical Internet Research, 22*(6), 18938.
25. Huff, C., & Martin, C. D., (1995). Computing consequences: A framework for teaching ethical computing. *Communications of the ACM, 38*(12), 75–84.
26. Kay, J., Barg, M., Fekete, A., Greening, T., Hollands, O., Kingston, J. H., & Crawford, K., (2000). Problem-based learning for foundation computer science courses. *Computer Science Education, 10*(2), 109–128.
27. Kosslyn, S. M., (1975). Information representation in visual images. *Cognitive Psychology, 7*(3), 341–370.
28. Lagesen, V. A., (2008). A cyberfeminist utopia? Perceptions of gender and computer science among Malaysian women computer science students and faculty. *Science, Technology, & Human Values, 33*(1), 5–27.
29. Leach, J. E., Triplett, L. R., Argueso, C. T., & Trivedi, P., (2017). Communication in the phytobiome. *Cell, 169*(4), 587–596.
30. Linn, M. C., (1995). Designing computer learning environments for engineering

and computer science: The scaffolded knowledge integration framework. *Journal of Science Education and Technology, 4*, 103–126.

31. Loui, M. C., (1995). Computer science is a new engineering discipline. *ACM Computing Surveys (CSUR), 27*(1), 31, 32.
32. Lu, H., Li, Y., Chen, M., Kim, H., & Serikawa, S., (2018). Brain intelligence: Go beyond artificial intelligence. *Mobile Networks and Applications, 23*, 368–375.
33. Makridakis, S., (2017). The forthcoming artificial intelligence (AI) revolution: Its impact on society and firms. *Futures, 90*, 46–60.
34. Mamei, M., Menezes, R., Tolksdorf, R., & Zambonelli, F., (2006). Case studies for self-organization in computer science. *Journal of Systems Architecture, 52*(8, 9), 443–460.
35. Margolis, J., Fisher, A., & Miller, F., (2000). The anatomy of interest: Women in undergraduate computer science. *Women's Studies Quarterly, 28*(1, 2), 104–127.
36. Master, A., Cheryan, S., & Meltzoff, A. N., (2016). Computing whether she belongs: Stereotypes undermine girls' interest and sense of belonging in computer science. *Journal of Educational Psychology, 108*(3), 424.
37. Mayer, R. E., (2017). Using multimedia for e learning. *Journal of Computer Assisted Learning, 33*(5), 403–423.
38. McConnell, J. J., (1996). Active learning and its use in computer science. In: *Proceedings of the 1st Conference on Integrating Technology into Computer Science Education, 1*(1), 52–54.
39. McLeod, S. A., (2007). *Stages of Memory-Encoding Storage and Retrieval* (Vol. 21, p. 2015).
40. Mottier, V., (2005). The interpretive turn: History, memory, and storage in qualitative research. In: *Forum Qualitative Sozialforschung/Forum: Qualitative Social Research* (Vol. 6, No. 2, p. 53).
41. Nakamura, Y., & Noda, A., (1982). On a hybrid network system of circuit switching and packet switching. *Electronics and Communications in Japan (Part I: Communications), 65*(6), 37–45.
42. Ouahbi, I., Kaddari, F., Darhmaoui, H., Elachqar, A., & Lahmine, S., (2015). Learning basic programming concepts by creating games with scratch programming environment. *Procedia-Social and Behavioral Sciences, 191*, 1479–1482.
43. Özsu, M. T., & Valduriez, P., (1996). Distributed and parallel database systems. *ACM Computing Surveys (CSUR), 28*(1), 125–128.
44. Parnas, D. L., (1999). Software engineering programs are not computer science programs. *IEEE Software, 16*(6), 19–30.
45. Posteguillo, S., (1999). The schematic structure of computer science research articles. *English for Specific Purposes, 18*(2), 139–160.
46. PVSSR, C. M., (2018). Adaptive, robust and blind digital watermarking using Bhattacharyya distance and bit manipulation. *Multimedia Tools and Applications, 77*, 5609–5635.

47. Roehrs, A., Da Costa, C. A., Da Rosa, R. R., & De Oliveira, K. S. F., (2017). Personal health records: A systematic literature review. *Journal of Medical Internet Research, 19*(1), 5876.

48. Rubin, F., (1976). Experiments in text file compression. *Communications of the ACM, 19*(11), 617–623.

49. Saeed, A. M., (2017). Role of database management systems (DBMS) in supporting information technology in sector of education. *International Journal of Science and Research (IJSR), 6*(5), 1462–1466.

50. Schwill, A., (1994). Fundamental ideas of computer science. *Bulletin-European Association for Theoretical Computer Science, 53*, 274.

51. Shackelford, R. L., & LeBlanc, R. J., (1997). Introducing computer science fundamentals before programming. In: *Proceedings Frontiers in Education 1997 27th Annual Conference, Teaching and Learning in an Era of Change* (Vol. 1, pp. 285–289). IEEE.

52. Stemler, L. K., (1997). Educational characteristics of multimedia: A literature review. *Journal of Educational Multimedia and Hypermedia, 6*, 339–360.

53. Stonebraker, M., (1981). Operating system support for database management. *Communications of the ACM, 24*(7), 412–418.

54. Tanenbaum, A. S., & Van, R. R., (1985). Distributed operating systems. *ACM Computing Surveys (CSUR), 17*(4), 419–470.

55. Taylor, J. M., Imamoglu, A., & Lukin, M. D., (2003). Controlling a mesoscopic spin environment by quantum bit manipulation. *Physical Review Letters, 91*(24), 246802.

56. Temple, B., & Edwards, R., (2002). Interpreters/translators and cross-language research: Reflexivity and border crossings. *International Journal of Qualitative Methods, 1*(2), 1–12.

57. Thostenson, E. T., & Chou, T. W., (1999). Microwave processing: Fundamentals and applications. *Composites Part A: Applied Science and Manufacturing, 30*(9), 1055–1071.

58. Vaishya, R., Javaid, M., Khan, I. H., & Haleem, A., (2020). Artificial intelligence (AI) applications for COVID-19 pandemic. *Diabetes & Metabolic Syndrome: Clinical Research & Reviews, 14*(4), 337–339.

59. Van, R. P., (2009). Programming paradigms for dummies: What every programmer should know. *New Computational Paradigms for Computer Music, 104*, 616–621.

60. Vanjani, M., & Aiken, M., (2020). A comparison of free online machine language translators. *J. Manag. Sci. Bus. Intell., 5*, 26–31.

61. Wang, F., (1990). Improving remote sensing image analysis through fuzzy information representation. *Photogrammetric Engineering and Remote Sensing, 56*(8), 1163–1169.

62. Wang, T., Bhuiyan, M. Z. A., Wang, G., Qi, L., Wu, J., & Hayajneh, T., (2019). Preserving balance between privacy and data integrity in edge-assisted internet of things. *IEEE Internet of Things Journal, 7*(4), 2679–2689.

63. Webb, M., Davis, N., Bell, T., Katz, Y. J., Reynolds, N., Chambers, D. P., & Sysło,

M. M., (2017). Computer science in K-12 school curricula of the 2I[st] century: Why, what and when? *Education and Information Technologies, 22*, 445–468.

64. Wilson, B. C., (2002). A study of factors promoting success in computer science including gender differences. *Computer Science Education, 12*(1, 2), 141–164.
65. Yadav, A., Gretter, S., Hambrusch, S., & Sands, P., (2016). Expanding computer science education in schools: Understanding teacher experiences and challenges. *Computer Science Education, 26*(4), 235–254.
66. Zhilyaev, A. P., & Langdon, T. G., (2008). Using high-pressure torsion for metal processing: Fundamentals and applications. *Progress in Materials Science, 53*(6), 893–979.
67. Zhulin, I. B., (2015). Databases for microbiologists. *Journal of Bacteriology, 197*(15), 2458–2467.

CHAPTER 2

FUNDAMENTALS OF DATA STRUCTURES AND ALGORITHMS

UNIT INTRODUCTION

Data structures and algorithms are fundamental concepts in computer science that form the building blocks of efficient software design and development. A data structure is a way of organizing and storing data in a computer so that it can be accessed and manipulated efficiently. Examples of data structures include arrays, linked lists, stacks, queues, trees, and graphs. An algorithm is a set of step-by-step instructions for solving a problem or performing a specific task. Algorithms can be used to manipulate data stored in data structures or to solve a variety of computational problems. The study of data structures and algorithms is important in computer science because it provides the foundation for understanding how data is organized and manipulated in computer systems. By understanding data structures and algorithms, software developers can design and implement efficient algorithms that can process large amounts of data quickly and accurately (Aggarwal & Vitter, 1988; Agrawal et al., 2004). They can also select appropriate data structures for a particular application, which can help improve the efficiency of their programs. Some common topics that are covered in the study of data structures and algorithms include complexity analysis, which is the study of how much time and space an algorithm requires to solve a problem, and algorithmic design techniques, such as brute force, greedy algorithms, and dynamic programming. Additionally, the study of data structures and algorithms is an active area of research, with ongoing efforts to develop new algorithms and data structures that can improve the efficiency and performance of computer systems.

Data Structures and Algorithms are fundamental concepts in computer science that are crucial for designing and developing efficient software systems. A data structure is a way of organizing and storing data in a computer so that it can be accessed and manipulated efficiently. An algorithm, on the other hand, is a step-by-step procedure for solving a problem or performing a specific task. These two concepts are intimately linked since algorithms can manipulate data stored in data structures or solve a variety of computational problems (Ahuja & Orlin, 1989; Ahuja et al., 1989).

Data structures are used to represent and manipulate data in computer systems. They allow us to store, retrieve, and manipulate data in an organized and efficient manner. For example, an array is a simple data structure that allows us to store a collection of elements of the same type in a contiguous block of memory. Linked lists are another type of data structure that allow us to store elements in a linear sequence, but with more flexibility in terms of insertion and deletion. Stacks and queues are data structures that allow us to manage data in a specific order, with a Last-In-First-Out (LIFO) policy for stacks and First-In-First-Out (FIFO) policy for queues. Trees and graphs are more complex data structures that allow us to represent hierarchical relationships and non-linear connections between data elements. Algorithms, on the other hand, are used to manipulate data stored in data structures or to solve a variety of computational problems. They are the driving force behind most software applications, ranging from simple arithmetic operations to complex machine learning algorithms. Common examples of algorithms include sorting algorithms, search algorithms, and graph algorithms (Szymanski & Van Wyk, 1983; Didier, 2009).

Learning Objectives

At the end of this chapter, readers will be able to:

- Define data structures and identify their different types, including arrays, linked lists, stacks, queues, trees, and graphs.
- Understand the operations that can be performed on data structures, such as traversals, insertions, deletions, searching, and sorting.
- Evaluate the pros and cons of each data structure and choose the most appropriate one for a given problem.
- Identify the basic types of algorithms, including searching algorithms, sorting algorithms, graph algorithms, and dynamic programming.
- Explain the strengths and weaknesses of each type of algorithm and choose the most appropriate one for a given problem.
- Describe the concept of algorithmic analysis and understand the different types of analysis, including worst-case analysis, average-case analysis, and best-case analysis.
- Use asymptotic notation, including Big-O notation, Omega notation, and Theta notation, to describe the time and space complexity of algorithms.

- Understand the common algorithmic techniques, including brute force, greedy algorithms, divide and conquer, and dynamic programming.
- Evaluate the strengths and weaknesses of each algorithmic technique and choose the most appropriate one for a given problem.
- Apply the concepts and techniques learned in this chapter to design and analyze algorithms and data structures for real-world problems in computer science.

Key Terms

- Data Structures
- Algorithms
- Complexity Analysis
- Asymptotic Notation
- Big-O Notation
- Omega Notation
- Theta Notation
- Brute Force
- Greedy Algorithms
- Dynamic Programming

2.1 THE IMPORTANCE OF DATA STRUCTURES AND ALGORITHMS

The importance of data structures and algorithms in computer science cannot be overstated. They are fundamental concepts that provide the foundation for developing efficient software systems. Here are some reasons why data structures and algorithms are important (Snyder, 1984):

Did you Know?

The origins of algorithms can be traced back to ancient Babylonians, who used mathematical algorithms to solve problems related to commerce, trade and taxation.

- Efficiency: The primary reason for using data structures and algorithms is o improve the efficiency of software systems. Data structures provide a way to organize and access data in a manner that minimizes the time and space required to perform operations on the data. Algorithms provide a way to process and manipulate data efficiently, thereby reducing the time and resources required to perform a task.
- Problem Solving: Data structures and algorithms are essential tools for solving a wide range of computational problems. Many problems in computer science can be formulated as data manipulation tasks that require the use of data structures and algorithms. For example, search algorithms are used to find a specific item in a collection of data, and sorting algorithms are used to arrange data in a specific order.
- Flexibility: Data structures and algorithms provide a flexible framework for software development. They allow us to model complex real-world systems in a way that is easy to manipulate and understand. By choosing the appropriate data structures and algorithms for a particular problem, we can create software systems that are robust and scalable.
- Reusability: Data structures and algorithms are reusable components that can be used in multiple software applications. Once a data structure or algorithm has been implemented, it can be used in different software applications, thereby saving time and resources in software development (Aki, 1989; Akra & Bazzi, 1998).
- Innovation: The study of data structures and algorithms is an active area of research that is constantly evolving. New algorithms and data structures are being developed that can improve the efficiency and performance of computer systems. By staying up-to-date with the latest advances in data structures and algorithms, software developers

can create innovative solutions to complex computational problems.

In conclusion, data structures and algorithms are fundamental concepts in computer science that are essential for designing and developing efficient software systems. They provide a flexible, reusable, and scalable framework for software development that can be used to solve a wide range of computational problems (Regli, 1992; Ajtai et al., 2001).

2.2 DATA STRUCTURES

Data structures are a way of organizing and storing data in a computer so that it can be accessed and manipulated efficiently. There are many types of data structures, including arrays, linked lists, stacks, queues, trees, and graphs. Each data structure has its own advantages and disadvantages, and the choice of data structure depends on the specific application and the types of operations that need to be performed on the data. Common operations on data structures include traversals, insertions, deletions, searching, and sorting. The study of data structures is essential for understanding how data is organized and manipulated in computer systems and is a fundamental concept in computer science (Alon, 1990).

Did you Know?

The concept of data structures can be traced back to the 1940s, when John von Neumann introduced the concept of a stored program computer.

A data structure is a way of organizing and storing data in a computer so that it can be accessed and manipulated efficiently. It provides a systematic way to manage and organize data, allowing us to store, retrieve, and manipulate data in an organized and efficient manner. The use of data structures is essential for efficient software design and development (Andersson & Thorup, 2000; Bakker et al., 2012).

2.2.1 Types of Data Structures

Following are the types of data structures:

- Arrays: An array is a simple data structure that stores a fixed-size sequential collection of elements of the same data type. The elements are stored in contiguous memory locations, and each element can be accessed using an index. Arrays are commonly used for storing and accessing data that is indexed, such as lists of items or records.
- Linked Lists: A linked list is a data structure that consists of a sequence of nodes, where each node contains data and

a pointer to the next node in the sequence. Linked lists are commonly used for implementing dynamic data structures, where the size of the data structure can change during program execution.

- Stacks: A stack is a data structure that follows the Last-In-First-Out (LIFO) principle. It allows access to only the top element of the stack, which is the last element added to the stack. Stacks are commonly used for implementing functions that need to keep track of the previous state, such as backtracking algorithms.
- Queues: A queue is a data structure that follows the First-In-First-Out (FIFO) principle. It allows access to both the first and last elements in the queue, with the first element being the oldest element in the queue. Queues are commonly used for implementing buffers, where data is stored in a queue until it can be processed.
- Trees: A tree is a data structure that consists of a collection of nodes connected by edges. Each node has a parent node and zero or more child nodes. Trees are commonly used for representing hierarchical relationships, such as the structure of a file system or the organization of a company.
- Graphs: A graph is a data structure that consists of a collection of nodes (also known as vertices) connected by edges. The edges can be directed or undirected and can be weighted or unweighted. Graphs are commonly used for representing complex relationships, such as social networks or transportation systems (Ramadge & Wonham, 1989; Amir et al., 2006).

Each data structure has its own advantages and disadvantages, and the choice of data structure depends on the specific application and the types of operations that need to be performed on the data. Common operations on data structures include traversals, insertions, deletions, searching, and sorting. The study of data structures is essential for understanding how data is organized and manipulated in computer systems and is a fundamental concept in computer science.

2.2.2 Operations on Data Structures

Once a data structure is created, it needs to be operated upon to insert, delete, search, sort or traverse the elements within it. Some of the most common operations performed on data structures are:

2.2.2.1 Traversals

Traversing a data structure means accessing each element in the data structure in a specific order. Traversal can be done in different ways depending on the type of data structure. For example, linear data structures such as arrays and linked lists can be traversed using a simple loop, whereas tree and graph data structures require more complex traversal algorithms such as depth-first search or breadth-first search. Traversal is useful when we need to perform an operation on all the elements of a data structure. For example, to find the minimum or maximum element in an array, we need to traverse the entire array (Dengiz et al., 1997; Berger & Barkaoui, 2004).

2.2.2.2 Insertions

Insertion refers to adding a new element to a data structure. Depending on the type of data structure, insertion can be simple or complex. For example, inserting an element into an array is a simple operation as we just need to find an empty space and place the new element there.

However, inserting an element into a linked list requires creating a new node and updating the pointers of the previous and next nodes. Insertion can also have different complexity levels depending on the location of the insertion. For example, inserting an element at the beginning of an array or linked list is simpler than inserting an element in the middle (Festa & Resende, 2002; Zhu & Wilhelm, 2006).

2.2.2.3 Deletions

Deletion refers to removing an element from a data structure. Similar to insertion, deleting an element can be simple or complex depending on the type of data structure and the location of the deletion. For example, deleting an element from the end of an array is a simple operation as we just need to decrement the size of the array. However, deleting an element from the middle of a linked list requires updating the pointers of the previous and next nodes. Deletion can also have different complexity levels depending on the type of data structure and the location of the deletion.

2.2.2.4 Searching

Searching refers to finding a specific element within a data structure. Depending on the type of data structure, different searching algorithms can be used such as linear search, binary search, or depth-first search. Linear search is used for linear data structures such as arrays and linked lists, whereas binary search is used for sorted arrays. Searching algorithms can be simple or complex depending on the size of the data structure and the algorithm used. For example, linear search has a time complexity of O(n) where n is the size of the data structure, whereas binary search has a time complexity of O(log n) (Wallace et al., 2004; Wang, 2008).

2.2.2.5 Sorting

Sorting refers to arranging the elements of a data structure in a specific order. Depending on the type of data structure, different sorting algorithms can be used such as bubble sort, insertion sort, quicksort, or merge sort. Sorting is important for organizing data and making it easier to search, access, and analyze. Sorting algorithms can have different time and space complexities depending on the size of the data structure and the algorithm used. For example, bubble sort has a time complexity of O(n^2), whereas quicksort has an average time complexity of O(n log n).

In conclusion, operations on data structures are essential for manipulating and organizing data in computer systems. Understanding the complexities of these operations is important for choosing the right data structure and algorithm for a specific task, and for designing and developing efficient software systems. Different data structures have different strengths and weaknesses, and choosing the appropriate data structure for a specific task is essential for developing efficient software systems.

2.2.3 Pros and Cons of each Data Structure

Here are some pros and cons of the different types of data structures:

2.2.3.1 Arrays

Following are the pros:

- Simple to use and implement
- Easy to access and manipulate elements using index
- Efficient for random access

Following are the cons:

- Fixed size, which means the size of the array cannot be changed after it is created
- Inefficient for inserting and deleting elements, especially in the middle of the array
- Can cause memory wastage if the array size is larger than the number of elements it contains

2.2.3.2 Linked Lists

Following are the pros:

- Dynamic size, which means elements can be added or removed easily

- Efficient for inserting and deleting elements, especially in the middle of the list
- Memory efficient as each element is stored in a separate node

Following are the cons:

- Not efficient for random access as elements need to be traversed sequentially
- Extra memory overhead due to storing pointers to the next node
- Requires additional complexity for implementation compared to arrays

2.2.3.3 Stacks

Following are the pros:

- Simple to use and implement
- Easy to understand and maintain a Last-In-First-Out (LIFO) order
- Efficient for adding and removing elements from the top of the stack

Following are the cons:

- Limited functionality as only the top element of the stack can be accessed
- Not efficient for random access or searching
- Not suitable for complex data structures or applications

2.2.3.4 Queues

Following are the pros:

- Simple to use and implement
- Easy to understand and maintain a First-In-First-Out (FIFO) order
- Efficient for adding and removing elements from the front and back of the queue

Following are the cons:

- Limited functionality as only the front and back elements can be accessed
- Not efficient for random access or searching
- Not suitable for complex data structures or applications

2.2.3.5 Trees

Following are the pros:

- Efficient for representing hierarchical relationships

- Can be used to implement various searching and sorting algorithms
- Easy to add or remove nodes dynamically

Following are the cons:

- Complex to implement and understand compared to simpler data structures
- Can be inefficient for storing data that does not have a hierarchical structure
- Requires additional memory overhead due to storing pointers to the parent and child nodes

2.2.3.6 Graphs

Following are the pros:

- Efficient for representing complex relationships between data elements
- Can be used to implement various searching and sorting algorithms
- Provides flexibility for storing and manipulating data in a non-linear manner

Following are the cons:

- Complex to implement and understand compared to simpler data structures
- Requires additional memory overhead due to storing pointers to the nodes and edges
- Can be inefficient for large graphs or complex algorithms

Table 2.1. Benefits and Drawbacks of Different Data Structures (Source: Robert Lafore, Creative Commons License)

Data Structure	Advantages	Disadvantages
Array	Quick insertion and access if the index is known.	Slow deletion, slow search, and fixed size.
Ordered array	Quicker than an unsorted array for searching.	Fixed-size, slow deletion, an insertion.
Stack	Access is last-in, first-out.	Accessing other objects slowly.
Queue	Gives access on a first-in, first-out basis.	Accessing other objects slowly.
Linked list	Quick addition and deletion.	Search slowly.

Binary tree	Quick insertion, search, and deletion (if the tree remains balanced).	Complex deletion algorithm.
Hash table	Fast access if the key is known. Speedy insertion.	Slow deletion, sluggish access if the key is unknown, and inefficient memory consumption.
Heap	Access to the largest item and quick insertion and deletion.	Accessing other objects slowly.

In conclusion, each type of data structure has its own strengths and weaknesses. The choice of data structure depends on the specific application and the types of operations that need to be performed on the data. Choosing the appropriate data structure for a specific task is essential for developing efficient software systems (Herr, 1980; Stock & Watson, 2001).

2.3 ALGORITHMS

Algorithms are a set of step-by-step instructions used to solve a specific problem or perform a specific task. In computer science, algorithms are used to manipulate data structures, perform complex computations, and solve problems that cannot be solved using simple, straightforward methods. There are many different types of algorithms, each with its own advantages and disadvantages. Common types of algorithms include sorting algorithms, searching algorithms, graph algorithms, and dynamic programming algorithms. The study of algorithms is essential for understanding how computers solve problems and for developing efficient software systems (Price, 1973; Berry & Howls, 2012).

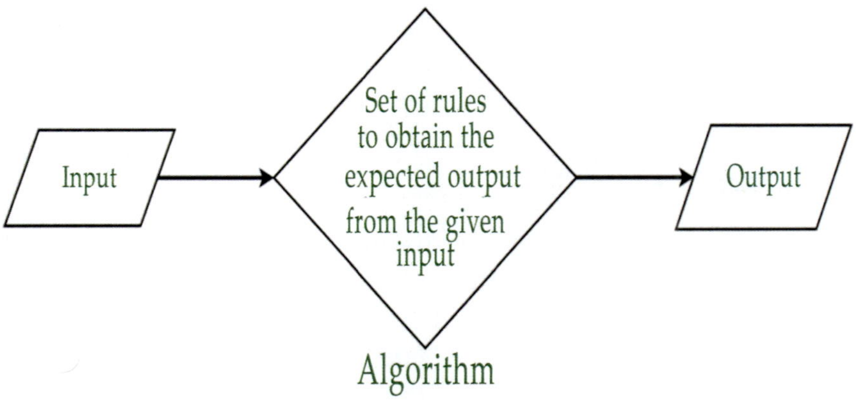

Figure 2.1. Schematic of the algorithm (Source: Geeks for Geeks, Creative Commons License).

An algorithm is a set of instructions designed to solve a specific problem or perform a specific task. It is a finite sequence of well-defined steps that can be executed to produce a desired output from a given input. In computer science, algorithms are used to manipulate data structures, perform complex computations, and solve problems that cannot be solved using simple, straightforward methods. An algorithm can be represented in various forms such as a flowchart, pseudocode, or a computer program (Bellare & Sudan, 1994; Friedl & Sudan, 1995).

Did you Know?

The world's first computer algorithm was written by Ada Lovelace, a mathematician and computer programmer who is widely regarded as the world's first computer programmer.

2.3.1 Types of Algorithms

Following are the types of algorithms:

2.3.1.1 Searching Algorithms

Searching algorithms are used to find the location of a particular element in a data structure. Common searching algorithms include linear search and binary search. Linear search is used for unsorted data structures such as arrays and linked lists, whereas binary search is used for sorted data structures such as arrays. Searching algorithms have different time complexities depending on the type of algorithm and the size of the data structure (Sudan, 1992; Arora & Lund, 1996).

2.3.1.2 Sorting Algorithms

Sorting algorithms are used to arrange the elements of a data structure in a specific order. Common sorting algorithms include bubble sort, insertion sort, selection sort, quicksort, and merge sort. Sorting algorithms have different time complexities depending on the type of algorithm and the size of the data structure. Efficient sorting algorithms are important for organizing data and making it easier to search, access, and analyze (Fredman & Willard, 1993; Raman, 1996).

2.3.1.3 Graph Algorithms

Graph algorithms are used to manipulate and traverse graphs, which are data structures that consist of a collection of nodes (vertices) connected by edges. Common graph algorithms include breadth-first search, depth-first search, Dijkstra's algorithm, and Bellman-Ford algorithm. Graph algorithms are important for solving problems that involve complex relationships between data elements, such as social networks or transportation systems (Polishchuk & Spielman, 1994; Thorup, 1997).

2.3.1.4 Dynamic Programming

Dynamic programming is a technique used to solve complex optimization problems by breaking them down into smaller subproblems and solving each subproblem only once. The solution to each subproblem is stored in memory and used to solve larger subproblems, eventually leading to the solution of the original problem. Dynamic programming is commonly used for problems such as the Knapsack problem, the Traveling Salesman problem, and the Longest Common Subsequence problem (Brodnik et al., 1997).

In conclusion, algorithms are essential for solving complex problems in computer science. Understanding the different types of algorithms and their strengths and weaknesses is important for choosing the appropriate algorithm for a specific problem or task. The study of algorithms is important for developing efficient software systems, as well as for advancing the field of computer science.

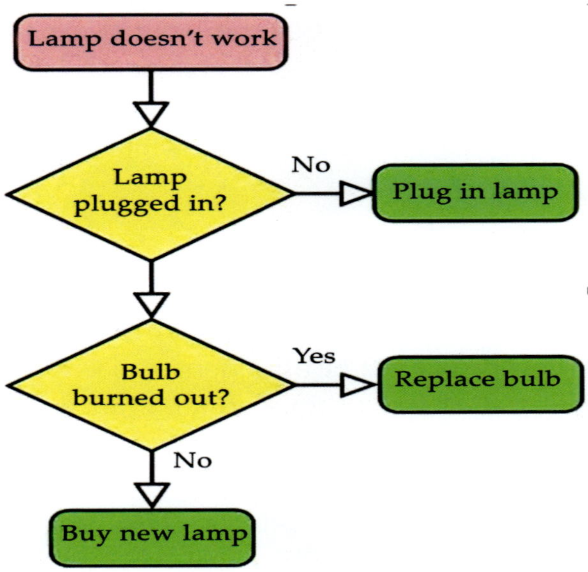

Figure 2.2 . Flowchart of algorithm application (Source: JT Newsome, Creative Commons License).

2.3.2 Complexity Analysis

Complexity analysis is the process of evaluating the efficiency of an algorithm in terms of time and space complexity. Time complexity refers to the amount of time an algorithm takes to complete its task, whereas space complexity refers to the amount of memory an algorithm requires to complete its task. Complexity analysis is important for understanding the efficiency of an algorithm and for choosing the appropriate algorithm for a specific task (Phillips & Westbrook, 1993; Ciurea & Ciupala, 2001).

2.3.2.1 Time Complexity

Time complexity is a measure of the amount of time an algorithm takes to complete its task. It is usually expressed in terms of the input size, which is the number of elements in the input data. The time complexity of an algorithm can be expressed using Big-O notation, which provides an upper bound on the number of operations an algorithm performs as the input size grows. Common time complexity classes include O(1), O(log n), O(n), O(n log n), O(n^2), O(2^n), and O(n!). Algorithms with lower time complexity are generally more efficient than algorithms with higher time complexity (Cheriyan & Hagerup, 1989).

2.3.2.2 Space Complexity

Space complexity is a measure of the amount of memory an algorithm requires to complete its task. It is usually expressed in terms of the input size or the size of the data structure being used. The space complexity of an algorithm can also be expressed using Big-O notation, which provides an upper bound on the amount of memory an algorithm uses as the input size or data structure size grows. Common space complexity classes include O(1), O(n), O(n^2), O(2^n), and O(n!). Algorithms with lower space complexity are generally more memory-efficient than algorithms with higher space complexity.

2.3.2.3 Big-O Notation

Big-O notation is a mathematical notation used to describe the upper bound of the growth rate of a function. In complexity analysis, Big-O notation is used to express the time or space complexity of an algorithm in terms of the input size or data structure size. For example, if an algorithm has a time complexity of O(n^2), it means that the number of operations the algorithm performs is proportional to the square of the input size. Big-O notation provides a simple way to compare the efficiency of different algorithms and to choose the most appropriate algorithm for a specific task (Roura, 2001; Drmota & Szpankowski, 2013).

In conclusion, complexity analysis is an essential tool for evaluating the efficiency of algorithms in terms of time and space complexity. Time complexity measures the amount of time an algorithm takes to complete its task, whereas space complexity measures the amount of memory an algorithm requires to complete its task. Big-O notation is used to express the time or space complexity of an algorithm in terms of the input size or data structure size. Understanding complexity analysis is important for choosing the appropriate algorithm for a specific task and for designing and developing efficient software systems (Igarashi et al., 1987; Park & Oldfield, 1993).

2.3.3 Common Algorithmic Techniques

2.3.3.1 Brute Force

Brute force is a simple algorithmic technique that involves trying every possible solution to a problem until the correct solution is found. It is commonly used for small or simple problems that can be solved in a reasonable amount of time. However, for large or complex problems, brute force can be inefficient and time-consuming. Brute force algorithms have a time complexity of O(2^n) or O(n!) and are often used as a benchmark for evaluating the efficiency of other algorithms.

2.3.3.2 Greedy Algorithms

Greedy algorithms are a type of algorithmic technique that make locally optimal choices at each step in the hope of finding a global optimum. Greedy algorithms are often used for optimization problems such as minimum spanning trees, shortest path algorithms, and scheduling problems. However, greedy algorithms do not always find the global optimum and can be inefficient for certain types of problems. Greedy algorithms have a time complexity of O(n log n) or O(n^2).

2.3.3.3 Divide and Conquer

Divide and conquer is a type of algorithmic technique that involves breaking down a problem into smaller subproblems, solving each subproblem independently, and combining the solutions to the subproblems to solve the original problem. Divide and conquer is often used for problems such as sorting, searching, and matrix multiplication. Divide and conquer algorithms have a time complexity of O(n log n) or O(n^2) depending on the specific algorithm and problem (Glasser & Austin Barron, 1983).

2.3.3.4 Dynamic Programming

Dynamic programming is a type of algorithmic technique that involves breaking down a problem into smaller subproblems and storing the solutions to the subproblems in memory. The solutions to the subproblems are used to solve larger subproblems, eventually leading to the solution of the original problem. Dynamic programming is commonly used for problems such as the Knapsack problem, the

Traveling Salesman problem, and the Longest Common Subsequence problem. Dynamic programming algorithms have a time complexity of O(n^2) or O(n^3) depending on the specific algorithm and problem. In conclusion, there are several common algorithmic techniques used in computer science such as brute force, greedy algorithms, divide and conquer, and dynamic programming. Each technique has its own strengths and weaknesses and is suitable for specific types of problems. Understanding these algorithmic techniques is important for designing and developing efficient software systems and for solving complex problems in computer science (Du & Atallah, 2001; Eppstein et al., 2005).

2.3.4 Pros and Cons of each Algorithm

Here are some pros and cons of each algorithmic technique:

2.3.4.1 Brute Force

Following are the pros:

- Simple to implement and understand
- Can be used for small or simple problems

Following are the cons:

- Inefficient and time-consuming for large or complex problems
- May not find the optimal solution for some problems
- Can require a large amount of memory

2.3.4.2 Greedy Algorithms

Following are the pros:

- Simple to implement and understand
- Can be used for optimization problems

Following are the cons:

- May not always find the global optimum
- Can be inefficient for certain types of problems
- Can be difficult to prove the correctness of the solution

2.3.4.3 Divide and Conquer

Following are the pros:

- Efficient for large or complex problems
- Can be used for problems such as sorting, searching, and matrix multiplication

- Can be parallelized for further optimization

Following are the cons:

- Can require additional memory for storing the solutions to subproblems
- Can be difficult to implement and understand for some problems
- May not be efficient for all types of problems

2.3.4.4 Dynamic Programming

Following are the pros:

- Efficient for problems with overlapping subproblems
- Can be used for problems such as the Knapsack problem, the Traveling Salesman problem, and the Longest Common Subsequence problem
- Can be parallelized for further optimization

Following are the cons:

- Can require additional memory for storing the solutions to subproblems
- Can be difficult to implement and understand for some problems
- May not be efficient for all types of problems

In conclusion, each algorithmic technique has its own strengths and weaknesses. The choice of algorithm depends on the specific problem or task that needs to be solved. Choosing the appropriate algorithmic technique is essential for developing efficient software systems and for solving complex problems in computer science.

2.4 ALGORITHMIC ANALYSIS

Algorithmic analysis is the process of evaluating the efficiency of an algorithm in terms of time and space complexity. It involves analyzing the algorithm to determine how its performance changes as the size of the input data increases. The goal of algorithmic analysis is to determine the worst-case, best-case, and average-case time and space complexity of an algorithm. This information can be used to compare different algorithms and to choose the most efficient algorithm for a specific problem or task. Algorithmic analysis is important for developing efficient software systems and for solving complex problems in computer science (Sardelis &Valahas, 1999; Dickerson et al., 2003).

2.4.1 Analysis of Algorithms

Analysis of algorithms is the process of evaluating the efficiency of an algorithm in terms of time and space complexity. It involves analyzing the algorithm to determine how its performance changes as the size of the input data increases. The goal of algorithmic analysis is to determine the worst-case, best-case, and average-case time and space complexity of an algorithm. This information can be used to compare different algorithms and to choose the most efficient algorithm for a specific problem or task. The most commonly used method for algorithmic analysis is asymptotic analysis, which provides an upper bound on the running time or space usage of an algorithm (Goodrich et al., 2005).

2.4.1.1 Worst-case Analysis

Worst-case analysis is a type of algorithmic analysis that considers the input data that causes the algorithm to take the longest time or require the most space. The worst-case time complexity of an algorithm is the maximum number of operations an algorithm performs on any input of size n. The worst-case space complexity of an algorithm is the maximum amount of memory an algorithm requires to solve any input of size n. Worst-case analysis provides a guaranteed upper bound on the running time or space usage of an algorithm.

2.4.1.2 Average-case Analysis

Average-case analysis is a type of algorithmic analysis that considers the expected time or space usage of an algorithm over all possible inputs of size n. It involves calculating the average number of operations an algorithm performs or the average amount of memory an algorithm requires for a given input size. Average-case analysis requires knowledge of the probability distribution of the input data, which can be difficult to determine in practice. However, average-case analysis can provide a more accurate estimation of the efficiency of an algorithm than worst-case analysis.

2.4.1.3 Best-case Analysis

Best-case analysis is a type of algorithmic analysis that considers the input data that causes the algorithm to take the shortest time or require the least space. The best-case time complexity of an algorithm is the minimum number of operations an algorithm performs on any input of size n. The best-case space complexity of an algorithm is the minimum amount of memory an algorithm requires to solve any input of size n. Best-case analysis is not useful for determining the efficiency of an algorithm in practice, as the best-case scenario may rarely or never occur.

In conclusion, analysis of algorithms is essential for evaluating the efficiency of algorithms in terms of time and space complexity. Worst-case analysis considers the input data that causes the algorithm to take the longest time or require the most space, whereas average-case analysis considers the expected time or space usage of an algorithm over all possible inputs. Best-case analysis considers the input data that causes the algorithm to take the shortest time or require the least space, but is not useful for determining the efficiency of an algorithm in practice. Understanding these types of algorithmic analysis is important for designing and developing efficient software systems and for solving complex problems in computer science (Eppstein et al., 2008; Acar, 2009).

2.4.2 Asymptotic Notation

Asymptotic notation is a mathematical notation used to describe the limiting behavior of a function as the input size or data structure size grows infinitely large. In algorithmic analysis, asymptotic notation is used to express the time or space complexity of an algorithm in terms of the input size or data structure size. Asymptotic notation provides a simple way to compare the efficiency of different algorithms and to choose the most appropriate algorithm for a specific task. The most commonly used types of asymptotic notation in algorithmic analysis are Big-O notation, Omega notation, and Theta notation.

2.4.2.1 Big-O Notation

Big-O notation is a type of asymptotic notation used to describe the upper bound of the growth rate of a function. In complexity analysis, Big-O notation is used to express the time or space complexity of an algorithm in terms of the input size or data structure size. For example, if an algorithm has a time complexity of O(n^2), it means that the number of operations the algorithm performs is proportional to the square of the input size. Big-O notation provides a simple way to compare the efficiency of different algorithms and to choose the most appropriate algorithm for a specific task (Amtoft et al., 2002; Ausiello et al., 2012).

2.4.2.2 Omega Notation

Omega notation is a type of asymptotic notation used to describe the lower bound of the growth rate of a function. In complexity analysis, Omega notation is used to express the best-case time or space complexity of an algorithm in terms of the input size or data structure size. For example, if an algorithm has a best-case time complexity of $\Omega(1)$, it means that the number of operations the algorithm performs is at least proportional to a constant. Omega notation provides a lower bound on the efficiency of an algorithm.

2.4.2.3 Theta Notation

Theta notation is a type of asymptotic notation used to describe both the upper and lower bounds of the growth rate of a function. In complexity analysis, Theta notation is used to express the tight bound of the time or space complexity of an algorithm in terms of the input size or data structure size. For example, if an algorithm has a time complexity of $\Theta(n)$, it means that the number of operations the algorithm performs is proportional to the input size. Theta notation provides a tight bound on the efficiency of an algorithm (Bailey et al., 1991; Baswana et al., 2002). In conclusion, asymptotic notation is an important tool for describing the limiting behavior of functions and for expressing the time or space complexity of algorithms. Big-O notation is used to describe the upper bound of the growth rate of a function, Omega notation is used to describe the lower bound of the growth rate of a function, and Theta notation is used to describe the tight bound of the growth rate of a function. Understanding asymptotic notation is essential for comparing the efficiency of different algorithms and for designing and developing efficient software systems.

ACTIVITY 2.1

Read latest case studies and research papers on data structures and algorithms in order to understand the real-world applications of data structures and algorithms.

2.4.3 Growth Rates of Functions

In algorithmic analysis, growth rates of functions are used to describe the time or space complexity of algorithms in terms of the input size or data structure size. Different types of functions have different growth rates, and the growth rate of a function is determined by the dominant term in the function.

2.4.3.1 Constant Time

Constant time refers to an algorithm that takes the same amount of time or space to complete its task, regardless of the input size. The time or space complexity of an algorithm with constant time is denoted as $O(1)$, indicating that the number of operations the algorithm performs is constant.

2.4.3.2 Logarithmic Time

Logarithmic time refers to an algorithm that takes time or space proportional to the logarithm of the input size to complete its task. The time or space complexity of an algorithm with logarithmic time is denoted as $O(\log n)$, indicating that the number of operations the algorithm performs increases logarithmically with the input size (Blasgen et al., 1977).

2.4.3.3 Linear Time

Linear time refers to an algorithm that takes time or space proportional to the input size to complete its task. The time or space complexity of an algorithm with linear time is denoted as O(n), indicating that the number of operations the algorithm performs increases linearly with the input size.

2.4.3.4 Quadratic Time

Quadratic time refers to an algorithm that takes time or space proportional to the square of the input size to complete its task. The time or space complexity of an algorithm with quadratic time is denoted as O(n^2), indicating that the number of operations the algorithm performs increases quadratically with the input size.

2.4.3.5 Exponential Time

Exponential time refers to an algorithm that takes time or space proportional to a constant raised to the power of the input size to complete its task. The time or space complexity of an algorithm with exponential time is denoted as O(c^n), where c is a constant greater than 1. Exponential time algorithms are generally considered to be inefficient and impractical for most real-world problems (Blelloch & Gibbons, 2004).

In conclusion, understanding the growth rates of functions is important for algorithmic analysis and for choosing the most efficient algorithm for a specific task. Constant time algorithms have the fastest growth rate, followed by logarithmic time, linear time, quadratic time, and exponential time. Choosing an algorithm with a lower growth rate can significantly improve the efficiency of a software system.

SUMMARY

The chapter on Fundamentals of Data Structures and Algorithms provides an introduction to the essential concepts and techniques used in computer science to design and analyze algorithms and data structures. The chapter starts with an explanation of data structures, including definitions and types such as arrays, linked lists, stacks, queues, trees, and graphs. It then discusses the operations on these data structures, such as traversals, insertions, deletions, searching, and sorting. The pros and cons of each data structure are also outlined. The chapter then covers the basic types of algorithms, including searching algorithms, sorting algorithms, graph algorithms, and dynamic programming. Each type of algorithm is explained in detail, including their strengths and weaknesses. The chapter also covers algorithmic analysis, including worst-case analysis, average-case analysis, and best-case analysis. It explains the different types of asymptotic notation, including Big-O notation, Omega notation, and Theta notation, used to describe the time and space complexity of algorithms. Lastly, the chapter covers common algorithmic techniques, such as brute force, greedy algorithms, divide and conquer, and dynamic programming. Each technique is discussed in detail, including their strengths and weaknesses. Overall, the chapter on Fundamentals of Data Structures and Algorithms provides a solid foundation for understanding the essential concepts and techniques used in computer science to design and analyze algorithms and data structures. This knowledge is essential for designing and developing efficient software systems and for solving complex problems in computer science.

REVIEW QUESTIONS

1. What are data structures, and why are they important in computer science?
2. What are the basic types of data structures, and what are the operations that can be performed on them?
3. What are the basic types of algorithms, and what are their strengths and weaknesses?
4. What is algorithmic analysis, and what are the different types of analysis that can be performed?
5. What is asymptotic notation, and how is it used to describe the time and space complexity of algorithms?
6. What are the common algorithmic techniques, and when is each technique best used?
7. What are the pros and cons of different data structures and algorithms, and how can they be evaluated for a specific problem?
8. How can the concepts and techniques learned in this chapter be applied to design and analyze algorithms and data structures for real-world problems in computer science?

MULTIPLE CHOICE QUESTIONS

1. **What is the best-case time complexity of an algorithm?**
   a. The maximum number of operations an algorithm performs on any input of size n
   b. The minimum number of operations an algorithm performs on any input of size n
   c. The expected time an algorithm takes to complete on any input of size n
   d. The average number of operations an algorithm performs on any input of size n
2. **Which data structure provides constant time access to its elements?**
   a. Linked List
   b. Queue
   c. Stack
   d. Array
3. **Which algorithmic technique makes the locally optimal choice at each step in the hope of finding a global optimum?**
   a. Brute Force
   b. Greedy Algorithm
   c. Divide and Conquer
   d. Dynamic Programming
4. **What is the worst-case time complexity of an algorithm?**
   a. The maximum number of operations an algorithm performs on any input of size n
   b. The minimum number of operations an algorithm performs on any input of size n
   c. The expected time an algorithm takes to complete on any input of size n
   d. The average number of operations an algorithm performs on any input of size n
5. **Which type of algorithm has a best-case time complexity of O(1)?**
   a. Linear Search
   b. Binary Search
   c. Bubble Sort
   d. Insertion Sort
6. **What is the growth rate of an algorithm with quadratic time complexity?**
   a. O(n)
   b. O(n log n)
   c. O(n^2)
   d. O(2^n)

7. Which type of asymptotic notation is used to describe the upper bound of the growth rate of a function?

a. Big-O Notation

b. Omega Notation

c. Theta Notation

d. None of the above

Answers to Multiple Choice Questions

1. (b) 2. (d) 3. (b) 4. (a) 5. (b)

6. (c) 7. (a)

REFERENCES

1. Abramowitz, M., & Stegun, I. A., (1965). *Handbook of Mathematical Functions with Formulas, Graphs, and Mathematical Table* (Vol. 2172, pp. 1–23). New York: Dover.
2. Acar, U. A., (2009). Self-adjusting computation: An overview. In: *Proceedings of the 2009 ACM SIGPLAN Workshop on Partial Evaluation and Program Manipulation* (pp. 1–6). ACM.
3. Ahuja, R. K., & Orlin, J. B., (1989). A fast and simple algorithm for the maximum flow problem. *Operations Research, 37*(5), 748–759.
4. Ahuja, R. K., Orlin, J. B., & Tarjan, R. E., (1989). Improved time bounds for the maximum flow problem. *SIAM Journal on Computing, 18*(5), 939–954.
5. Ajtai, M., Megiddo, N., & Waarts, O., (2001). Improved algorithms and analysis for secretary problems and generalizations. *SIAM Journal on Discrete Mathematics, 14*(1), 1–27.
6. Aki, S. G., (1989). *The Design and Analysis of Parallel Algorithms, 1*, 10.
7. Akra, M., & Bazzi, L., (1998). On the solution of linear recurrence equations. *Computational Optimization and Applications, 10*(2), 195–210.
8. Alon, N., (1990). Generating pseudo-random permutations and maximum flow algorithms. *Information Processing Letters, 35*(4), 201–204.
9. Amir, A., Aumann, Y., Benson, G., Levy, A., Lipsky, O., Porat, E., & Vishne, U., (2006). Pattern matching with address errors: Rearrangement distances. In: *Proceedings of the Seventeenth Annual ACM-SIAM Symposium on Discrete Algorithm* (Vol. 1, pp. 1221–1229). Society for Industrial and Applied Mathematics.
10. Amtoft, T., Consel, C., Danvy, O., & Malmkjær, K., (2002). The abstraction and instantiation of string-matching programs. In: *The Essence of Computation* (pp. 332–357). Springer, Berlin, Heidelberg.
11. Andersson, A. A., & Thorup, M., (2000). Tight(er) worst-case bounds on dynamic

searching and priority queues. In: *Proceedings of the Thirty-Second Annual ACM Symposium on Theory of Computing* (Vol. 1, pp. 335–342). ACM.

12. Arge, L., (2001). External memory data structures. In: *European Symposium on Algorithms* (pp. 1–29). Springer, Berlin, Heidelberg.
13. Arora, S., & Lund, C., (1996). Hardness of approximations. In: *Approximation Algorithms for NP-Hard Problems* (pp. 399–446). PWS Publishing Co.
14. Arora, S., (1994). *Probabilistic Checking of Proofs and Hardness of Approximation Problems*. Doctoral dissertation, Princeton University, Department of Computer Science.
15. Arora, S., Lund, C., Motwani, R., Sudan, M., & Szegedy, M., (1998). Proof verification and the hardness of approximation problems. *Journal of the ACM (JACM), 45*(3), 501–555.
16. Aslam, J. A., (2001). *A Simple Bound on the Expected Height of a Randomly Built Binary Search Tree*, 1(1), 5-10.
17. Ausiello, G., Crescenzi, P., Gambosi, G., Kann, V., Marchetti-Spaccamela, A., & Protasi, M., (2012). *Complexity and Approximation: Combinatorial Optimization Problems and Their Approximability Properties*. Springer Science & Business Media.
18. Avidan, S., & Shamir, A., (2007). Seam carving for content-aware image resizing. In: *ACM Transactions on Graphics (TOG)* (Vol. 26, No. 3, p. 10). ACM.
19. Babaioff, M., Immorlica, N., Kempe, D., & Kleinberg, R., (2007). A knapsack secretary problem with applications. In: *Approximation, Randomization, and Combinatorial Optimization; Algorithms and Techniques* (pp. 16–28). Springer, Berlin, Heidelberg.
20. Bach, E., & Shallit, J. O., (1996). *Algorithmic Number Theory: Efficient Algorithms* (Vol. 1). MIT press.
21. Bach, E., (1990). Number-theoretic algorithms. *Annual Review of Computer Science, 4*(1), 119–172.
22. Bailey, D. H., Lee, K., & Simon, H. D., (1991). Using Strassen's algorithm to accelerate the solution of linear systems. *The Journal of Supercomputing, 4*(4), 357–371.
23. Bakker, M., Riezebos, J., & Teunter, R. H., (2012). Review of inventory systems with deterioration since 2001. *European Journal of Operational Research, 221*(2), 275–284.
24. Baswana, S., Hariharan, R., & Sen, S., (2002). Improved decremental algorithms for maintaining transitive closure and all-pairs shortest paths. In: *Proceedings of the Thirty-Fourth Annual ACM Symposium on Theory of Computing* (pp. 117–123). ACM.
25. Bateni, M., Hajiaghayi, M., & Zadimoghaddam, M., (2010). Submodular secretary problem and extensions. In: *Approximation, Randomization, and Combinatorial Optimization; Algorithms and Techniques* (pp. 39–52). Springer, Berlin, Heidelberg.
26. Bayer, R., (1972). Symmetric binary B-trees: Data structure and maintenance algorithms. *Acta Informatica, 1*(4), 290–306.
27. Beauchemin, P., Brassard, G., Crépeau, C., Goutier, C., & Pomerance, C., (1988).

The generation of random numbers that are probably prime. *Journal of Cryptology, 1*(1), 53–64.

28. Bellare, M., & Sudan, M., (1994). Improved non-approximability results. In: *Proceedings of the Twenty-Sixth Annual ACM Symposium on Theory of Computing* (pp. 184–193). ACM.
29. Bender, M. A., Demaine, E. D., & Farach-Colton, M., (2000). Cache-oblivious B-trees. In: *Foundations of Computer Science, 2000; Proceedings 41st Annual Symposium* (pp. 399–409). IEEE.
30. Ben-Or, M., (1983). Lower bounds for algebraic computation trees. In: *Proceedings of the Fifteenth Annual ACM Symposium on Theory of Computing* (pp. 80–86). ACM.
31. Bent, S. W., & John, J. W., (1985). Finding the median requires 2n comparisons. In: *Proceedings of the Seventeenth Annual ACM Symposium on Theory of Computing* (pp. 213–216). ACM.
32. Bentley, J. L., Haken, D., & Saxe, J. B., (1980). A general method for solving divide-and-conquer recurrences. *ACM SIGACT News, 12*(3), 36–44.
33. Berger, J., & Barkaoui, M., (2004). A parallel hybrid genetic algorithm for the vehicle routing problem with time windows. *Computers & Operations Research, 31*(12), 2037–2053.
34. Berry, M. V., & Howls, C. J., (2012). *Integrals with Coalescing Saddles, 36*, 775–793.
35. Bienstock, D., & McClosky, B., (2012). Tightening simple mixed-integer sets with guaranteed bounds. *Mathematical Programming, 133*(1), 337–363.
36. Bienstock, D., (2008). Approximate formulations for 0-1 knapsack sets. *Operations Research Letters, 36*(3), 317–320.
37. Blasgen, M. W., Casey, R. G., & Eswaran, K. P., (1977). An encoding method for multifield sorting and indexing. *Communications of the ACM, 20*(11), 874–878.
38. Blelloch, G. E., & Gibbons, P. B., (2004). Effectively sharing a cache among threads. In: *Proceedings of the Sixteenth Annual ACM Symposium on Parallelism in Algorithms and Architectures* (pp. 235–244). ACM.
39. Blelloch, G. E., & Greiner, J., (1996). A provable time and space efficient implementation of NESL. In: *ACM SIGPLAN Notices* (Vol. 31, No. 6, pp. 213–225). ACM.
40. Blelloch, G. E., & Maggs, B. M., (1996). Parallel algorithms. *ACM Computing Surveys (CSUR), 28*(1), 51–54.
41. Blelloch, G. E., Hardwick, J. C., Sipelstein, J., Zagha, M., & Chatterjee, S., (1994). Implementation of a portable nested data-parallel language. *Journal of Parallel and Distributed Computing, 21*(1), 4–14.
42. Bloom, N., & Van, R. J., (2002). Patents, real options and firm performance. *The Economic Journal, 112*(478).
43. Blumofe, R. D., & Leiserson, C. E., (1999). Scheduling multithreaded computations by work stealing. *Journal of the ACM (JACM), 46*(5), 720–748.

44. Bollerslev, T., Engle, R. F., & Nelson, D. B., (1994). ARCH models. *Handbook of Econometrics, 4*, 2959–3038.
45. Brassard, G., & Bratley, P., (1996). *Fundamentals of Algorithmics* (Vol. 33). Englewood Cliffs: Prentice Hall.
46. Brent, R. P., (1974). The parallel evaluation of general arithmetic expressions. *Journal of the ACM (JACM), 21*(2), 201–206.
47. Brodnik, A., Miltersen, P. B., & Munro, J. I., (1997). Trans-dichotomous algorithms without multiplication—Some upper and lower bounds. In: *Workshop on Algorithms and Data Structures* (pp. 426–439). Springer, Berlin, Heidelberg.
48. Buchbinder, N., Jain, K., & Singh, M., (2010). Secretary problems via linear programming. In: *International Conference on Integer Programming and Combinatorial Optimization* (pp. 163–176). Springer, Berlin, Heidelberg.
49. Buhler, J. P., Lenstra, H. W., & Pomerance, C., (1993). Factoring integers with the number field sieve. In: *The Development of the Number Field Sieve* (pp. 50–94). Springer, Berlin, Heidelberg.
50. CHAN, T. H., (2000). HOMFLY polynomials of some generalized Hopf links. *Journal of Knot Theory and Its Ramifications, 9*(07), 865–883.
51. Chen, L. T., & Davis, L. S., (1990). A parallel algorithm for list ranking image curves in O (log N) time. In: *DARPA Image Understanding Workshop* (pp. 805–815).
52. Cheriyan, J., & Hagerup, T., (1989). A randomized maximum-flow algorithm. In: *Foundations of Computer Science, 1989., 30th Annual Symposium* (pp. 118–123). IEEE.
53. Cheriyan, J., & Hagerup, T., (1995). A randomized maximum-flow algorithm. *SIAM Journal on Computing, 24*(2), 203–226.
54. Cheriyan, J., Hagerup, T., & Mehlhorn, K., (1990). Can a maximum flow be computed in o (nm) time? In: *International Colloquium on Automata, Languages, and Programming* (pp. 235–248). Springer, Berlin, Heidelberg.
55. Cheriyan, J., Hagerup, T., & Mehlhorn, K., (1996). An o(n^3)-time maximum-flow algorithm. *SIAM Journal on Computing, 25*(6), 1144–1170.
56. Ciurea, E., & Ciupala, L., (2001). Algorithms for minimum flows. *Computer Science Journal of Moldova, 9*(3), 27.
57. Conforti, M., Wolsey, L. A., & Zambelli, G., (2010). Projecting an extended formulation for mixed-integer covers on bipartite graphs. *Mathematics of Operations Research, 35*(3), 603–623.
58. Courcoubetis, C., Vardi, M., Wolper, P., & Yannakakis, M., (1992). Memory-efficient algorithms for the verification of temporal properties. *Formal Methods in System Design, 1*(2, 3), 275–288.
59. D'Aristotile, A., Diaconis, P., & Newman, C. M., (2003). Brownian motion and the classical groups. *Lecture Notes-Monograph Series*, 97–116.
60. Damgård, I., Landrock, P., & Pomerance, C., (1993). Average case error estimates

for the strong probable prime test. *Mathematics of Computation, 61*(203), 177–194.

61. Dehling, H., & Philipp, W., (2002). Empirical process techniques for dependent data. In: *Empirical Process Techniques for Dependent Data* (pp. 3–113). Birkhäuser, Boston, MA.
62. Dengiz, B., Altiparmak, F., & Smith, A. E., (1997). Efficient optimization of all-terminal reliable networks, using an evolutionary approach. *IEEE Transactions on Reliability, 46*(1), 18–26.
63. Dickerson, M., Eppstein, D., Goodrich, M. T., & Meng, J. Y., (2003). Confluent drawings: Visualizing non-planar diagrams in a planar way. In: *International Symposium on Graph Drawing* (pp. 1–12). Springer, Berlin, Heidelberg.
64. Didier, F., (2009). *Efficient Erasure Decoding of Reed-Solomon Codes* (Vol. 1, pp. 1–22). arXiv preprint arXiv:0901.1886.
65. Drmota, M., & Szpankowski, W., (2013). A master theorem for discrete divide and conquer recurrences. *Journal of the ACM (JACM), 60*(3), 16.
66. Du, W., & Atallah, M. J., (2001). Protocols for secure remote database access with approximate matching. In: *E-Commerce Security and Privacy* (pp. 87–111). Springer, Boston, MA.
67. Duda, R. O., Hart, P. E., & Stork, D. G., (1973). *Pattern Classification* (Vol. 2). New York: Wiley.
68. Eppstein, D., Goodrich, M. T., & Sun, J. Z., (2005). The skip quadtree: A simple dynamic data structure for multidimensional data. In: *Proceedings of the Twenty-First Annual Symposium on Computational Geometry* (pp. 296–305). ACM.
69. Eppstein, D., Goodrich, M. T., & Sun, J. Z., (2008). Skip quadtrees: Dynamic data structures for multidimensional point sets. *International Journal of Computational Geometry & Applications, 18*(1, 2), 131–160.
70. Faenza, Y., & Sanità, L., (2015). On the existence of compact ε-approximated formulations for knapsack in the original space. *Operations Research Letters, 43*(3), 339–342.
71. Festa, P., & Resende, M. G., (2002). GRASP: An annotated bibliography. In: *Essays and Surveys in Metaheuristics* (Vol. 1, pp. 325–367). Springer, Boston, MA.
72. Fourier, J. B. J., (1890). From Works of Fourier, G. Darboux Gauthier-Villars, Paris,2, 38–42.
73. Fourier, J.B.J. (1973). report in: "Analysis of the work of the Royal Academy of Sciences of the Institut de France" 7 (1827) xlvii-lv. Partial English translation in: DA Kohler," translation of a Report by Fourier on his work on Linear Inequalities", Opsearch, 10, 38-42.
74. Fredman, M. L., & Willard, D. E., (1993). Surpassing the information theoretic bound with fusion trees. *Journal of Computer and System Sciences, 47*(3), 424–436.
75. Friedl, K., & Sudan, M., (1995). Some improvements to total degree tests. In: *Theory of Computing and Systems, 1995; Proceedings Third Israel Symposium* (pp. 190–198). IEEE.

76. Frigo, M., Leiserson, C. E., & Randall, K. H., (1998). The implementation of the cilk-5 multithreaded language. *ACM Sigplan Notices, 33*(5), 212–223.
77. Fussenegger, F., & Gabow, H. N., (1979). A counting approach to lower bounds for selection problems. *Journal of the ACM (JACM), 26*(2), 227–238.
78. Glasser, K. S., & Austin, B. R. H., (1983). The d choice secretary problem. *Sequential Analysis, 2*(3), 177–199.
79. Goodrich, M. T., Atallah, M. J., & Tamassia, R., (2005). Indexing information for data forensics. In: *International Conference on Applied Cryptography and Network Security* (pp. 206–221). Springer, Berlin, Heidelberg.
80. Graefe, G., (2011). Modern B-tree techniques. *Foundations and Trends® in Databases, 3*(4), 203–402.
81. Hall, M., Frank, E., Holmes, G., Pfahringer, Badel'son-Vel'skii, G. M., & Landis, E. M., (1962). *Partial Differential Equations of Elliptic Type* (Vol. 1, pp. 1–22). Springer, Berlin.
82. Herr, D. G., (1980). On the history of the use of geometry in the general linear model. *The American Statistician, 34*(1), 43–47.
83. Icking, C., Klein, R., & Ottmann, T., (1987). Priority search trees in secondary memory. In: *International Workshop on Graph-Theoretic Concepts in Computer Science* (pp. 84–93). Springer, Berlin, Heidelberg.
84. IGARASHI, Y., SADO, K., & SAGA, K., (1987). Fast parallel sorts on a practical sized mesh-connected processor array. *IEICE Transactions (1976–1990), 70*(1), 56–64.
85. John, J. W., (1988). A new lower bound for the set-partitioning problem. *SIAM Journal on Computing, 17*(4), 640–647.
86. Kim, S. H., & Pomerance, C., (1989). The probability that a random probable prime is composite. *Mathematics of Computation, 53*(188), 721–741.
87. King, D. J., (1995). Functional binomial queues. In: *Functional Programming, Glasgow 1994* (Vol. 1, pp. 141–150). Springer, London.
88. Kirkpatrick, D. G., (1981). A unified lower bound for selection and set partitioning problems. *Journal of the ACM (JACM), 28*(1), 150–165.
89. Kwong, Y. S., & Wood, D., (1982). A new method for concurrency in B-trees. *IEEE Transactions on Software Engineering,* (3), 211–222.
90. Leighton, T., (1996). *Notes on Better Master Theorems for Divide-and-Conquer Recurrences.* Manuscript. Massachusetts Institute of Technology.
91. Maurer, S. B., (1985). The lessons of Williamstown. In: *New Directions in Two-Year College Mathematics* (Vol. 1, pp. 255–270). Springer, New York, NY.
92. Meijer, H., & Akl, S. G., (1987). Optimal computation of prefix sums on a binary tree of processors. *International Journal of Parallel Programming, 16*(2), 127–136.
93. Meijer, H., & Akl, S. G., (1988). Bit serial addition trees and their applications. *Computing, 40*(1), 9–17.

94. Monier, L., (1980). Evaluation and comparison of two efficient probabilistic primality testing algorithms. *Theoretical Computer Science, 12*(1), 97–108.

95. Morain, F., (1988). *Implementation of the Atkin-Goldwasser-Kilian Primality Testing Algorithm.* Doctoral dissertation, INRI).

96. Munro, J. I., & Poblete, P. V., (1982). *A Lower Bound for Determining the Median.* Faculty of Mathematics, University of Waterloo.

97. Nelson, D. B., & Foster, D. P., (1992). *Filtering and Forecasting with Misspecified ARCH Models II: Making the Right Forecast with the Wrong Model*, 67(2), 303-335.

98. Nievergelt, J., (1974). Binary search trees and file organization. *ACM Computing Surveys (CSUR), 6*(3), 195–207.

99. Park, T. G., & Oldfield, J. V., (1993). Minimum spanning tree generation with content-addressable memory. *Electronics Letters, 29*(11), 1037–1039.

100. Phillips, S., & Westbrook, J., (1993). Online load balancing and network flow. In: *Proceedings of the Twenty-Fifth Annual ACM Symposium on Theory of Computing* (pp. 402–411). ACM.

101. Polishchuk, A., & Spielman, D. A., (1994). Nearly-linear size holographic proofs. In: *Proceedings of the Twenty-Sixth Annual ACM Symposium on Theory of Computing* (pp. 194–203). ACM.

102. Prechelt, L., (1993). *Measurements of MasPar MP-1216A Communication Operations.* Univ., Fak. für Informatik.

103. Price, G. B., (1973). Telescoping sums and the summation of sequences. *The Two-Year College Mathematics Journal, 4*(2), 16–29.

104. Ramadge, P. J., & Wonham, W. M., (1989). The control of discrete event systems. *Proceedings of the IEEE, 77*(1), 81–98.

105. Raman, R., (1996). Priority queues: Small, monotone and trans-dichotomous. In: *European Symposium on Algorithms* (pp. 121–137). Springer, Berlin, Heidelberg.

106. Regli, W. C., (1992). *A Survey of Automated Feature Recognition Techniques, 1*, 1–22.

107. Roura, S., (2001). Improved master theorems for divide-and-conquer recurrences. *Journal of the ACM (JACM), 48*(2), 170–205.

108. Sardelis, D. A., & Valahas, T. M., (1999). Decision making: A golden rule. *The American Mathematical Monthly, 106*(3), 215–226.

109. Schönhage, A., Paterson, M., & Pippenger, N., (1976). Finding the median. *Journal of Computer and System Sciences, 13*(2), 184–199.

110. Shen, Z., & Marston, C. M., (1995). A study of a dice problem. *Applied Mathematics and Computation, 73*(2, 3), 231–247.

111. Smith, R. S., (1986). Rolle over Lagrange—Another shot at the mean value theorem. *The College Mathematics Journal, 17*(5), 403–406.

112. Snyder, L., (1984). *Parallel Programming and the Poker Programming Environment*

(No. TR-84-04-02, pp. 1–30). Washington Univ Seattle Dept of Computer Science.

113. Stock, J. H., & Watson, M. W., (2001). Vector autoregressions. *Journal of Economic Perspectives, 15*(4), 101–115.
114. Sudan, M., (1992). Efficient checking of polynomials and proofs and the hardness of approximation problems. *Lecture Notes in Computer Science*, 1001.
115. Szymanski, T. G., & Van, W. C. J., (1983). Space efficient algorithms for VLSI artwork analysis. In: *Proceedings of the 20th Design Automation Conference* (pp. 734–739). IEEE Press.
116. Szymanski, T. G., (1975). *A Special Case of the Maximal Common Subsequence Problem*. Technical Report TR-170, Computer Science Laboratory, Princeton University.
117. Thorup, M., (1997). *Faster Deterministic Sorting and Priority Queues in Linear Space* (pp. 550–555). Max-Planck-Institut für Informatik.
118. Vanderbei, R. J., (1980). The optimal choice of a subset of a population. *Mathematics of Operations Research, 5*(4), 481–486.
119. Verma, R. M., (1994). A general method and a master theorem for divide-and-conquer recurrences with applications. *Journal of Algorithms, 16*(1), 67–79.
120. Verma, R. M., (1997). General techniques for analyzing recursive algorithms with applications. *SIAM Journal on Computing, 26*(2), 568–581.
121. Wallace, L., Keil, M., & Rai, A., (2004). Understanding software project risk: A cluster analysis. *Information & Management, 42*(1), 115–125.
122. Wang, Y., (2008). Topology control for wireless sensor networks. In: *Wireless Sensor Networks and Applications* (Vol. 1, pp. 113–147). Springer, Boston, MA.
123. Wilf, H. S., (1984). A bijection in the theory of derangements. *Mathematics Magazine, 57*(1), 37–40.
124. Williamson, J., (2002). Probability logic. In: *Studies in Logic and Practical Reasoning* (Vol. 1, pp. 397–424). Elsevier.
125. Wilson, J. G., (1991). Optimal choice and assignment of the best m of n randomly arriving items. *Stochastic Processes and Their Applications, 39*(2), 325–343.
126. Winograd, S., (1970). On the algebraic complexity of functions. In: *Actes du Congres International des Mathématiciens* (Vol. 3, pp. 283–288).
127. Wunderlich, M. C., (1983). A performance analysis of a simple prime-testing algorithm. *Mathematics of Computation, 40*(162), 709–714.
128. Xiaodong, W., & Qingxiang, F., (1996). A frame for general divide-and-conquer recurrences. *Information Processing Letters, 59*(1), 45–51.
129. Yap, C., (2011). A real elementary approach to the master recurrence and generalizations. In: *International Conference on Theory and Applications of Models of Computation* (pp. 14–26). Springer, Berlin, Heidelberg.
130. Zhu, X., & Wilhelm, W. E., (2006). Scheduling and lot sizing with sequence-dependent setup: A literature review. *IIE Transactions, 38*(11), 987–1007.

CHAPTER 3

OPERATING SYSTEMS

UNIT INTRODUCTION

An Operating System (OS) is a collection of software that manages the execution of application programs and serves as a mediator between a computer user and the computer hardware. The Operating System (OS) is a type of software responsible for managing the computer hardware and creating a platform for the execution of application programs. Operating Systems (OS) such as Windows, Windows/NT, OS/2, and MacOS are commonly used in computing (Stankovic & Rajkumar, 2004) (Figure 3.1).

The primary aim of an operating system (OS) is:

1. To enhance the user experience by providing a user-friendly and accessible computer system.
2. To optimize the utilization of computer hardware resources.
3. To facilitate the resolution of user issues.

The computer system can be categorized into four components: hardware, operating system, application programs, and users. Figure 3.1 depicts the abstract representation of the system components.

1. The hardware components of a computer system include the central processing unit (CPU), memory, and input/output (I/O) devices.

2. The operating system is a crucial component that facilitates the efficient utilization of hardware in computer operations, analogous to the role of a government.
3. Application programs are designed to address users' computing issues, including Compilers, database systems, and web browsers.
4. In computing, "users" refers to individuals, devices, or other computer systems interacting with a given system or network.

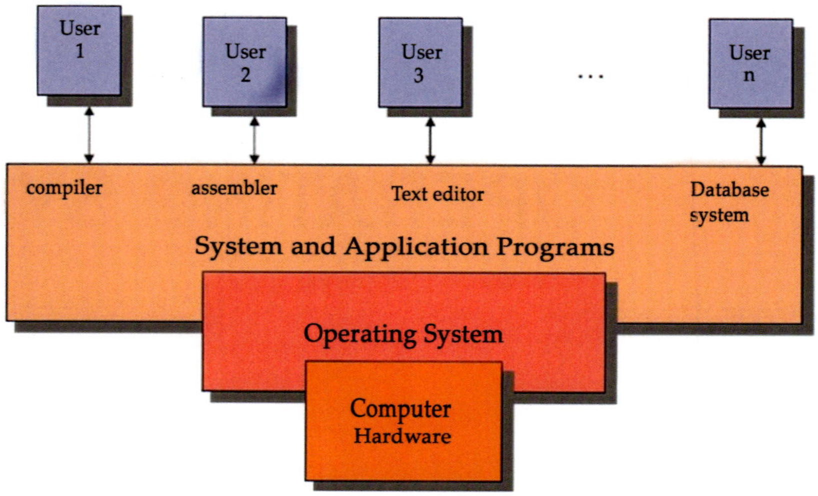

Figure 3.1. Schematic of the computer systems (Source: Qasim Mohammed Hussein, Creative Commons License).

Learning Objectives

After this chapter, readers will understand the following:

- Understand the operation of a computer system
- Acquire knowledge of the storage architecture of operating systems
- Describe the operating system functions
- Identify and describe the various operating system types
- Differentiate and describe the computer and mobile device operating systems
- Identify and explain the operating system components
- Selecting the optimal operating system for the enterprise

Key Terms

- Operating System
- Storage Structure
- Computer Operating System

- Smartphone Operating System
- Kernel
- User Interface
- Virtual Memory
- File Management
- Distributed Systems

3.1. COMPUTER-SYSTEM OPERATION

A contemporary computer system that serves various purposes comprises one or multiple central processing units (CPUs) and several device controllers that are interconnected through a unified bus, which facilitates access to shared memory (as depicted in Figure 3.2). Every device controller manages a distinct category of devices, such as disk drives, audio devices, and video displays. The central processing unit (CPU) and the device controllers can perform simultaneous execution, resulting in competition for memory cycles. To maintain organized access to the shared memory, a memory controller is employed to synchronize the access to said memory (Austin et al., 2002).

For a computer to initiate its operations, such as during power-up or reboot, it must possess an initial program to execute. This initial program, or bootstrap program, tends to be simple. The customary practice is to retain it in read-only memory (ROM) or "electrically erasable programmable read-only memory" (EEPROM), which is collectively referred to as firmware situated within the computer hardware. The process initializes all system components, including but not limited to the CPU registers, device controllers, and memory contents. The bootstrap program must possess the knowledge of loading the operating system and commencing the execution of a said system. To achieve this objective, the bootstrap routine is required to identify and retrieve the operating system kernel, loading it into the system's memory. Subsequently, the operating system initiates the execution of the foremost process, denoted as "init." It remains in a state of anticipation for a specific event (Rosenblum et al., 1995) (Figure 3.2).

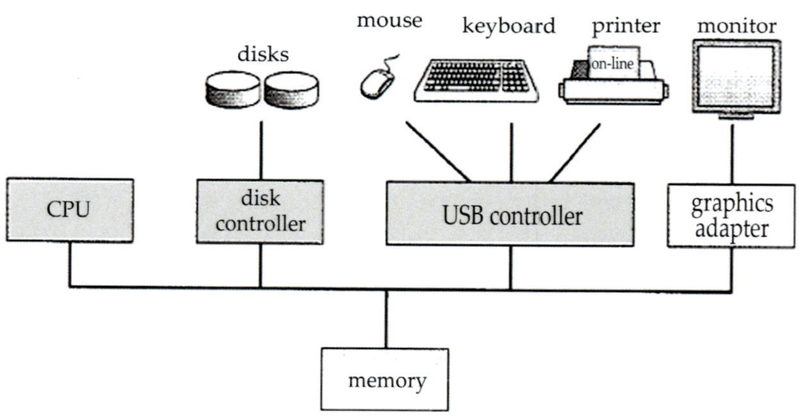

Figure 3.2. Illustration of a modern computer system (Source: Tikrit University, Creative Commons License).

3.2. STORAGE STRUCTURE

To execute computer programs, they must reside in the primary memory, commonly referred to as Random Access Memory (RAM). The processor has direct access to the main memory, the sole significant storage area. An array of memory words is generated. Every individual word possesses a unique address. Interaction is accomplished by executing load or store instructions that target particular memory locations. The load instruction facilitates the transfer of a word from the primary memory to an internal register within the central processing unit. Conversely, the store instruction enables the transfer of the contents of a register to the primary memory (Pereira et al., 2009).

The instruction-execution cycle encompasses the following components:

1. The process involves retrieving an instruction from memory and storing it in the instruction register. Furthermore, it is necessary to increase the program counter register.
2. Encoding instructions may result in the retrieval of operands from memory and their storage in an internal register.
3. Perform the given command and save the output in the computer's storage.

The programs and data are not permanently stored in main memory due to two reasons:

1. The main memory capacity is often insufficient to accommodate all the required programs and data. The data is permanently stored.
2. Main memory is a type of storage device that is volatile in nature, meaning that it tends to lose its stored data when the power supply is turned off or lost due to other reasons.

Most computer systems offer secondary storage to permanently expand primary memory to store substantial amounts of data (Zhai et al., 2016).

The organization of storage systems in a computer system can be structured hierarchically, as depicted in Figure 3.3. The primary distinctions among diverse storage systems pertain to their velocity, expense, magnitude, and susceptibility to volatility. Although the upper tiers have a higher price tag, they offer faster performance (Sharda et al., 2006) (Figure 3.3).

TIPS

Restarting your computer regularly can help keep it running smoothly and prevent performance issues.

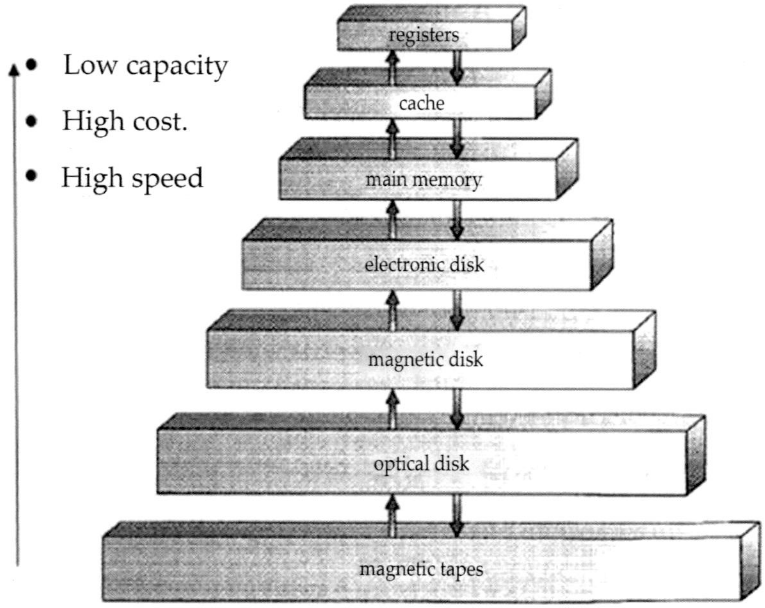

Figure 3.3. Schematic of Storage device hierarchy (Source: Tikrit University, Creative Commons License).

The computer system comprises central processing units (CPUs), and several device controllers interconnected via a shared bus. The device controller facilitates data transfer between the peripheral devices under its jurisdiction and the local buffer storage it manages. It is customary for operating systems to possess a device driver designated for every device controller (Dropsho et al., 2002).

Initiating an input/output operation involves loading relevant registers within the device controller by the device driver. The device's controller scrutinizes the contents of said registers to ascertain the appropriate course of action. The controller initiates the process of data transfer from the device to its local buffer. Upon data transfer completion, the device controller notifies the device driver through an interrupt, indicating the conclusion of its operation. Subsequently, the device driver relinquishes command to the operating system. The device driver provides status information for additional operations (Befikadu, 2014).

Direct Memory Access (DMA) transfers large amounts of data. Upon configuring buffers, pointers, and counters for the input/output (I/O) device, the controller autonomously moves a complete data block to or from its designated buffer storage to memory, without requiring involvement from the central processing unit (CPU). A solitary interrupt is produced for each block to notify the device driver that the operation has been finalized, as opposed to the multiple interrupts per byte generated for low-speed devices (Zhu et al., 2019). Computer systems can be categorized based on the number of processors utilized in their design:

1. A solitary central processing unit is responsible for executing instructions in a single-processor system.
2. A multiprocessor system comprises multiple processors that share a bus, clock, physical memory, and peripheral devices. Multiprocessors offer several benefits, such as:
   i) Enhance the rate of output.
   ii) Economy scale refers to the reduction in cost per unit of production as the volume of output increases.
   iii) Increases its reliability.
3. A clustered system comprises several interconnected computer systems via a local area network.

Operating systems have been evolving through the years.

Remember

Operating systems are like the conductors of a digital orchestra, ensuring all the different instruments (programs and processes) play together in harmony.

3.3. FUNCTIONS OF OPERATING SYSTEMS

3.3.1. Batch system

In this operating system, users regularly submit jobs on a predetermined schedule (such as daily, weekly, or monthly) to a centralized location, where the user does not directly interact with the computer system. To optimize processing efficiency, tasks with comparable requirements were consolidated into batches and executed collectively by the computer. Therefore, the programmer would entrust the programs to the operator. The output generated by each task would be directed to the corresponding software developer. This task category's primary objective was to facilitate the automatic transfer of control from one job to another (Lang et al., 2017).

One of the drawbacks of the batch processing system is that it may result in a longer turnaround time from the user's perspective. Similarly, the program presents challenges in terms of debugging.

3.3.2. Time-Sharing System

An interactive system is a type of operating system that facilitates real-time communication between the user and the system. The user can provide instructions directly and receive immediate feedback. The time-sharing system enables multiple users to share a computer system concurrently. The central processing unit (CPU) is efficiently shared among multiple programs through rapid multiplexing. These programs are stored in the computer's memory and disk. The program underwent a process of swapping between memory and disk (Ritchie & Thompson, 1978).

The implementation of a time-sharing system decreases the utilization of CPU idle time. The drawback presents a greater level of intricacy.

3.3.3. Real-time Operating System

Real-time systems are distinguished by their ability to provide instantaneous responses. The implementation of this measure ensures the timely completion of essential tasks. This category of computer programs requires predetermined time constraints for the execution of each function. Real-time systems are employed in situations where strict temporal constraints govern the functioning of a processor or the movement of data. Additionally, real-time systems may serve as a control mechanism in a specialized application (Shukla et al., 2018).

The airline's reservation system exemplifies this category.

3.3.4. On-line and Off-line Operation

A device controller, a distinct subroutine for each input/output (I/O) device, was developed. Certain input/output (I/O) devices have been outfitted for either online functionality, linked to the processor, or offline functionality, whereby the control unit operates them.

3.3.5. Buffering

A buffer refers to a designated region of primary storage that temporarily stores data while it is being transferred during input/output operations. The data is stored in the buffer by an I/O channel upon receiving input. Once the transfer is finished, the processor may then access the data. The buffing process can be carried out in either a single or double manner (Hartman et al., 2001).

3.3.6. Spooling (Simultaneously Peripheral Operation On-Line)

The process of spooling involves utilizing the disk as a sizable buffer. Spooling is advantageous as it enables devices to access data at varying rates. The buffer is a temporary storage location where information can be stored in abeyance while a comparatively slower device can process it.

Spooling enables the concurrent execution of a job's computation and another job's input/output operations (Kaplan, 1978).

3.3.7. Multiprogramming

In multiprogramming, multiple programs are retained in the main memory simultaneously, and the CPU switches between them; consequently, the CPU constantly has a program to run. When an operating system initiates the execution of a program from memory, and if the program requires a waiting period, such as an input/output operation, the operating system will switch to another program. The utilization of the CPU is enhanced by multiprogramming. Multiprogramming systems optimize the utilization of system resources, yet they do not facilitate interaction by users with the computer system (Dijkstra, 1968).

(i) Advantages:

a. One advantage is the achievement of high CPU utilization.

b. It seems that numerous programs are allocated CPU resources in close temporal proximity.

(ii) Disadvantages:

a. One of the drawbacks is that CPU scheduling is necessary.

b. Memory management is necessary to facilitate the storage of numerous jobs in memory.

3.3.8. Parallel System

The system comprises multiple processors. The processors are interconnected through the computer bus, clock, memory, and I/O devices (Elliott et al., 2014).

The benefit lies in the enhancement of throughput, which refers to the number of programs accomplished within a given time frame.

3.3.9. Distributed System

Utilize multiple physical processors to distribute the computation. The process entails establishing a communication link between two or more autonomous computer systems. Each processor is equipped with its operating system and local memory. Inter-processor communication is facilitated through various communication channels, including high-speed buses and telephone lines (Gärtner et al., 1999) (Figure 3.4).

Figure 3.4. Illustration of the Distributed System (Source: Qasim Mohammed Hussein, Creative Commons License).

Advantages:

a. One of the benefits of distributed systems is the ability to share resources such as files and printers.

b. Computation acceleration can be achieved by partitioning a task into smaller segments, allowing multiple processors to execute them simultaneously, thereby enabling load sharing.

c. The attribute of reliability is demonstrated by the ability of the remaining processors to continue functioning seamlessly in the event of a single processor failure.

d. The communications category includes electronic mail and file transfer protocol (FTP).

3.3.10. Personal Computer

Personal computers refer to computer systems designed and intended for the use of a single user. Personal computer operating systems lacked both multi-user and multi-tasking capabilities. Personal computer operating systems aimed to optimize user convenience and responsiveness rather than prioritizing maximizing CPU and I/O utilization (Mayer & Argyres, 2004).

The two computing systems being compared are Microsoft Windows and Apple Macintosh.

An operating system offers services to both software applications and their end-users. The operating system typically offers a range of standard services to users (Pfaffenberger, 1988):

1. Program execution involves loading a program into the memory by the operating system, followed by the execution of the program. The software application must be able to

terminate its operation, either in a standard or non-standard manner.

2. I/O operations: which can involve accessing files or utilizing various I/O devices. During program execution, an input/output device may be necessary. An operating system must furnish the necessary input/output capabilities.
3. File system manipulation: specifically reading or writing a file. The operating system grants authorization to a program to perform operations on a file.
4. Communication: necessary for transferring data between two processes over a certain period. Both processes are executed on a single computer or on separate computers interconnected through a computer network.

There are two methods by which communication can be implemented (Bardini & Horvath, 1995):

a. The method of shared memory.
b. Message passing mechanism.

Errors can arise in the central processing unit, input/output devices, or memory hardware. The operating system must maintain constant vigilance regarding potential errors. Proper measures must be taken to guarantee accurate and uniform computing.

3.3.11. Memory Management

Memory management pertains to the administration of Primary or Main Memory. The primary storage of a computer system is comprised of a vast collection of words or bytes, with each word or byte being assigned a unique address (Nilakanta et al., 2006).

The primary function of main memory is to offer a high-speed storage medium that can be directly accessed by the central processing unit (CPU). A program must be in the primary memory for it to be carried out. The Operating System performs various functions related to memory management, including:

1. The system monitors primary memory allocation, including identifying active users and unused portions.
2. In multiprogramming, the allocation of memory to processes is determined by the operating system, which determines both the timing and quantity of memory allocation.
3. The allocation of memory occurs upon a process's request.
4. Releasing memory when a program no longer requires it or has been dismissed is known as deallocation.

3.3.12. Processor Management

Within a multiprogramming environment, the operating system is responsible for determining the allocation of the processor to individual processes, including the timing and duration of such allocations. The operation above is commonly referred to as process scheduling. The Operating System performs various tasks related to managing the processor, including (Rhee et al., 2012):

1. The system monitors the processor and process status. The system is accountable for this function and is commonly called a traffic controller.
2. Assigning the central processing unit (CPU) to a specific process.
3. The processor is deallocated upon the termination of a process.

3.3.13. Device Management

Managing device communication through their corresponding drivers is a fundamental function of an Operating System. The functions above pertain to the management of devices (Miocinovic et al., 2020).

1. The task involves monitoring and recording the status of all electronic devices. The I/O controller is the program accountable for this task.
2. A decision-making process determines the allocation of the device and its duration of use.
3. The device is allocated efficiently.
4. The process of deallocating devices.

3.3.14. File Management

Typically, a file system is structured into directories to facilitate efficient navigation and utilization. The directories have the potential to store both files and additional instructions. The Operating System performs various tasks related to the management of files (Dinneen & Julien, 2020):

1. The system maintains records of data about information, location, utilization, condition, and other relevant factors. The term "file system" is commonly used to refer to shared facilities.
2. Determines the allocation of resources.
3. The process of allocating resources is undertaken.
4. The process of releasing or freeing up resources.

3.3.15. Other Important Activities

The Operating System executes a variety of crucial functions, including the following activities (Gori et al., 2020):

1. Implementing passwords and other relevant techniques serves as a measure to restrict unapproved access to data and programs, thereby ensuring security.
2. The ability to manage system performance by measuring the time lapse between initiating a service request and the corresponding system response.
3. Job accounting refers to monitoring and recording the duration and resources utilized by different jobs and users.
4. One of the techniques used in software development is the creation of error-detecting aids such as dumps, error messages, traces, and other debugging tools. These aids are designed to assist in recognizing and fixing errors that may occur during the software development process.
5. The effective coordination of compilers, interpreters, assemblers, and other software among computer system users is crucial.

Without an operating system, each program necessitates a mechanism to manage every part of a computer and hardware. The aforementioned entails the requirement of a mechanism to receive user inputs through the use of a keyboard and mice, to produce hard copies of documents, to perform read and write operations on memory sticks, to maintain temporal records, to display output on the screen, and to facilitate communication over a network. This would result in each program being significantly voluminous and burdensome (Kühn et al., 2011).

3.4. TYPES OF OPERATING SYSTEMS

Operating systems have continuously evolved since their inception to support increasingly complex operations. The present discourse aims to examine prevalent operating systems that are currently in use.

3.4.1. Batch Operating System

The present operating system involves the user's preparation of a job, which is subsequently submitted to a computer operator through a device such as a punch card. The individual responsible for operating the computer would categorize the tasks based on their computational demands and perform them in groups to optimize processing efficiency. This software is most appropriate for applications requiring extended computation periods and minimal user interaction, such as the statistical examination of substantial data sets (García-Muñoz et al., 2008).

Several issues are linked to these operating systems, such as inadequate user-computing job interaction, challenges in task prioritization based on urgency, extended turnaround times, and elevated CPU idle time due to the sluggishness of mechanical devices for input and output (Rey-Martínez et al., 2021).

3.4.2. Multiprogramming Operating System

A multiprogramming operating system is defined as one that can concurrently execute multiple programs. Its primary objective is to enhance the utilization of resources and system efficiency. The objective above is accomplished by implementing a system that arranges computational tasks in a way that guarantees the constant availability of a task for the central processing unit to execute (Hays et al., 1990).

The aforementioned operating systems are commonly denoted as multitasking due to their capability to enable the concurrent execution of two or more processes. This implies that multiple data sets can be concurrently stored in the primary memory.

3.4.3. Time-Sharing Operating System

A distinct form of multiprogramming characterizes the operating system in question. Similar to a conventional multiprogramming operating system, this system enables the simultaneous execution of multiple tasks. This feature is distinctive in that it has been specifically devised to cater to the needs of numerous users. This implies that numerous users can utilize identical computer resources. One advantageous aspect of this operating system is that it eliminates the need for users to wait in line to access the available resources (Oppenheimer & Weizer, 1968).

Each user perceives the utilization of a personal computer, despite multiple users sharing a single computer. The fast response times are attributed to the CPU's frequent job switching.

The operating system above optimizes CPU utilization by minimizing idle time while preventing software redundancy. Data communication can pose a challenge when multiple users concurrently access or modify the same programs and data. Consequently, the issue of reliability may arise (Ritchie, 1984).

3.4.4. Distributed Operating Systems

The presence of multiple central processors characterizes distributed operating systems. The processors above cater to multiple users concurrently operating various real-time applications. To clarify, these operating systems integrate multiple individual computers into a cohesive unit, operating as a singular entity.

The utilization of these operating systems commenced with the advent of computer networks, which facilitated communication between independent computer systems. The implementation of this technology facilitated the sharing of resources and significantly enhanced the exchange of data among various locations. Distributed operating systems are designed to alleviate the computational burden on the host machine, even when executing intensive tasks (Thekkath et al., 1994).

3.4.5. Network Operating System

The operating system in question operates on a server and facilitates access to computing resources for networked computers, as implied by its nomenclature. The administration of users, data, applications, and security is performed on the server (Badotra & Panda, 2020).

The present operating system facilitates the exchange of files and printers among multiple computers within a network. The operating as mentioned earlier system offers enhanced system security and stability. The expenses related to the acquisition and operation of a server may be considered steep for small enterprises.

3.4.6. Real-Time Operating Systems

In the context of these operating systems, the expeditious reception and processing of inputs are of utmost importance. Consequently, the operating system must ensure the timely processing of events. Certain systems may facilitate the execution of multiple tasks simultaneously, albeit by utilizing specialized algorithms for task scheduling. This approach guarantees task switching occurs according to their priorities, ensuring the timely completion of all tasks (Shukla et al., 2018).

Real-time operating systems (RTOS) are utilized in various applications, such as systems for air traffic control, weapon control, medical imaging, industrial control, and scientific experiments.

Real-time operating systems can be classified into two distinct types. The initial category is denoted as hard real-time operating systems, ensuring crucial operations are executed within a specified timeframe. The alternative category is a "soft real-time operating system," which allocates precedence to a specific task without ensuring it will be accomplished within a predetermined timeframe. The prioritization of the critical task will take precedence over all other tasks (Anh & Tan, 2009). Currently, a plethora of operating systems is in use. Various prominent technology companies have developed operating systems for their clientele, each with distinct advantages and drawbacks depending on their applications. Consequently, certain entities have garnered greater popularity relative to their counterparts. The following discourse examines five of the most widely used operating systems for computers and smartphones.

3.5. COMPUTER OPERATING SYSTEMS

Every computer operating system possesses a dedicated group of supporters who firmly believe that no alternative operating system can match its capabilities. Nonetheless, the subsequent five options were consistently evaluated as having a significant computer market share (Yan et al., 2010).

3.5.1. Windows

A significant proportion of individuals who utilize computers have had an experience with the Windows OS at a certain juncture. Microsoft is the developer of the Windows operating system. The installed base of Windows 10 has exceeded 350 million devices, with a target of reaching 1 billion by 2018. By 2011, over 1.25 billion computers had been installed on an edition of the Windows OS worldwide.

Unsurprisingly, Windows OS has historically held a market share of over 90%, as evidenced by recent trends. The prevalence of Windows 7 has decreased due to the rizing prominence of Windows 10, despite the former's enduring popularity (Vömel & Freiling, 2011) (Figure 3.5).

Figure 3.5. Windows Operating System (Source: Richard Nwanekezie, Creative Commons License).

The most recent version of the operating system that runs

on Windows is Windows 11. The previous versions encompass Windows 8.1, Windows 8, Windows 7, Windows Vista, Windows XP, and Windows 2000. The widespread adoption of Windows operating systems can be partially ascribed to the triumph of the Microsoft Office Suite, which presently boasts a user base exceeding 1.2 billion. The product has a global reach, accessible in 140 nations and utilizing 107 different languages (Martinovic et al., 2012).

Windows devices exhibit extensive compatibility with hardware and software, encompassing a broad spectrum of price points ranging from affordable entry-level devices to costly high-performance gaming machines.

Operating systems are not devoid of drawbacks. The meticulousness observed in the construction of Mac computers is not typically evident in the design of Windows computers. This phenomenon is observable in the construction standards of the hardware components, including the trackpads and the display, which exhibit a higher degree of excellence in Macintosh computers.

An additional disadvantage pertains to the proliferation of malicious software. Due to its widespread usage, Windows-based computers are a preferred target for malicious actors, resulting in most malware being developed for this operating system. It can be inferred that Windows computers may pose a higher level of vulnerability than alternative operating systems (Vömel & Freiling, 2011).

3.5.2. Mac OS

The operating system above has been created by Apple Inc. specifically for utilizing their proprietary computer systems. The software is pre-installed on all Macintosh computers. The antecedent operating system for Macintosh computers was Mac OS, which was subsequently superseded by the present-day Mac OS X. From 1984 until 1999, Mac OS served as the primary operating system for Apple. However, in 1999, Apple introduced Mac OS X Server 1.0, specifically designed for server usage (Kukreja et al., 2006).

Shortly after, Apple introduced a desktop iteration of OS X that was pre-installed on Macintosh computers in 2001. Before the launch of OS X 10.7, commonly referred to as "Lion," Apple had been manufacturing separate versions of OS X for server and client purposes. These two editions were merged in OS X 10.7 and all later editions (Figure 3.6).

Did you Know?

Mac OS has a significantly lower market share compared to Windows, but it is popular among creative professionals and is known for its sleek design and user-friendly interface.

Figure 3.6. Illustration of the MacOS (Source: Cam Ranger, Creative Commons License).

A distinguishing characteristic of Mac OS and OS X is their lucidity and precision. The operating system has been developed specifically for desktop use and fulfills that purpose effectively. Given this consideration, it is unlikely that any of the issues stemming from Windows 8's "Metro" interface will occur (Kakar, 2015).

The operating system's interface has been meticulously crafted, resulting in a highly favorable user experience. Considerable deliberation has been devoted to the design of the computers, thereby rendering it arduous to abstain from deriving pleasure from their usage. The devices exhibit exceptional battery longevity, a user-friendly touchpad interface, and superior hardware proficiency. Modern MacBook laptops can surpass high-end ultrabooks in terms of performance for the average user.

Nonetheless, this operating system also presents certain drawbacks. The primary factor to consider is the cost. As the operating system exclusively operates on Apple hardware, acquiring an Apple computer is necessary to utilize the OS. Regrettably, these computing devices are not accessible within the low or mid-range financial plan. Suppose one's financial constraints limit their budget to below $500. In that case, the prospect of owning a Macintosh computer may be unattainable unless they are willing to consider purchasing a previously owned and restored device, the functionality of which may be uncertain (Singh, 2014).

Another disadvantage pertains to the software. Despite the availability of essential office and creative applications such as the Microsoft Office Suite and Adobe Creative Suite on this platform, it remains incomparable to the vast array of software accessible to Windows users. Fortuitously, owing to the burgeoning prominence of internet-dependent software, this operating system is progressively becoming more efficacious in contrast to its antecedent iterations.

However, compromises will need to be made regarding gaming as this platform is lagging significantly behind.

3.5.3. Linux

Linux is an OS that caters to proficient users with technical expertise in computer hardware and software. A variety of vendors offer Linux laptops for purchase. However, obtaining a complimentary version of the operating system and installing it on an alternative computer is also possible. Nonetheless, the installation process is run independently; there is no assurance that all of the hardware will function as anticipated (Haris et al., 2018).

Linus OSes are widely utilized by developers and technology enthusiasts who favor a UNIX-based operating system. Although the integration of web-based software has enhanced the usability and functionality of Linux for the general user, it remains challenging to endorse a Linux-based computer to individuals not specifically seeking this platform, despite its prevalence in Macs.

3.5.4. Chrome OS

The operating system under consideration predominantly depends on the Chrome web browser developed by Google. The Chromebook operating system is ubiquitous across all devices. While it offers a range of desktop-based applications, a significant portion of its functionality is executed through the Chrome browser.

Consequently, it is necessary to locate a Chrome application that corresponds to the desired task to expand the range of capabilities. The platform in question does not support the execution of desktop software designed for Windows or Mac operating systems. However, this limitation is not expected to pose a significant challenge, as a plethora of Chrome applications can effectively facilitate the completion of virtually any task. To utilize Linux desktop software on Chromebook, it is necessary to transition the device to developer mode (Tracy, 2012).

Notwithstanding these obstacles, there are advantages. One notable aspect is the affordability of Chromebooks. A viable option can be acquired within the price range of $200 to $300, and they possess a user-friendly interface (Tracy, 2012). In addition, users will experience the advantage of being free from malware concerns, as opposed to Windows-based computers.

This operating system is suitable for individuals whose work can be accomplished solely through the Chrome web browser. The user will be provided with a straightforward interface at an affordable cost.

3.5.5. Android

Despite being primarily recognized as a mobile device operating system, Android warrants discussion in the context of convertible tablets due to its prevalence in this market. An exemplary illustration is provided by the Asus Transformer devices, which operate as tablets but can be categorized as comprehensive Android computers upon integration of the keyboard.

Although Android is a highly robust smartphone operating system, most individuals may not find it suitable for computing purposes. The laptop's user experience may not align with the expectations of the majority of computer users. Initially, access will be restricted solely to utilizing mobile applications, thereby precluding the use of desktop applications with windowed interfaces. The mobile application version of the browser presents a less user-friendly interface than its desktop counterpart (Chinetha et al., 2015).

However, this option may be suitable if one seeks flexibility and mobility. Typing on a keyboard is more efficient and expeditious when as opposed to typing on a tablet screen.

3.6. SMARTPHONE OPERATING SYSTEMS

Like computers, smartphone operating systems have dedicated enthusiasts who can provide numerous justifications for why their OS is superior. This paper examines 5 of the most prevalent operating systems currently utilized in smartphones.

3.6.1. Google Android

The Android mobile operating system was developed by Google and was founded on the Linux kernel. Android is the most widely used mobile operating system worldwide, commanding a market share exceeding 80%. Although it may not be widely embraced in the realm of computing, it remains a preferred option for a significant number of individuals in the smartphone industry. The software is user-friendly and offers extensive options for customization (Matos & Grasser, 2010) (Figure 3.7).

The Android operating system's popularity can be attributed to the significant presence of app developers. This guarantees that users are constantly equipped with an application-based solution for any issue. The platform's minimal restrictions give developers greater flexibility to enhance application functionality. This elucidates the vast array of applications present on the Android Play Store that are accessible to end-users.

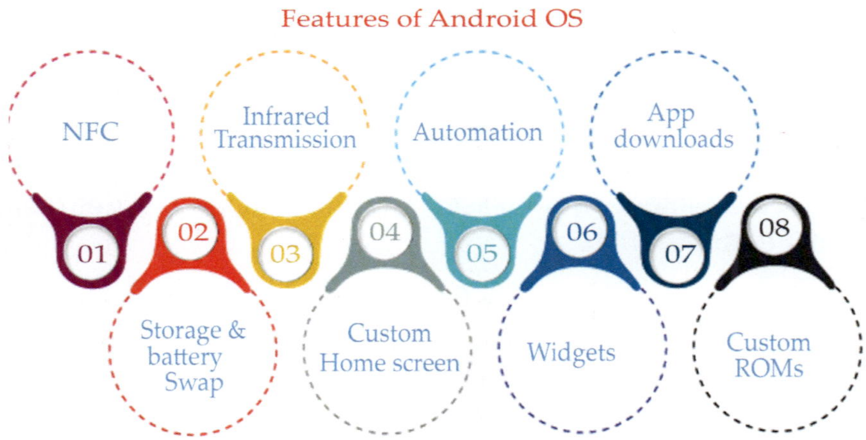

Figure 3.7. Schematic of the features of the Android OS (Source: Java T Point, Creative Commons License).

The widespread availability of this operating system to multiple smartphone manufacturers has contributed to its increased global popularity. This phenomenon enhances accessibility to a wider audience, as individuals with limited financial resources can also procure Android devices (Shaheen et al., 2017).

3.6.2. Apple iOS

The operating system mentioned above is pre-installed on every iPhone manufactured by Apple Inc. Like Mac OS, the operating system is exclusively accessible on devices produced by its manufacturer and is not compatible with devices from other manufacturers. The implication is that the organization can monitor the caliber of the products introduced to the market, resulting in substantial quality improvement.

The operating system above is a multitasking system compatible with various Apple devices such as the iPad, iPhone, Apple TV, and iPod. It possesses the second most extensive global user population on mobile devices. Regarding applications, iOS users are provided with access to a vast array of applications, numbering in the millions, through the Apple App Store. The community comprises many developers who consistently contribute additional applications to the existing ones available in the store.

The primary obstacle confronting this particular operating system is identical to the challenge encountered by the Mac OS. Given that the operating system is exclusively accessible on Apple devices, ownership of an Apple device is a prerequisite for utilization. Regrettably, the organization caters exclusively to the premium market segment, rendering the devices unaffordable to users with limited financial resources (Foulad et al., 2013).

3.6.3. Windows Mobile

Windows Mobile, formerly Windows Phone, ranks third among the most widely used mobile operating systems. Microsoft is the developer of this software, which has been released in six versions to date. The operating system in question has employed an interface reminiscent of the Windows 8 Metro since its initial release in February 2010.

Although Windows OS is widely used in computers, the software giant Microsoft has not achieved comparable success in smartphones. A significant proportion of users, including those utilizing Windows-based computing systems, prefer the Android or iOS operating systems.

The operating system boasts several key benefits, such as its user-friendly interface and visually engaging animated graphics. Additionally, the operating system exhibits a low RAM consumption, facilitating the seamless execution of resource-intensive applications (Grispos et al., 2011).

A notable drawback of this operating system is its comparatively limited assortment of applications available on the Windows Store, in contrast to the Apple App Store and Android Play Store. This platform's acceptance level among developers is comparatively lower than that observed in both app stores. Nonetheless, the figure above exhibits a consistent upward trend, while end-users retain access to satisfactory applications.

3.6.4. Blackberry OS

RIM (Research In Motion), a company renowned for producing Blackberry smartphones, owns the operating system in question. The operating system mentioned earlier was among the initial ones developed for smartphones; however, it was rapidly surpassed by Windows Mobile, Android, and iOS. Nevertheless, it remains highly prevalent worldwide, as many initial adopters continue to adhere to it.

The operating system mentioned above has encountered a considerable number of obstacles over the course of the last twenty years. However, it remains one of the leading five widely used smartphone operating systems in the current market. The application is highly favored for its utility in business contexts and has managed to maintain its market presence despite facing significant competition from Apple and Android.

A significant proportion of present-day users of this particular operating system are individuals who have remained loyal since its heyday as one of the most prevalent mobile platforms globally.

3.6.5. Firefox OS

Firefox OS is an open-source operating system developed by Mozilla, responsible for the widely-used Firefox web browser. The primary impetus for creating the OS is the company's aspiration to enhance the competitiveness of the open web and challenge the dominance of individual vendors (Figure 3.8).

Figure 3.8. Illustration of the Firefox OS (Source: Shawn Knight, Creative Commons License).

3.7. COMPONENTS OF AN OPERATING SYSTEM

The distinct constituents of an OS facilitate its function of enabling the various components of a computer to collaborate. Let us examine the functions of each of these components.

3.7.1. Kernel

The kernel is an essential component in the foundational structure of an OS. The process of managing computer hardware devices involves the determination of hardware assets that will be allocated to various programs. This process guarantees that the central processing unit (CPU) is consistently functioning at its maximum efficiency (Cheriton & Duda, 1995).

3.7.2. Process Management

Numerous programs are concurrently executed on a computer system. During typical usage, a computer undergoes numerous processes ranging from background-running apps to applications that users actively engage with. Given that contemporary operating systems support multi-tasking, it is incumbent upon the operating system to allocate the resources among all active processes.

3.7.3. Memory Management

Modern computers are equipped with various types of memory. The components encompass the central processing unit cache, random access memory, and disk storage. The operating system's memory manager is responsible for monitoring the availability of memory and facilitating the transfer of data between memory locations. This practice guarantees the allocation of the maximum available memory to each process, enhancing the execution speed. The operating system guarantees the allocation of virtual memory addresses to each process to prevent any interference between processes that are concurrently present in memory (Nilakanta et al., 2006).

3.7.4. Security

Given that the operating system is responsible for managing computing resources, it must be able to differentiate between permissible and impermissible requests. This encompasses endogenous requests from the computer system and exogenous requests from other computer systems within the network. In addition, auditing options are provided to inform users about the individuals who have accessed various files and any modifications that may have been implemented.

3.7.5. Networking

Networking facilitates the sharing of resources among operating systems through various connections. The TCP/IP protocol is widely recognized as the prevailing networking protocol.

3.7.6. File Systems and Disk Access

One of the fundamental functions of operating systems is to regulate access to data that is stored on various disks within a computer system. The operating system is responsible for ensuring that files are kept in a way that facilitates rapid access and maximizes dependability. Furthermore, they facilitate efficient utilization of the existing disk space. The file system refers to the specific method of organizing and storing files on a disk. The process of assigning names and features to files and organizing them systematically into directories is facilitated by file management.

3.8. CHOOSING AN OPERATING SYSTEM FOR A BUSINESS

Having acknowledged that individual operating systems possess distinct advantages and disadvantages, the following section discusses selecting the optimal one for an enterprise.

3.8.1. Ease of Use

Consider the varying user interfaces provided by distinct operating systems. Each user will experience a learning curve. However, the extent of this learning curve may vary among individuals. Consider the professional experience and qualifications of the personnel. With what OS are the majority of individuals acquainted? Select the option that will present the least difficulty for personnel. Ensuring a seamless experience for one's customers is paramount (Palme et al., 2010).

3.8.2. Availability of Software and Applications

It is imperative to ensure that the software utilized in service delivery is readily accessible. Typically, the Windows operating system offers a diverse array of software options; however, the primary consideration in selecting an operating system is not the availability of software. The vast array of available programs is unnecessary. One should prioritize acquiring resources that facilitate the provision of their services. Select the OS that provides comprehensive support and regular updates, encompassing all the necessary features.

ACTIVITY 3.1.

You're a graphic designer working on a Mac OS platform and your computer suddenly freezes while you're working on a time-sensitive project. You're not sure what to do next to fix the issue and avoid losing your progress?

3.8.3. Note What Customers Use

It is imperative to consider the prevalent operating system among one's clientele to mitigate compatibility issues while transmitting or receiving files. Services can be effectively provided without issues by ensuring a seamless connection with clients.

3.8.4. Security

When contemplating security measures, it is necessary to take into account the level of technological proficiency possessed by one's personnel. If a significant proportion of the users are inexperienced with computers, it would be advisable to procure an operating system with high security. Windows exhibits a comparatively higher susceptibility to security breaches. Provided that personnel are trained in secure browsing practices, it is plausible that a significant proportion of these attacks can be prevented. Ultimately, verifying that the computer systems fall within the designated financial parameters is imperative. When procuring computers for the entire organization, it is imperative to ensure the cost is within budgetary limits. Apple computers typically command a higher price point than other brands, while Windows-based machines offer a broader selection of options. In comparison to Mac, Windows is considered to have lower security measures (Chesbrough & Schwartz, 2007).

SUMMARY

This section introduces operating systems and describes how they control computer components. The chapter's goals are to familiarize readers with the inner workings of a computer system, the storage structure of operating systems, the functions of operating systems, the types of operating systems, the differences between computer and smartphone operating systems, the components of operating systems, and the process of selecting the best operating system for a business. Beginning with a discussion of what is known as "primary memory," "secondary memory," and "virtual memory," this chapter details the storage structure of operating systems. It then discusses how operating systems do tasks, including managing processes, memory, devices, and files. Next, the chapter breaks down the many OSes available, including batch, real-time, interactive, and network OSes. It also compares and contrasts the operating systems used by computers and mobile devices without naming specific platforms. This chapter also breaks down the OS into parts, such as the kernel, the UI, and the device drivers. Finally, it offers advice on selecting the optimal OS for a company without recommending any particular one. In general, the chapter thoroughly introduces computer operating systems without focusing on one in particular. It discusses the different kinds of storage, their uses, and their components, as well as the similarities and differences between desktop and mobile operating systems. The chapter also includes advice on selecting the optimal OS for a company..

REVIEW QUESTIONS

1. Explain the basic functions of an operating system.
2. What are the different types of operating systems?
3. What is the difference between computer and smartphone operating systems?
4. Describe the storage structure of an operating system.
5. What are the components of an operating system?
6. What is the kernel of an operating system, and what is its function?
7. How do you choose the best operating system for a business?

MULTIPLE CHOICE QUESTIONS

1. What is the purpose of an operating system?

a. To manage hardware resources
b. To manage software resources
c. To manage both hardware and software resources
d. None of the above

2. **Which of the following is not a type of operating system?**
   a. Batch
   b. Real-time
   c. Interactive
   d. Terminal
3. **Which of the following is not a component of an operating system?**
   a. CPU
   b. Memory management
   c. Device drivers
   d. Application software
4. **Which type of operating system is used in smartphones?**
   a. Windows
   b. Linux
   c. iOS
   d. macOS
5. **What is the function of the kernel in an operating system?**
   a. To manage the user interface
   b. To manage system resources
   c. To manage application software
   d. None of the above
6. **What is virtual memory?**
   a. A type of secondary memory
   b. A type of primary memory
   c. A technique used to make primary memory appear larger than it is
   d. A technique used to make secondary memory appear smaller than it is
7. **Which operating system is best for a business that requires high security?**
   a. Windows
   b. macOS
   c. Linux
   d. Android

Answers to Multiple Choice Questions

1. (c) 2. (d) 3. (d) 4. (c) 5. (b)

6. (c) 7. (c)

REFERENCES

1. Ali, A. S. Y., (2016). Choosing the components of distributed information systems as a multi-criteria optimization problem. *International Journal of Computer Applications, 975*, 8887.
2. Anh, T. N. B., & Tan, S. L., (2009). Real-time operating systems for small microcontrollers. *IEEE Micro, 29*(5), 30–45.
3. Austin, T., Larson, E., & Ernst, D., (2002). SimpleScalar: An infrastructure for computer system modeling. *Computer, 35*(2), 59–67.
4. Badotra, S., & Panda, S. N., (2020). Evaluation and comparison of OpenDayLight and open networking operating system in software-defined networking. *Cluster Computing, 23*, 1281–1291.
5. Bardini, T., & Horvath, A. T., (1995). The social construction of the personal computer user. *Journal of Communication, 45*(3), 40–65.
6. Befikadu, D., (2014). Factors affecting quality of grain stored in Ethiopian traditional storage structures and opportunities for improvement. *International Journal of Sciences: Basic and Applied Research, 18*(1), 235–257.
7. Besen, S. M., & Farrell, J., (1994). Choosing how to compete: Strategies and tactics in standardization. *Journal of Economic Perspectives, 8*(2), 117–131.
8. Cheriton, D. R., & Duda, K. J., (1995). A caching model of operating system kernel functionality. *ACM SIGOPS Operating Systems Review, 29*(1), 83–86.
9. Chesbrough, H., & Schwartz, K., (2007). Innovating business models with co-development partnerships. *Research-Technology Management, 50*(1), 55–59.
10. Chinetha, K., Joann, J. D., & Shalini, A., (2015). An evolution of android operating system and its version. *International Journal of Engineering and Applied Sciences, 2*(2), 257997.
11. Dijkstra, E. W., (1968). The structure of the "THE"-multiprogramming system. *Communications of the ACM, 11*(5), 341–346.
12. Dinneen, J. D., & Julien, C. A., (2020). The ubiquitous digital file: A review of file management research. *Journal of the Association for Information Science and Technology, 71*(1), 1–32.
13. Dropsho, S., Buyuktosunoglu, A., Balasubramonian, R., Albonesi, D. H., Dwarkadas, S., Semeraro, G., & Scottt, M. L., (2002). Integrating adaptive on-chip storage structures for reduced dynamic power. In: *Proceedings International Conference on Parallel Architectures and Compilation Techniques, 1*(1), 141–152. IEEE.
14. Elliott, J., Kelly, D., Chryssanthacopoulos, J., Glotter, M., Jhunjhnuwala, K., Best, N., & Foster, I., (2014). The parallel system for integrating impact models and sectors (pSIMS). *Environmental Modeling & Software, 62*, 509–516.
15. Fiarni, C., Sipayung, E. M., & Tumundo, P. B., (2019). Academic decision support system for choosing information systems sub majors programs using decision tree algorithm. *J. Inf. Syst. Eng. Bus. Intell., 5*(1), 57.

16. Foulad, A., Bui, P., & Djalilian, H., (2013). Automated audiometry using apple iOS-based application technology. *Otolaryngology–Head and Neck Surgery, 149*(5), 700–706.
17. García-Muñoz, S., MacGregor, J. F., Neogi, D., Latshaw, B. E., & Mehta, S., (2008). Optimization of batch operating policies. Part II. Incorporating process constraints and industrial applications. *Industrial & Engineering Chemistry Research, 47*(12), 4202–4208.
18. Gärtner, F. C., (1999). Fundamentals of fault-tolerant distributed computing in asynchronous environments. *ACM Computing Surveys (CSUR), 31*(1), 1–26.
19. Gori, J., Han, H. L., & Beaudouin-Lafon, M., (2020). FileWeaver: Flexible file management with automatic dependency tracking. In: *Proceedings of the 33rd Annual ACM Symposium on User Interface Software and Technology, 1*, 22–34.
20. Grispos, G., Storer, T., & Glisson, W. B., (2011). A comparison of forensic evidence recovery techniques for a windows mobile smart phone. *Digital Investigation, 8*(1), 23–36.
21. Haris, M., Jadoon, B., Yousaf, M., & Khan, F. H., (2018). Evolution of android operating system: A review. *Asia Pacific Journal of Contemporary Education and Communication Technology, 4*(1), 178–188.
22. Hartman, IV. J. L., Garvik, B., & Hartwell, L., (2001). Principles for the buffering of genetic variation. *Science, 291*(5506), 1001–1004.
23. Hays, J. H., Miller, L., Othmer, B., & Saeed, M., (1990). Simulation of process and resource management in a multiprogramming operating system. *ACM SIGCSE Bulletin, 22*(1), 125–128.
24. Johnson, H. T., (2012). Lean dilemma: Choose system principles or management accounting controls—Not both. *Lean Accounting: Best Practices for Sustainable Integration*, 1–16.
25. Kakar, A. K., (2015). Why do users speak more positively about Mac OS X but are more loyal to Windows 7? *Computers in Human Behavior, 44*, 166–173.
26. Kaplan, H. L., (1978). An output spooling system for continuous data-logging paradigms. *Behavior Research Methods & Instrumentation, 10*(2), 285–290.
27. Kühn, S., Keizer, A. W., Colzato, L. S., Rombouts, S. A., & Hommel, B., (2011). The neural underpinnings of event-file management: Evidence for stimulus-induced activation of and competition among stimulus–response bindings. *Journal of Cognitive Neuroscience, 23*(4), 896–904.
28. Kukreja, U., Stevenson, W. E., & Ritter, F. E., (2006). RUI: Recording user input from interfaces under Windows and Mac OS X. *Behavior Research Methods, 38*(4), 656–659.
29. Lang, M., Bischl, B., & Surmann, D., (2017). Batchtools: Tools for R to work on batch systems. *Journal of Open Source Software, 2*(10), 135.
30. Martinovic, G., Balen, J., & Cukic, B., (2012). Performance evaluation of recent

windows operating systems. *J. Univers. Comput. Sci., 18*(2), 218–263.

31. Matos, V., & Grasser, R., (2010). Building applications for the Android OS mobile platform: A primer and course materials. *JCSC (Journal of Circuits, Systems, and Computers), 26*(1), 23.
32. Mayer, K. J., & Argyres, N. S., (2004). Learning to contract: Evidence from the personal computer industry. *Organization Science, 15*(4), 394–410.
33. Miocinovic, S., Ostrem, J. L., Okun, M. S., Bullinger, K. L., Riva-Posse, P., Gross, R. E., & Buetefisch, C. M., (2020). Recommendations for deep brain stimulation device management during a pandemic. *Journal of Parkinson's Disease, 10*(3), 903–910.
34. Nilakanta, S., Miller, L. L., & Zhu, D., (2006). Organizational memory management: Technological and research issues. *Journal of Database Management (JDM), 17*(1), 85–94.
35. Oppenheimer, G., & Weizer, N., (1968). Resource management for a medium scale time-sharing operating system. *Communications of the ACM, 11*(5), 313–322.
36. Palme, E., Tan, C. H., Sutanto, J., & Phang, C. W., (2010). Choosing the smart phone operating system for developing mobile applications. In: *Proceedings of the 12th International Conference on Electronic Commerce: Roadmap for the Future of Electronic Business, 1*, 146–152.
37. Pereira, T., Guo, Z., Nieh, S., Arias, J., & Hahn, H. T., (2009). Energy storage structural composites: A review. *Journal of Composite Materials, 43*(5), 549–560.
38. Pfaffenberger, B., (1988). The social meaning of the personal computer: Or, why the personal computer revolution was no revolution. *Anthropological Quarterly, 1*, 39–47.
39. Rey-Martínez, N., Barreiro-López, A., Guisasola, A., & Baeza, J. A., (2021). Comparing continuous and batch operation for high-rate treatment of urban wastewater. *Biomass and Bioenergy, 149*, 106077.
40. Rhee, K., Jeon, W., & Won, D., (2012). Security requirements of a mobile device management system. *International Journal of Security and Its Applications, 6*(2), 353–358.
41. Ritchie, D. M., & Thompson, K., (1978). The UNIX time-sharing system. *Bell System Technical Journal, 57*(6), 1905–1929.
42. Ritchie, D. M., (1984). The UNIX system: The evolution of the UNIX time-sharing system. *AT&T Bell Laboratories Technical Journal, 63*(8), 1577–1593.
43. Rosenblum, M., Herrod, S. A., Witchel, E., & Gupta, A., (1995). Complete computer system simulation: The SimOS approach. *IEEE Parallel & Distributed Technology: Systems & Applications, 3*(4), 34–43.
44. Shaheen, J. A., Asghar, M. A., & Hussain, A., (2017). Android OS with its architecture and Android application with Dalvik virtual machine review. *International Journal of Multimedia and Ubiquitous Engineering, 12*(7), 19–30.
45. Sharda, V. N., Kurothe, R. S., Sena, D. R., Pande, V. C., & Tiwari, S. P., (2006). Estimation of groundwater recharge from water storage structures in a semi-arid

climate of India. *Journal of Hydrology, 329*(1, 2), 224–243.

46. Shukla, A. K., Sharma, R., & Muhuri, P. K., (2018). A review of the scopes and challenges of the modern real-time operating systems. *International Journal of Embedded and Real-Time Communication Systems (IJERTCS), 9*(1), 66–82.
47. Singh, R., (2014). An overview of android operating system and its security. *Int. Journal of Engineering Research and Applications, 4*(2), 519–521.
48. Stankovic, J. A., & Rajkumar, R., (2004). Real-time operating systems. *Real-Time Systems, 28*(2, 3), 237–253.
49. Thekkath, C. A., Levy, H. M., & Lazowska, E. D., (1994). Separating data and control transfer in distributed operating systems. *ACM SIGOPS Operating Systems Review, 28*(5), 2–11.
50. Tracy, K. W., (2012). Mobile application development experiences on Apple's iOS and Android OS. *IEEE Potentials, 31*(4), 30–34.
51. Vömel, S., & Freiling, F. C., (2011). A survey of main memory acquisition and analysis techniques for the windows operating system. *Digital Investigation, 8*(1), 3–22.
52. Wu, M. S., (1988). Choosing PC software for decision-making. *Journal of Systems Management, 39*(12), 19.
53. Yan, K. K., Fang, G., Bhardwaj, N., Alexander, R. P., & Gerstein, M., (2010). Comparing genomes to computer operating systems in terms of the topology and evolution of their regulatory control networks. *Proceedings of the National Academy of Sciences, 107*(20), 9186–9191.
54. Zaher, M., & Molnár, S., (2022). A comparative and analytical study for choosing the best suited SDN network operating system for cloud data center. *Annals of Emerging Technologies in Computing (AETiC), 6*(1), 43–59.
55. Zhai, S., Karahan, H. E., Wei, L., Qian, Q., Harris, A. T., Minett, A. I., & Chen, Y., (2016). Textile energy storage: Structural design concepts, material selection and future perspectives. *Energy Storage Materials, 3*, 123–139.
56. Zhu, X., Xu, J., Luo, Y., Fu, Q., Liang, G., Luo, L., & Zhao, X. S., (2019). $MoNb_{12}O_{33}$ as a new anode material for high-capacity, safe, rapid and durable Li^+ storage: Structural characteristics, electrochemical properties and working mechanisms. *Journal of Materials Chemistry A, 7*(11), 6522–6532.

CHAPTER 4

TELECOMMUNICATION AND NETWORKS

UNIT INTRODUCTION

Telecommunication and networks are essential components of modern computer science that enable people and organizations to communicate and share information over long distances. Telecommunication refers to the transmission of information and data through different types of communication channels, including wired, wireless, and satellite networks. Networks, on the other hand, are collections of interconnected devices that can communicate and share resources such as data, applications, and services (Dewett & Jones, 2001).

In today's world, telecommunication and networks have become increasingly important due to the rise of globalization, mobile devices, and the internet. They play a critical role in enabling people and organizations to communicate and collaborate across different locations, making the world a smaller and more connected place. For businesses, telecommunication and networks are essential for enabling remote work, conducting online transactions, and providing customer support. They also play a vital role in the delivery of essential services such as healthcare, education, and emergency response (Grover et al., 1996).

Overall, telecommunication and networks have become a fundamental aspect of modern society, shaping the way people interact and conduct business on a global scale. Their importance is likely to continue growing as technology continues to evolve and new innovations emerge, leading to new possibilities for communication, collaboration, and data sharing (Subba, 2004).

Learning Objectives

At the end of this chapter, readers will be able to learn:

- Define and explain the concept of telecommunication and networks in computer science.
- Identify the different types of telecommunication and networks, as well as their components and protocols.
- Understand the advantages and examples of using telecommunication and networks in computer science, including email, video conferencing, and cloud computing.
- Recognize the challenges and risks associated with telecommunication and networks in computer science, such as security, reliability, and cost, as well as the potential risks of hacking, data breaches, and cyber-attacks.
- Explore the future trends of telecommunication and networks in computer science, such as 5G, IoT, and AI, and their implications on society and computer science development.
- Emphasize the importance of telecommunication and networks in computer science for future development and progress, and their role in modern society.

Key Terms

- Telecommunication
- Networks
- Wired communication
- Wireless communication
- Satellite communication
- Transmission media
- Protocols
- Video conferencing
- Cloud computing
- Data breaches

4.1. A FOUNDATION FOR TELECOMMUNICATION AND NETWORK MANAGEMENT

In the late 1980s, the International Telecommunications Union (ITU) and the International Organization for Standardization (ISO) collaborated to release network and system management standards known as the OSI Reference Model. The Telecommunication Management Network (TMN) was established as a framework based on this model and has since become a popular reference framework for network and system management (Gupta et al., 1999).

The ISO model introduced fundamental concepts in network management, defining a network management system as an application with the aim of analyzing, controlling, and managing network and service infrastructure. The model differentiates between management entities and agent entities, with agents representing network resources or end systems and providing management information to the network managers, who monitor the agents and make management and control decisions accordingly (Raman, 1998).

While the ISO model still serves as a foundation for network management, the role of managers and agents has become less distinct with advancements in distributed system architectures and peer-to-peer based systems, and more intelligence is being distributed into networks. However, the terms manager and agent are still used conceptually to describe the roles entities play in given operations or functions. The OSI reference model also emphasizes the distinction between managed entities, which are physical resources or end systems being managed, and managed objects, which refer to the informational view of the entity and provide relevant management information and capacities. A common information model is necessary to present such information in a consistent manner, and a common communication medium is needed for conveying management information to the managers.

The OSI reference model defines a management system based on functional, communicational, and informational aspects, with five functional areas of management: configuration, fault, performance, accounting, and security (FCAPS). These areas have helped structure network management research efforts (Schwartz, 1995). Telecommunication networks are complex infrastructures spanning over networks, services, users, and business entities. Effective management of these networks involves various functions such as

Did you Know?

According to the International Telecommunication Union (ITU), as of 2021, there are over 5.27 billion mobile phone users worldwide, with mobile broadband penetration reaching 79% globally.

configuration, fault detection and recovery, performance monitoring, accounting, and security. The Open Systems Interconnection (OSI) model defines these management functions, while the Telecommunication Management Network (TMN) framework adds layers for element management, network management, service management, and business management (Haggerty & Seetharaman, 1998) (Figure 4.1).

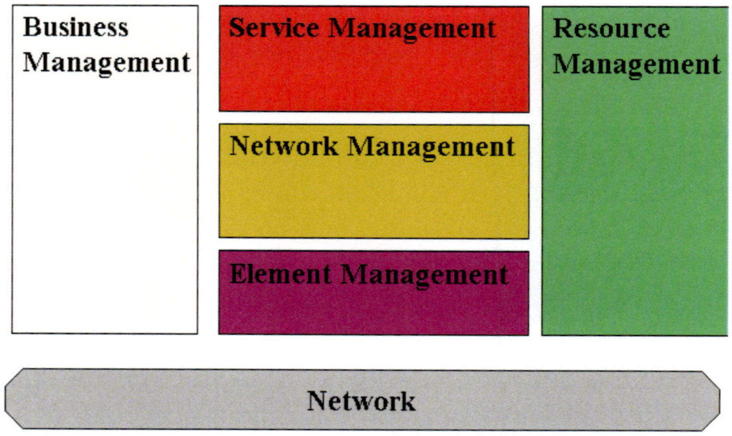

Figure 4.1. Illustration of Telecommunications Network – Network Management Architecture (Source: Martin John Baker, Creative Commons License).

The element management layer provides a view of the collection of network elements and mediates data between the network element and the network manager. It is device and network technology specific. The network management layer provides an end-to-end network view of the managed resources and devices, and it is device neutral. The service management layer provides contacts with customers and service providers, quality of service assurances, service orders, billing information, and trouble ticketing. The business management layer focuses on product and human resource planning and provides a business-level view of the services and financial concerns.

However, as the telecommunication infrastructures have evolved over the past fifteen years, the community's view of the upper layers of management has changed substantially. There is no representation of customers in the TMN model, but as service differentiation and customization have grown, customers have become increasingly important in management. There is also an increasing need for user profiling for location and context tracking. The service layer has grown more complex as well, with a mix of multimedia services, personalized user services, and third-party applications (Hunt, 1997). The constant evolution of telecommunication networks has brought about new challenges and opened new issues in old problems. This has led to changes in network management research and a need to address new challenges in configuration, fault management, performance monitoring, accounting, and security.

4.2. TELECOMMUNICATION

Telecommunication refers to the process of transmitting and receiving information over a distance through the use of different types of communication channels, such as wired, wireless, and satellite networks. The information being transmitted can include voice, data, images, and video (Al-Mamary et al., 2014).

4.2.1. Types of Telecommunications

There are several types of telecommunications, including (Grover et al., 1994) (Figure 4.2):

1. Wired Telecommunication: This type of telecommunication uses physical cables, such as copper or fiber optic cables, to transmit information. Examples of wired telecommunications include traditional telephone systems and wired internet connections.
2. Wireless Telecommunication: This type of telecommunication uses radio waves to transmit information wirelessly over the air. Examples of wireless telecommunications include mobile phones, Wi-Fi, and Bluetooth.

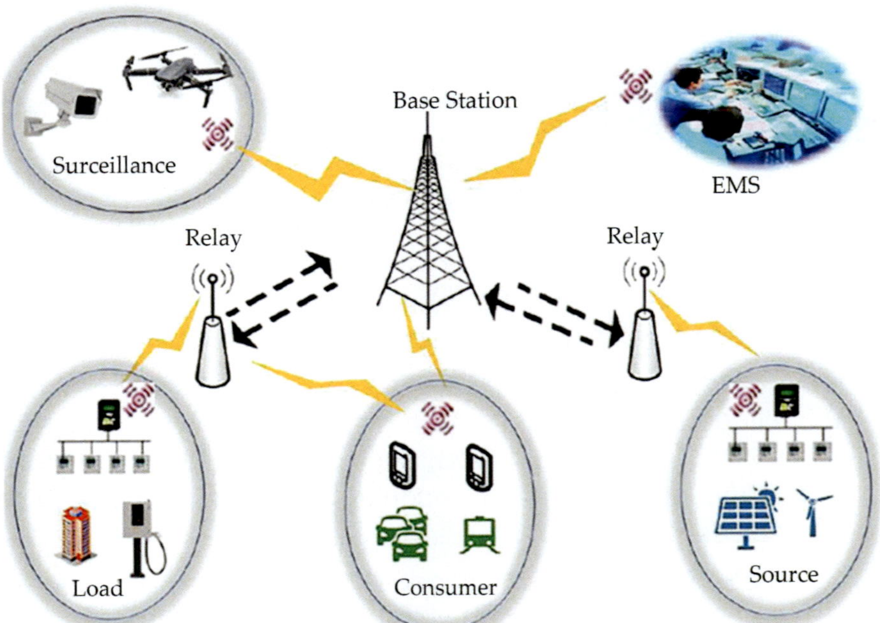

Figure 4.2. Schematic of the wireless communication networks (Source: Xiurong Zhang, Creative Commons License).

3. Satellite Telecommunication: This type of telecommunication uses satellites in space to transmit information over long distances. Examples of satellite telecommunications include satellite TV and satellite-based internet connections.

4.2.2. Components of Telecommunication

The components of telecommunication include (Kim et al., 2011):

1. Transmission Media: This refers to the physical channels used to transmit information. Examples of transmission media include cables, radio waves, and satellite signals.
2. Equipment: This refers to the physical devices used to transmit and receive information. Examples of equipment include telephones, modems, routers, and antennas.
3. Protocols: This refers to the set of rules and procedures used to transmit and receive information. Protocols ensure that the information being transmitted is delivered accurately and efficiently. Examples of protocols include TCP/IP, HTTP, and SMTP.

Remember

Networks are a crucial component of information systems as they facilitate communication and data transfer between devices and users. It is important to design and maintain secure, efficient, and reliable networks to ensure the smooth operation of information systems and prevent potential security breaches.

4.3. NETWORK

A network refers to a collection of interconnected devices, such as computers, servers, printers, and storage devices, that can communicate and share resources with each other. Networks can be used for various purposes, such as sharing information, accessing resources, and collaborating on projects (Ben-Akiva et al., 1991).

4.3.1. Types of Networks

There are several types of networks, including (Zachman, 1987) (Figure 4.3):

1. Local Area Network (LAN): A LAN is a network that connects devices within a limited geographic area, such as a home, school, or office building.
2. Wide Area Network (WAN): A WAN is a network that spans a larger geographic area, such as a city, state, or country. WANs are often used to connect multiple LANs or remote offices.
3. Metropolitan Area Network (MAN): A MAN is a network that connects devices within a city or metropolitan area.

MANs are often used by organizations that have multiple locations within a city.

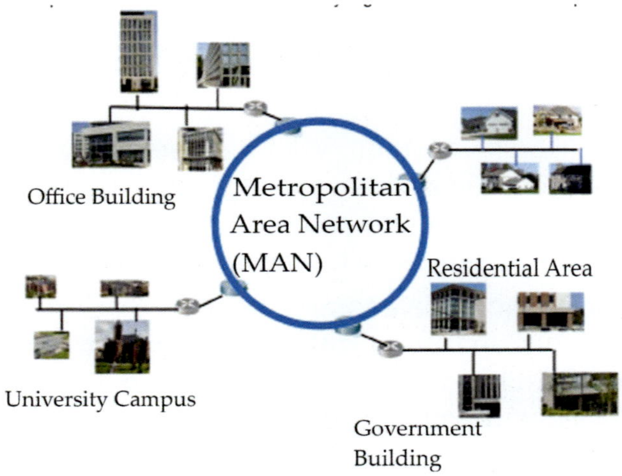

Figure 4.3. Diagram representing Metropolitan Area Network (MAN) (Source: Eric Conrad, Creative Commons License).

4.3.2. Components of Networks

The components of networks include (Mahmassani & Peeta, 1993):

1. Nodes: Nodes are the devices that are connected to a network, such as computers, servers, printers, and storage devices.
2. Links: Links are the communication channels used to connect nodes in a network. Examples of links include Ethernet cables, wireless signals, and satellite connections.
3. Protocols: Protocols are the rules and procedures used to transmit data between nodes in a network. Examples of protocols include TCP/IP, HTTP, and FTP.

Overall, networks are essential for enabling communication and resource sharing among devices and users. They play a critical role in facilitating business operations, enhancing collaboration, and enabling access to information and resources. Different types of networks and their associated components are used in various contexts, depending on the scale and requirements of the organization (Hanseth et al., 2004).

4.4. TELECOMMUNICATION AND NETWORKS IN COMPUTER SCIENCE

Telecommunication and networks are crucial components of modern computer science. They enable individuals and organizations to communicate and share information across long distances and facilitate the use of various resources and services (Al-Mamary et al., 2014).

Telecommunication and networks in computer science offer several advantages, including:

1. Faster Communication: With the use of telecommunication and networks, individuals and organizations can communicate and share information more quickly and efficiently, leading to improved productivity and faster decision-making.
2. Wider Reach: Telecommunication and networks allow individuals and organizations to connect with people and resources from different geographic locations, leading to a wider reach and greater access to information and resources.
3. Better Collaboration: Telecommunication and networks enable individuals and organizations to collaborate and work together in real-time, regardless of their physical location. This leads to better teamwork, improved innovation, and greater creativity.
4. Examples of telecommunication and networks in computer science include:
5. Email: Email is a form of telecommunication that enables individuals and organizations to send and receive messages, documents, and other information electronically over the internet.
6. Video Conferencing: Video conferencing is a type of telecommunication that enables individuals and organizations to conduct meetings and conferences in real-time, regardless of their physical location. This is made possible through the use of video and audio communication tools.
7. Cloud Computing: Cloud computing is a type of network-based computing that allows individuals and organizations to store and access data and applications over the internet. This enables them to access their resources from any location, leading to improved collaboration and greater efficiency.

TIPS

Stay up-to-date with the latest trends in telecommunication and networks such as 5G, IoT, and AI to remain competitive and take advantage of new opportunities in information systems development.

Overall, the use of telecommunication and networks in computer science plays a vital role in enabling communication, collaboration, and access to resources and services. The advantages offered by these technologies are increasingly important in today's world, where remote work, globalization, and the internet have made it essential for individuals and organizations to be connected and efficient (Sheldon, 1993). Networks are essential in computer science because they enable the sharing and transfer of data and information between different devices, systems, and locations. Here are some of the reasons why networks are necessary in computer science:

1. Data and information sharing: Networks enable the sharing of data and information between different devices and systems. This allows individuals and organizations to access and use data from different locations, leading to improved collaboration and productivity.
2. Resource sharing: Networks also enable the sharing of resources such as printers, storage devices, and servers. This means that multiple users can access the same resources, leading to cost savings and increased efficiency.
3. Communication: Networks enable communication between devices, systems, and individuals. This means that individuals can communicate and collaborate with each other regardless of their location, leading to improved collaboration and productivity.
4. Centralized management: Networks allow for centralized management of devices and systems. This means that IT professionals can manage and monitor multiple devices and systems from a single location, leading to improved efficiency and security.
5. Scalability: Networks are scalable, meaning they can easily accommodate additional devices and systems as needed. This means that organizations can easily expand their computer science as their needs grow and change.

Overall, networks are necessary in computer science because they enable data and information sharing, resource sharing, communication, centralized management, and scalability. These benefits lead to improved collaboration, productivity, and efficiency for individuals and organizations (Kim et al., 2011).

4.5. CHALLENGES AND RISKS IN TELECOMMUNICATION AND NETWORKS

While telecommunication and networks play a crucial role in modern computer science, they also come with their own set of challenges and risks.

4.5.1. Challenges

Following are the challenges:

1. Security: Telecommunication and networks are vulnerable to security threats such as unauthorized access, malware, and data breaches.

Organizations need to implement robust security measures to protect against these threats (Atay & Masera, 2011).

2. Reliability: The reliability of telecommunication and networks is critical for the smooth operation of computer science. Network downtime, slow internet speeds, and other issues can lead to reduced productivity and lost revenue.
3. Cost: Building and maintaining a network can be expensive, particularly for small businesses or organizations with limited resources. The cost of hardware, software, and network maintenance can be a significant challenge.

4.5.2. Risks

Following are the risks:

1. Hacking: Hackers can gain unauthorized access to networks and computer science, leading to data theft, system disruption, and other issues.
2. Data Breaches: Data breaches can occur when sensitive information is stolen or accessed without authorization. This can lead to loss of revenue, legal liability, and damage to the reputation of the organization.
3. Cyber Attacks: Cyber-attacks can take many forms, including malware, phishing, and denial-of-service attacks. These attacks can cause significant damage to networks and computer science, leading to data loss, system disruption, and other issues (Figure 4.4).

Figure 4.4. Various cybersecurity attacks in computer science (Source: Reciprocity, Creative Commons License).

In summary, while telecommunication and networks offer many benefits to computer science, they also pose significant challenges and risks. Organizations need to take proactive steps to address these issues, including implementing robust security measures, maintaining network reliability, and managing costs. By doing so, they can ensure that their networks and computer science remain secure, efficient, and productive (Smith et al., 2011).

The future of telecommunication and networks in computer science is promising and full of exciting possibilities. Some of the significant trends that are expected to shape the future of computer science include:

1. 5G Technology: 5G is the latest wireless technology that offers significantly faster speeds, lower latency, and improved capacity compared to the previous 4G technology. This will enable the development of new and innovative applications that rely on fast and reliable networks, such as augmented reality and virtual reality.
2. Internet of Things (IoT): IoT refers to the interconnectedness of everyday objects and devices through the internet. The use of IoT is expected to grow rapidly, with devices such as smart home appliances, medical devices, and industrial sensors becoming more prevalent (Figure 4.5).

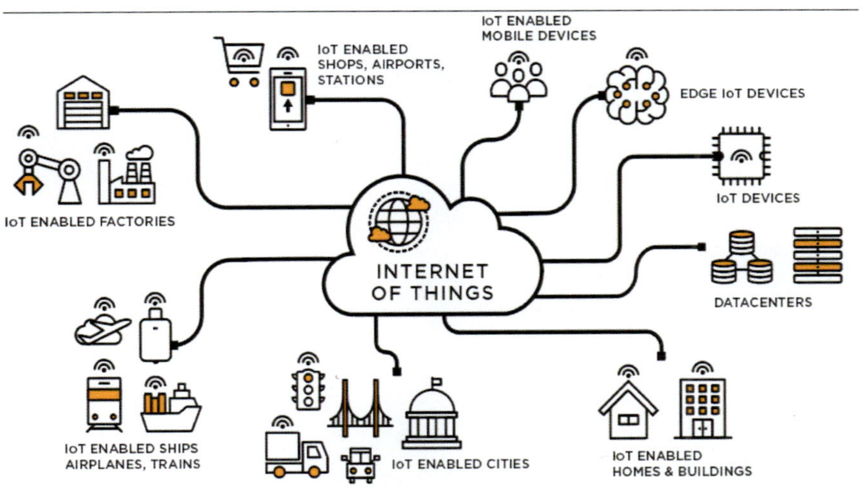

Figure 4.5. Illustration of internet of things (IoT) (Source: TIBCO, Creative Commons License).

3. Artificial Intelligence (AI): AI is expected to play a significant role in the future of computer science. AI technologies such as machine learning and natural language processing are already being used in various applications, including virtual assistants, autonomous vehicles, and intelligent decision-making systems.

The implications of these future trends on computer science and society are numerous. Some of the key implications include (Hawilo et al., 2014):

ACTIVITY 5.1

How will the widespread adoption of 5G, IoT, and AI impact the future of transportation and logistics systems, and what challenges and opportunities will arise for information systems development in these industries?

1. Greater Efficiency: The use of advanced networks and technologies will lead to greater efficiency and productivity in computer science, with tasks being completed faster and with fewer errors.
2. New Business Opportunities: The emergence of new technologies and applications will create new business opportunities and revenue streams for organizations that can take advantage of them.
3. Improved Quality of Life: The use of IoT and AI technologies is expected to improve the quality of life for individuals, with smart homes, healthcare devices, and other applications leading to greater convenience, safety, and comfort.

However, there are also potential risks associated with these future trends, including privacy and security concerns, as well as the displacement of jobs and changes to the way people live and work. It will be essential for organizations and individuals to take proactive steps to address these risks and ensure that the benefits of these future trends are realized while minimizing the potential negative impacts (Ravi et al., 2004).

SUMMARY

In conclusion, telecommunication and networks play a critical role in computer science. They enable the transmission of information and data between devices, systems, and networks, leading to faster communication, wider reach, better collaboration, cost savings, and improved productivity and efficiency.

Telecommunication and networks are necessary in computer science because they enable data and information sharing, resource sharing, communication, centralized management, and scalability. They also provide a platform for future developments and progress, such as the integration of emerging technologies like 5G, IoT, and AI, which will further enhance the capabilities and potential of computer science.

As technology continues to advance and organizations increasingly rely on digital infrastructure, the importance of telecommunication and networks in computer science will only continue to grow. It is therefore essential that individuals and organizations understand the benefits and challenges of these technologies and take steps to ensure their proper implementation and management in order to achieve optimal results.

REVIEW QUESTIONS

1. What is telecommunication, and why is it important in modern society?
2. What are the different types of telecommunication, and what are some examples of each type?
3. What are the components of a network, and how do they work together to facilitate communication and data transfer?
4. How are telecommunication and networks used in computer science, and what are some advantages of using these technologies?
5. What are some challenges and risks associated with telecommunication and networks in computer science, and how can they be mitigated?

MULTIPLE CHOICE QUESTIONS

1. What is the main advantage of using telecommunication and networks in computer science?

a. Slower communication

b. Limited reach

c. Better collaboration

d. Higher cost

2. Which type of network covers the largest geographic area?

a. LAN

b. WAN
c. MAN
d. WLAN

3. Which of the following is an example of wired telecommunication?
a. Wi-Fi
b. Bluetooth
c. Ethernet
d. Infrared

4. What is one of the main challenges of telecommunication and networks in computer science?
a. Low cost
b. High reliability
c. Low security
d. High speed

5. Which of the following is a future trend in telecommunication and networks in computer science?
a. 6G
b. 5G
c. 4G
d. 2G

Answers to Multiple Choice Questions

1. (c) 2. (b) 3. (c) 4. (c) 5. (b)

REFERENCES

1. Ahn, J. H., & Skudlark, A. E., (1997). Resolving conflict of interests in the process of an information system implementation for advanced telecommunication services. *Journal of Information Technology, 12*(1), 3–13.
2. Al-Mamary, Y. H., Shamsuddin, A., & Aziati, N., (2014). The meaning of management computer science and its role in telecommunication companies in Yemen. *American Journal of Software Engineering, 2*(2), 22–25.
3. Assegie, T. A., & Nair, P. S., (2019). A review on software defined network security risks and challenges. *TELKOMNIKA (Telecommunication Computing Electronics and Control), 17*(6), 3168–3174.
4. Atay, S., & Masera, M., (2011). Challenges for the security analysis of next generation networks. *Information Security Technical Report, 16*(1), 3–11.

5. Batalla, J. M., Andrukiewicz, E., Gomez, G. P., Sapiecha, P., Mavromoustakis, C. X., Mastorakis, G., & Imran, M., (2020). Security risk assessment for 5G networks: National perspective. *IEEE Wireless Communications, 27*(4), 16–22.
6. Ben-Akiva, M., De Palma, A., & Isam, K., (1991). Dynamic network models and driver computer science. *Transportation Research Part A: General, 25*(5), 251–266.
7. Benzaid, C., & Taleb, T., (2020). AI-driven zero touch network and service management in 5G and beyond: Challenges and research directions. *IEEE Network, 34*(2), 186–194.
8. Chen, A. J., Boudreau, M. C., & Watson, R. T., (2008). Computer science and ecological sustainability. *Journal of Systems and Information Technology, 10*(3), 186–201.
9. Dewett, T., & Jones, G. R., (2001). The role of information technology in the organization: A review, model, and assessment. *Journal of Management, 27*(3), 313–346.
10. Grover, V., Cheon, M. J., & Teng, J. T., (1994). A descriptive study on the outsourcing of computer science functions. *Information & Management, 27*(1), 33–44.
11. Grover, V., Cheon, M. J., & Teng, J. T., (1996). The effect of service quality and partnership on the outsourcing of computer science functions. *Journal of Management Computer Science, 12*(4), 89–116.
12. Gupta, A., Stahl, D. O., & Whinston, A. B., (1999). The economics of network management. *Communications of the ACM, 42*(9), 57–63.
13. Haggerty, P., & Seetharaman, K., (1998). The benefits of CORBA-based network management. *Communications of the ACM, 41*(10), 73–79.
14. Hanseth, O., Aanestad, M., & Berg, M., (2004). Guest editors' introduction: Actor network theory and computer science. What's so special? *Information Technology & People, 17*(2), 116–123.
15. Hawilo, H., Shami, A., Mirahmadi, M., & Asal, R., (2014). NFV: State of the art, challenges, and implementation in next generation mobile networks (vEPC). *IEEE Network, 28*(6), 18–26.
16. Hellström, T., (2003). Systemic innovation and risk: Technology assessment and the challenge of responsible innovation. *Technology in Society, 25*(3), 369–384.
17. Hunt, R., (1997). SNMP, SNMPv2 and CMIP—The technologies for multivendor network management. *Computer Communications, 20*(2), 73–88.
18. Kim, K. K., Ryoo, S. Y., & Jung, M. D., (2011). Inter-organizational computer science visibility in buyer–supplier relationships: The case of telecommunication equipment component manufacturing industry. *Omega, 39*(6), 667–676.
19. Mahmassani, H. S., & Peeta, S., (1993). Network performance under system optimal and user equilibrium dynamic assignments: Implications for advanced traveler computer science. *Transportation Research Record, 1408*, 83.
20. Raman, L., (1998). OSI systems and network management. *IEEE Communications Magazine, 36*(3), 46–53.

21. Ravi, S., Raghunathan, A., Kocher, P., & Hattangady, S., (2004). Security in embedded systems: Design challenges. *ACM Transactions on Embedded Computing Systems (TECS), 3*(3), 461–491.
22. Schwartz, M., (1995). Network management and control issues in multimedia wireless networks. *IEEE Personal Communications, 2*(3), 8–16.
23. Sheldon, P. J., (1993). Destination computer science. *Annals of Tourism Research, 20*(4), 633–649.
24. Smith, P., Hutchison, D., Sterbenz, J. P., Schöller, M., Fessi, A., Karaliopoulos, M., & Plattner, B., (2011). Network resilience: A systematic approach. *IEEE Communications Magazine, 49*(7), 88–97.
25. Subba, R. S., (2004). Role of ICTs in India's rural community computer science. *Info, 6*(4), 261–269.
26. Watson, R. T., Kelly, G. G., Galliers, R. D., & Brancheau, J. C., (1997). Key issues in computer science management: An international perspective. *Journal of Management Computer Science, 13*(4), 91–115.
27. Zachman, J. A., (1987). A framework for computer science architecture. *IBM Systems Journal, 26*(3), 276–292.
28. Zio, E., & Aven, T., (2011). Uncertainties in smart grids behavior and modeling: What are the risks and vulnerabilities? How to analyze them? *Energy Policy, 39*(10), 6308–6320.

CHAPTER 5

ARTIFICIAL INTELLIGENCE

UNIT INTRODUCTION

Artificial intelligence (AI) has experienced several false starts and pauses. It is part-time because people do not fully grasp what AI is about or what it could achieve. The fact that films, tv programs, and novels have all collaborated to create unrealistic expectations regarding the potential of AI is a significant contributor to the problem. In contrast, the human propensity to anthropomorphize or attribute human attributes to technology creates the impression that artificial intelligence must do tasks beyond its capabilities. Therefore, the most effective method for beginning this work is describing what (Charniak, 1985).

What AI is, what it's not, and how it relates to computers in the present day are all discussed. Naturally, the base for what you want from AI is a composite of how you describe AI, your technologies for implementing AI, and your objectives towards AI. This is because how you define AI influences the technologies you have available to implement AI. As a direct result, everyone has a unique perspective on AI. This book adopts an approach somewhat within the middle, looking at artificial intelligence from as many angles as possible. To provide you with the most accurate picture of artificial intelligence as technological advancement, it neither participates in the hyperbole advocated by AI's supporters nor wallows in the pessimism backed by the technology's critics.

Consequently, you may discover that you possess relatively different perceptions than many of those who face inside this book, which is excellent; nonetheless, you must examine what the technologies can genuinely achieve for you instead of expecting something they can't (Wang, 2019) (Figure 5.1).

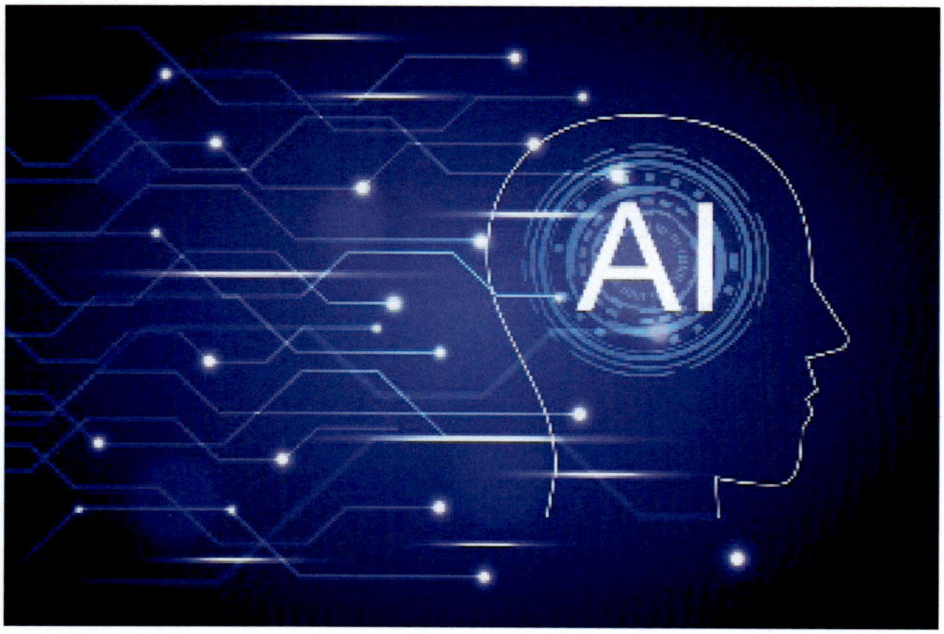

Figure 5.1. An Overview of AI (Source: UiB, Creative Commons License).

Learning Objectives

By the end of this chapter, students will be able to learn the following:

- What is AI?
- Differentiate between AI and discerning intelligence
- Four ways of defining AI
- History of AI.

Key Terms

- Artificial Intelligence
- Discerning Intelligence
- Dartmouth
- AI Hype
- AI Winters
- Simulation Potential
- Human Tool

5.1. DEFINING THE TERM AI

A phrase's definition is necessary before it can be utilized in any relevant or practical context. Since no one can agree on a definition, the term ultimately has no meaning and is merely a group of characters (Figure 5.2).

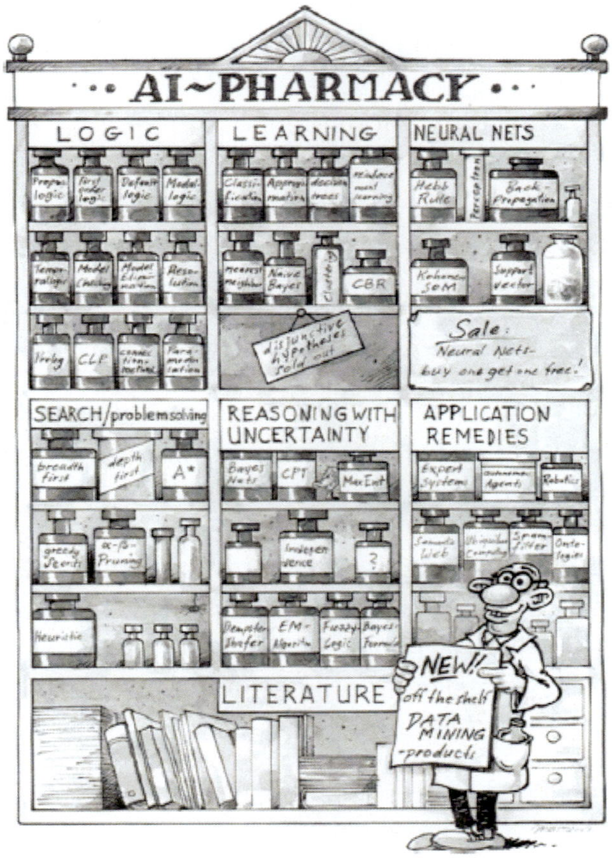

Figure 5.2. A short selection of the options provided by AI (Source: Wolfgang Ertel, Creative Commons License).

Using technical terminology that has garnered a lot of press attention at various points and in different ways, it's crucial to define the idiom (a phrase whose meaning is unclear from the definitions of its constituent parts). The fact that there are several debates and controversies surrounding the words "*artificial intelligence*" is because saying that it is artificial intelligence doesn't tell us anything useful. Yes, you could claim that what happens is unnatural because it didn't originate from such a natural source. The intelligence component, however, is, at best equivocal. Although if you don't particularly agree with the concept of AI as it is used in the subsections that follow, understanding it will make it easier for you to grasp the rest of the material (Schmidt, 2020).

5.2. DISCERNING INTELLIGENCE

A variety of people have different ideas of what intelligence is. However, you might assert that intelligence entails mental processes made up of the following processes:

- **Learning:** Possessing the capacity to gather and process new data.
- **Reasoning:** Being able to use the information to its fullest potential.
- **Understanding:** Considering the effects of information manipulation.
- **Grasping truths:** Evaluating the accuracy of the modified data.
- **Seeing relationships:** Determining the relationship between validated data and other data.
- **Considering meanings:** Applying principles to specific circumstances in a way that is consistent with how they relate.
- **Separating fact from belief:** Assessing whether the information is sufficiently supported by verifiable sources, which can always be reliable (Schuurman, 2019).

Did you Know?

In 1956 John McCarthy coined the term 'artificial intelligence' and had the first AI conference.

Also, this list, which has the potential to be lengthy, is open to interpretation by those who take it seriously. But as anyone can see from lists, intelligence typically behaves in a manner that a computer program may imitate as a way of a simulated world:

1. Decide on a target based on your needs or desires.
2. Evaluate the importance of any knowledge that is currently known to help achieve the goal.
3. Obtain new data that can help you achieve your aim.
4. Change the data to take on a form like the information already available.
5. Define the connections and truth levels between the old and new data.
6. Check to see if the objective was accomplished.
7. Adapt the objective by considering the new information and its impact on the likelihood of success.
8. If necessary, repeat Steps 2 through 7 until the objective is met (found to be confirmed) or all options have been explored (found false) (Jani et al., 2021).

Computers can facilitate this process by creating algorithms and giving users data access, but their capacity for intelligence is severely constrained. For instance, a computer cannot comprehend anything as it depends mainly on mechanical machine operations to modify data utilizing pure math. Similarly, computers struggle to distinguish between truth and lies. A machine could fully implement none of the mental processes included in the listing that characterizes intelligence. Classifying intelligence helps determine what intelligence entails. To complete tasks, humans need a variety of intelligence rather than just one. Knowing these categories of intelligence, as described by Harvard professor Howard Gardner, makes it easier to connect these to the types of activities a computer can replicate as intelligence (Gyory & Cagan, 2022).

5.3. DISCOVERING WAYS TO DEFINE AI

The first idea that needs to be understood would be that AI doesn't have anything in common with human intellect, as was covered in the section above. Yes, some artificial intelligence (AI) is modeled like human intelligence, but that's all it is: a simulation. Consider the interaction between goal-seeking, data processing to attain the goal, and data collecting to improve understanding of the objective when considering AI. AI uses algorithms to produce a result that could or could not be related to human objectives or means of reaching those objectives. Considering this, there are four categories in which to place AI (Langley & Zytkow, 1989).

5.3.1. Acting Humanly

The Turing test, which determines whether a computer can successfully perform when it is impossible to distinguish it from a human, is best represented by a computer that behaves like a human. The media's portrayal of AI is also reflected in this category. It is used in fields including machine learning, automated reasoning, information retrieval, and natural language processing (all four of which are necessary to be current to pass the test) (Laborie, 2003).

There was no physical interaction in the initial Turing Test. The machine must use machine learning and robots to pass the more recent Total Turing Test, which would involve a physical connection in the form of wise ability inquiry. Modern methods incorporate attaining the goal instead of closely emulating humans. For instance, the Wright Brothers didn't succeed in building an airplane by precisely replicating the flight of birds; rather, the birds offered inspiration for the development of aerodynamics, which ultimately led to human flight. To fly is the aim. Both birds and people succeed in achieving this objective, but they go about it differently (Weitz et al., 2021).

5.3.2. Thinking Humanly

Whenever a computer thinks like a human, it may complete jobs like driving a car which requires intelligence from such a person in contrast to rote operations. The cognitive modeling technique defines a strategy for figuring out how humans know, which is necessary to establish whether software thinks like such a human.

5.3.3. Introspection

Identifying and recording the strategies employed to accomplish objectives by keeping an eye on one's cognitive processes.

5.3.4. Psychological Testing

Monitoring a person's behavior and entering it into a database of behaviors from other people who had a comparable mix of situations, objectives, resources, and environmental factors (among other things).

5.3.5. Brain Imaging

Directly observing brain activity using various mechanical techniques, such as Computerized Axial Tomography (CAT), Positron Emission Tomography (PET), Magnetic Resonance Imaging (MRI), and Magnetoencephalography (MEG) (Malandraki-Miller & Riley, 2021).

The subcategories used to characterize AI provide a way to think about numerous applications or purposes for AI. A few methods used to categorize AI are imprecise and lack distinction. For instance, some organizations have strong opinions about AI (general intelligence, which can adjust to a wide range of settings) or weak opinions about AI (specific intelligence designed to perform a specific task well). Strong AI has the drawback of performing no task well, but weak AI is too general to carry out tasks independently (Langley & Zytkow, 1989).

Even so, using just two type categories won't be sufficient. A more robust foundation for comprehending AI is provided by the four classification kinds advocated by Arend Hintze:

Reactive machines are those you see winning chess games or participating in game shows. Reactive devices lack memory and experience on which to draw knowledge. Instead, it recreates each judgment using only processing power and clever algorithms. This is an illustration of a subpar AI employed for a specific objective.

5.3.6. Limited Memory

An autonomous robot or self-driving automobile cannot spare the time necessary to make every choice from scratch. These devices rely on a small amount of storage to provide practical experience in various circumstances. Whenever the machine encounters the same condition, it can depend on expertise to speed up decision-making and offer more resources for unheard-of decisions. This demonstrates the current state of powerful AI (Nagarajan et al., 2019).

5.3.7. Theory of Mind

A machine with this kind of awareness is somewhat currently possible but not available in any commercial form. It can evaluate its set objectives and the future goals of many other entities in a similar environment. However, that level of AI needs to be fully developed before self-driving cars can achieve genuine autonomy. A self-driving car must understand where it needs to travel, but it also needs to anticipate how other drivers' objectives might conflict with its own and respond appropriately.

Remember

Artificial intelligence (AI) is currently one of the hottest buzzwords in tech, and with good reason. The last few years have seen several innovations and advancements that have previously been solely in the realm of science fiction slowly transform into reality.

5.3.8. Self-Awareness

This kind of AI is what you typically see in films. However, since such a robot could have a feeling of self-awareness, this would require technology that is not even remotely feasible. Additionally, this kind of machine would've been able to deduce the intention of others depending on experiential knowledge rather than only guessing their aims based on the environment as well as the responses of other entities (Sahoo et al., 2021).

5.4. UNDERSTANDING THE HISTORY OF AI

You can better appreciate intelligence from a human point of view and how hopelessly incompetent modern computers are even to simulate human intelligence, far less truly develop intelligence themselves, by reading the earlier sections of such a chapter.

But the ambition to build sentient machines—or, in earlier times, idols—is as old as humans. There is a great need not to be isolated in the cosmos and to have a communication partner free from other people's flaws. The background of modern AI efforts is briefly reviewed in the following parts because a single book obviously cannot cover the entirety of human history (Cetinic & She, 2022) (Figure 5.3).

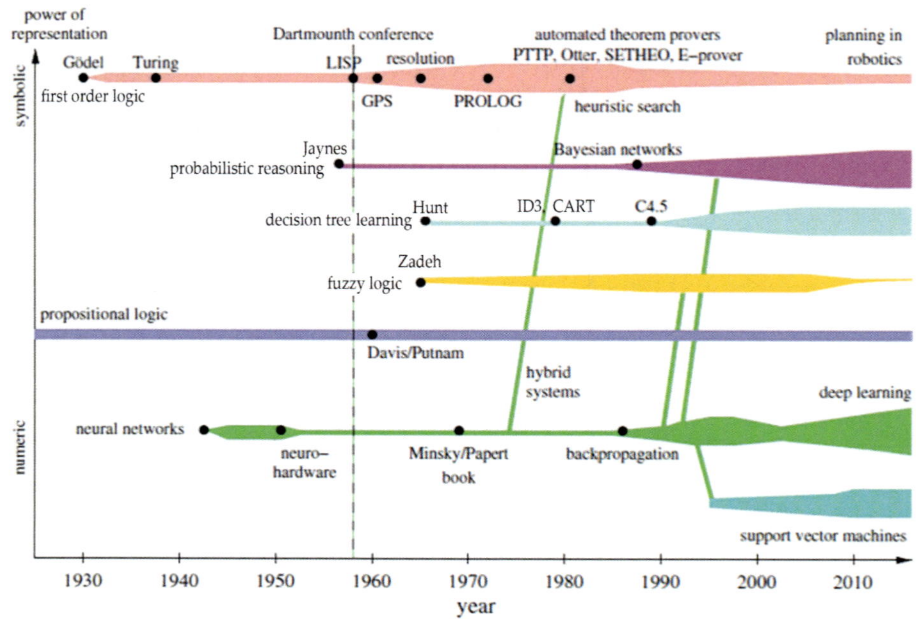

Figure 5.3. History of the many AI fields. The width of the bars represents the frequency of application of the procedure (Source: Wolfgang Ertel, Creative Commons License).

5.5. STARTING WITH SYMBOLIC LOGIC AT DARTMOUTH

The first computers were merely computing tools. They emulated how we can manipulate signs to execute simple math operations like addition. Later, the capacity for quantitative reasoning through comparisons was introduced to logical reasoning (such as deciding whether one value is better than another). However, humans were still required to specify the computation's algorithm, supply the necessary data in the proper format, and then evaluate the outcome. Several scientists gathered for a workshop on the Dartmouth College campus in the summer of 1956 to take further action. They projected that it would take, at most, a generation to create robots that might reason as well as humans. They were mistaken. Only recently have we recognized that machines are capable of reasoning mathematically and logically just as well as human beings (which means that computers necessarily master at least six more intelligence before reaching whatever is even close to human intelligence) (Kline, 2010) (Figure 5.4).

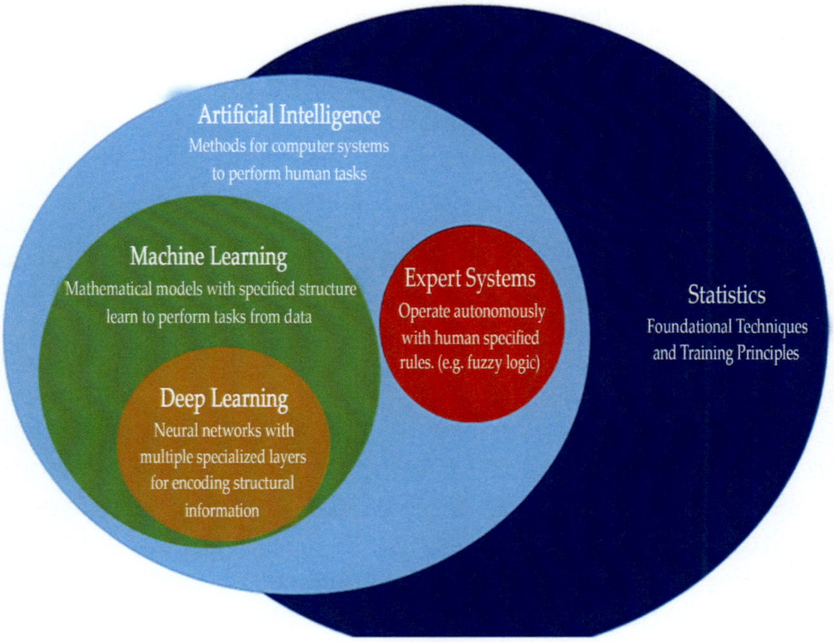

Figure 5.4. Relationships between AI, ML, DL, expert systems, and statistics are shown in a Venn diagram (Source: American Meteorological, Creative Commons License).

The hardware issue with Dartmouth College and other period projects is the processing power needed to complete computations to construct a simulation quickly. But that's not the entire issue. Hardware plays a role in the equation, but you can't imitate a process you don't fully comprehend. The hardware has improved sufficiently to support the necessary calculations, which is why AI is somewhat immediately effective (Fogelin, 2005).

The primary issue with all these initial attempts, still a significant issue today—is that we don't comprehend human reasoning well enough to develop any simulation, presuming that such a simulation of guidance is even feasible. Remember the problems with managed flying that were mentioned previously in the chapter. The Wright brothers developed the subject of aerodynamics by studying the processes used by birds rather than by replicating them.

As a result, whenever anyone claims that the next significant advancement in AI is just around the corner but that there isn't a solid dissertation outlining the methods involved, the advancement is anything but imminent (Goncharov & Knight, 2014).

5.6. CONTINUING WITH EXPERT SYSTEMS

Utilize experts' expertise and lessen AI's computing demands; expert systems first surfaced in the 1970s and then again in the 1980s. There were several expert system depictions, such as rule-based, frame-based, and logic-based. Rule-based expert systems use if-then declarations to base decisions on a rule of thumb. In contrast, frame-based expert systems use databases arranged into connected hierarchies of generic information called frames (which rely on set theory to find relationships). Expert systems are a significant development because they represent AI's first real successful and usable applications (McKinion & Lemmon, 1985).

Although they aren't termed expert systems anymore, you can still observe them. For instance, expert systems include punctuation and grammar checks in your application. Mainly the grammar checker is heavily rule-based. It helps to take a closer look at potential new applications for expert systems in the real world.

Expert systems have the drawback of being challenging to develop and maintain. Initial users must master specialist programming languages like Prolog or List Processing (LisP). Some companies recognized a chance to use solutions like VPExpert, which depends on the rule-based methodology, to give rookie or less experienced programmers' access to expert systems. These systems, however, typically offered very little usefulness when leveraging modest knowledge bases. The term "expert system" started to fade in the 1990s. Although it did seem as though expert systems were just a failure, the truth is that they were so effective that they were integrated into the applications for which they were created. For instance, when using a word processor, you had to purchase a separate grammar-checking program like Right Writer. However, due to their success, grammar checks are now included in word processors (if not always correct) (Dillard & Yuthas, 2001).

5.7. OVERCOMING THE AI WINTERS

The phrase "AI winter" describes a time when AI development funding was low. In general, advocates of AI have overstated what is feasible, leading those with a large amount of cash but little technical expertise to invest in the technology. When AI falls short of expectations, a phase of criticism is followed by a funding cut. These cycles have happened several times over the years, each destructive to real advancement (Gonsalves, 2019).

Machine learning, a tool that enables computers to learn from data, is why AI is experiencing a new buzz phase. When a computer learns from data, its operations (tasks) are derived directly through examples that demonstrate how the computer ought to act rather than being predetermined by a human programmer. It's like teaching a baby by modeling good behavior. Because careless instruction might lead to the computer learning how to perform things properly, machine learning has drawbacks (Grudin, 2009). Five scientific tribes are working on machine-learning algorithms, every with a unique perspective (for more information, read the "Avoiding AI Hype" part later in the chapter). Deep learning, a method that aims to mimic the human brain, is presently the most effective approach. Large datasets generated by the digitization of our culture, access to powerful computers, intelligent algorithms, and massive investments from companies like Google, Amazon, Facebook, and others who leverage the AI revolution within their businesses have made deep learning conceivable.

People claim that deep learning has ended the AI winter, and they are correct for the time being. However, it's clear from observing how people regard AI today that if proponents don't temper their hyperbole, another wave of criticism will soon emerge. AI is capable of astounding feats, but they are the kind of banal feats that are recounted in the next chapter (Kautz, 2022).

5.8. CONSIDERING AI USES

Today, AI is present in a wide range of applications. The only issue is that you are unaware of the technology's existence because it functions perfectly. You might even be astonished to see how many appliances in your home currently employ AI. For instance, certain smart thermostats automatically develop routines depending on how you physically adjust the temperature. Similarly, voice input commands gadgets that pick up on your speech patterns to improve communication. Your car most likely has AI, and the office is more so. Even when they are dramatic, AI has millions of applications safely hidden from view. Here are a few examples of how artificial intelligence may be used (Kampf & Fashakin, 2021).

5.8.1. Fraud Detection

A credit card company contacts you and inquires whether you made a specific purchase. The credit card issuer isn't interested; it's merely warning you that someone else might use your card to make purchases. The AI included in the credit card provider's code noticed an unusual spending trend and notified someone about it.

5.8.2. Resource Scheduling

Many companies need to plan their resource usage. For instance, a hospital might need to choose a patient's location based on the patient's needs, the accessibility of qualified specialists, and the anticipated length of stay indicated by the doctor.

5.8.3. Complex Analysis

With sophisticated analysis, humans frequently require assistance since there are too many variables to consider. The same signs, for instance, might point to multiple issues. To preserve a patient's life, a physician or other professional could require assistance in quickly reaching a diagnosis.

5.8.4. Automation

AI can be included in any automation system to handle unforeseen events or adjustments. A drawback of some modern automation is that it could be stopped by an unforeseen circumstance, like an object placed in the wrong location. By incorporating AI, automation may be able to deal with unforeseen circumstances and carry on as usual (Kwon & Kim, 2021).

5.8.5. Customer Service

You might not even reach a live person on the customer support line you're calling. The automation can handle most of your queries using multiple resources and scripts. You may not be able to recognize that you're speaking with a machine if the vocal inflection is good (supplied by AI as well).

5.8.6. Safety Systems

Several safety features featured in modern machines rely upon AI to take control of the vehicle in an emergency. For instance, many autonomous braking systems use artificial intelligence (AI) to stop the car depending on all the data that a vehicle can offer, such as the path of a skid.

5.8.7. Machine Efficiency

AI can assist in controlling a machine to achieve optimal efficiency. The AI manages resource usage to prevent the system from exceeding speed or other objectives. Every watt of energy is used precisely when necessary to deliver the services required (Ranschaert, 2018).

5.9. AVOIDING AI HYPE

AI hype is frequently mentioned in this chapter. However, the chapter barely scratches the surface of the unrest that has been created. You could think AI is more advanced than it is if you see films like her and Ex Machina. The issue is that AI is still in its infancy, and any use cases like those in films result from an overly creative imagination. You may be familiar with the singularities, which serve as the basis for the speculative assertions made in media and films.

The five types of learning employed in machine learning are all included in the singularity, which is a master algorithm. According to the seven types of intelligence covered in the chapter's opening "Discerning intelligence" section, the machine has to be capable of learning as a person would accomplish what all these sources indicate it must be capable of doing. The five developmental tribes are as follows (Hendler, 2008):

- **Symbolists:** This tribe has a logical and philosophical foundation. This team uses inverse deduction to find solutions.
- **Connectionists:** This tribe has its roots in neurobiology and uses a back-propagation algorithm to find solutions to issues.
- **Evolutionaries:** The tribe of evolutionists derives from evolutionary biology and uses genetic programming to resolve issues (Tandon, 2019).
- **Bayesians:** This tribe has statistical roots and uses probabilistic reasoning to resolve issues.
- **Analogies:** This tribe has its roots in psychology. To fix issues, the group uses kernel machines.

To build a unique algorithm (the master algorithm) that can learn everything, machine learning's ultimate objective is to merge the techniques and ideologueies used by the five tribes. Of course, it will take a while to accomplish that goal. However, researchers like Pedro Domingo's are presently focusing on that objective (Sandkuhl, 2019).

The five tribes might not be capable of providing enough data to adequately address the issue of human intelligence, making the situation even less noticeable.

As a result, developing master algorithms for each of the five tribes might not result in singularity. It would help if you were astounded at this point at how little individuals know about their beliefs or why they believe the way they do. Any rumors about AI enslaving humanity or eventually surpassing them are untrue (Strachna & Asan, 2021).

TIPS

Artificial Intelligence is a method of making a computer, a computer-controlled robot, or a software think intelligently like the human mind.

5.10. CONNECTING AI TO THE UNDERLYING COMPUTER

You could use a computing system such as an application with the necessary software and a level of knowledge to observe AI in action. The computing system might be any device with a chip inside; in reality, a smartphone performs as effectively as a desktop computer for some tasks. Of course, whether you're Amazon and wish to offer guidance on a specific person's upcoming purchase, a smartphone won't cut it; you'll need a potent computer (Hendler, 2008).

The quantity of work you anticipate the AI to complete depends on the computer network size. The application's size, functionality, and sometimes even locations can change. A server-based application could be used, for instance, if you run a business and would like to analyze customer data to find a way of making a sales pitch. The application does not exist on your computer; instead, you contact through an internet application hosted on Amazon's servers. If you're a consumer and want to search for items on Amazon, go along with your present buy items (Perez Cruz & Treisman, 2018).

The information base differs in size and location. The more complicated the information, the more information you can extract from it, yet more manipulation is required. When it relates to knowledge management, there are no free meals. It's also crucial to consider how time and place interact. You may access a sizable body of knowledge online with the help of a data connection; however, the connectivity latency makes it time-consuming. Localized databases frequently lack details, even if they are quick (Sandkuhl, 2019).

ACTIVITY 5.1.

A local coffee shop wants to implement an AI-driven chatbot to assist with customer service and automate the process of taking orders. As a computer science student, you are tasked with designing this chatbot.

1. What are the key features and functionalities that this AI-driven chatbot should have to effectively handle customer inquiries and process orders?
2. What natural language processing techniques would you consider using to ensure the chatbot can understand and respond to customer messages accurately?
3. How would you train and test the chatbot to improve its performance over time and ensure it meets the needs of the coffee shop and its customers?

SUMMARY

1. What is AI?

This chapter introduces the readers to the introduction of AI. It explains that Artificial intelligence (AI) is the ability of a digital computer or computer-controlled robot to perform tasks often associated with intelligent beings.

2. Four ways to define AI

This also summarizes the four ways that can define AI. Those four ways are

i. Acting Humanly
ii. Thinking humanly
iii. Introspection
iv. Psychological Testing

3. AI winters

This chapter summarizes that an AI winter is a phase in the history of artificial intelligence characterized by decreased interest in artificial intelligence research and financing for that research.

REVIEW QUESTIONS

1. Define AI
2. Differentiate between AI and discerning intelligence
3. What do you know about the history of AI?
4. What are those four ways which define AI?
5. Explain avoiding AI hype.

MULTIPLE CHOICE QUESTIONS

1. What is the full form of "AI"?

a. Artificially Intelligent
b. Artificial Intelligence
c. Artificially Intelligence
d. Advanced Intelligence

2. What is Artificial Intelligence?

a. Artificial Intelligence is a field that aims to make humans more intelligent
b. Artificial Intelligence is a field that aims to improve the security

c. Artificial Intelligence is a field that aims to develop intelligent machines
d. Artificial Intelligence is a field that aims to mine the data

3. Who is the inventor of Artificial Intelligence?

a. Geoffrey Hinton
b. Andrew Ng
c. John McCarthy
d. Jürgen Schmid Huber

4. Which of the following is the branch of Artificial Intelligence?

a. Machine Learning
b. Cyber forensics
c. Full-Stack Developer
d. Network Design

5. What is the goal of Artificial Intelligence?

a. To solve artificial problems
b. To extract scientific causes
c. To explain various sorts of intelligence
d. To solve real-world problems

Answers to Multiple Choice Questions

1. (b) 2. (c) 3. (c) 4. (a) 5. (c)

REFERENCES

1. Adam, A. E., (1990). What can the history of AI learn from the history of science? *AI & Society, 4*(3), 232–241.
2. Akerkar, R., (2014). *Introduction to Artificial Intelligence*. PHI Learning Pvt. Ltd.
3. Alsheibani, S. A., Cheung, D., & Messom, D., (2019). *Factors Inhibiting the Adoption of Artificial Intelligence at Organizational-Level: A Preliminary Investigation, 1(1), 5-10.*
4. Bench-Capon, T., Araszkiewicz, M., Ashley, K., Atkinson, K., Bex, F., Borges, F., & Wyner, A. Z., (2012). A history of AI and law in 50 papers: 25 years of the international conference on AI and law. *Artificial Intelligence and Law, 20*(3), 215–319.
5. Bokovnya, A. Y., Begishev, I. R., Khisamova, Z. I., Narimanova, N. R., Sherbakova, L. M., & Minina, A. A., (2020). Legal approaches to artificial intelligence concept and essence definition. *Revista San Gregorio*, (41), 115–121.
6. Bosse, J., Glancy, C., McDaniels, J., Provaznik, D., & Wisniewski, J., (2018). *Origins of Intelligence: Discerning Corroboration vs. Replication in Open-Source Intelligence*

Production 1(1), 6-16.

7. Buchanan, B. G., (2005). A (very) brief history of artificial intelligence. *Ai Magazine, 26*(4), 53–53.
8. Cai, C. J., Winter, S., Steiner, D., Wilcox, L., & Terry, M., (2019). "Hello AI": Uncovering the onboarding needs of medical practitioners for human-AI collaborative decision-making. *Proceedings of the ACM on Human-computer Interaction, 3*(CSCW), 1–24.
9. Cetinic, E., & She, J., (2022). Understanding and creating art with AI: Review and outlook. *ACM Transactions on Multimedia Computing, Communications, and Applications (TOMM), 18*(2), 1–22.
10. Champagne, D., Chilukuri, S., Imprialou, M., Rathore, S., & VanLare, J., (2018). *Machine Learning and Therapeutics 2.0: Avoiding Hype, Realizing Potential.* McKinsey & Company.
11. Chang, C. L., Cheng, B. W., & Su, J. L., (2004). Using case-based reasoning to establish a continuing care information system of discharge planning. *Expert Systems with Applications, 26*(4), 601–613.
12. Charniak, E., (1985). *Introduction to Artificial Intelligence*. Pearson Education India.
13. Coppin, B., (2004). *Artificial Intelligence Illuminated*. Jones & Bartlett Learning.
14. DePold, H. R., & Gass, F. D., (1999). *The Application of Expert Systems and Neural Networks to Gas Turbine Prognostics and Diagnostics, 78668, 98-101.*
15. Dillard, J. F., & Yuthas, K., (2001). A responsibility ethics for audit expert systems. *Journal of Business Ethics, 30*(4), 337–359.
16. Duan, Y., Edwards, J. S., & Dwivedi, Y. K., (2019). Artificial intelligence for decision making in the era of big data–evolution, challenges and research agenda. *International Journal of Information Management, 48*, 63–71.
17. Ertel, W., (2018). *Introduction to Artificial Intelligence*. Springer.
18. Flasiński, M., (2016). *Introduction to Artificial Intelligence*. Switzerland: Springer International Publishing.
19. Fogelin, R., (2005). The logic of deep disagreements. *Informal Logic, 25*(1).
20. Foucault, M., & Blasius, M., (1993). About the beginning of the hermeneutics of the self: Two lectures at Dartmouth. *Political Theory, 21*(2), 198–227.
21. Frawley, W. J., Piatetsky-Shapiro, G., & Matheus, C. J., (1992). Knowledge discovery in databases: An overview. *AI Magazine, 13*(3), 57.
22. Gaines, B., (1988). Knowledge acquisition systems for rapid prototyping of expert systems. *INFOR: Information Systems and Operational Research, 26*(4), 256–285.
23. Goncharov, H., & Knight, M., (2014). Skordev, for his thesis entitled, Computability in partial algebraic systems. Starting in 1986, a series of international conferences organized by the department of mathematical logic at Sofia university took place at which prominent scientists from around the world participated. It was at one of these conferences that Soskov met Yian-nis Moschovakis, from UCLA. Moschovakis had

invented the notions of prime and search. *The Bulletin of Symbolic Logic, 20*(1).
24. Gonsalves, T., (2019). The summers and winters of artificial intelligence. In: *Advanced Methodologies and Technologies in Artificial Intelligence, Computer Simulation, and Human-Computer Interaction* (pp. 168–179). IGI Global.
25. Grudin, J., (2009). AI and HCI: Two fields divided by a common focus. *Ai Magazine, 30*(4), 48.
26. Gupta, T., & Ghosh, B. K., (1989). A survey of expert systems in manufacturing and process planning. *Computers in Industry, 11*(2), 195–204.
27. Gyory, J. T., Kotovsky, K., & Cagan, J., (2022). Is it human or is it artificial intelligence? Discerning the impact and effectiveness of process managers based on the manager's identity. *Proceedings of the Design Society, 2*, 1579–1588.
28. Hendler, J., (2008). Avoiding another AI winter. *IEEE Intelligent Systems, 23*(02), 2–4.
29. Jani, V., Danford, D. A., Thompson, W. R., Schuster, A., Manlhiot, C., & Kutty, S., (2021). The discerning ear: Cardiac auscultation in the era of artificial intelligence and telemedicine. *European Heart Journal-Digital Health, 2*(3), 456–466.
30. Kampf, C. E., & Fashakin, O. K., (2021). The social responsibility of AI: A framework for considering ethics and DEI. In: *Public Relations for Social Responsibility* (pp. 121–133). Emerald Publishing Limited.
31. Kautz, H., (2022). The third AI summer: AAAI Robert S. Engelmore memorial lecture. *AI Magazine, 43*(1), 93–104.
32. Kline, R., (2010). Cybernetics, automata studies, and the Dartmouth conference on artificial intelligence. *IEEE Annals of the History of Computing, 33*(4), 5–16.
33. Kushniruk, A., & Borycki, E., (2021). The human factors of AI in healthcare: Recurrent issues, future challenges and ways forward. In: *Multiple Perspectives on Artificial Intelligence in Healthcare* (pp. 3–12). Springer, Cham.
34. Kwon, K., Lee, S., & Kim, S., (2021). AI-based home energy management system considering energy efficiency and resident satisfaction. *IEEE Internet of Things Journal, 9*(2), 1608–1621.
35. Laborie, P., (2003). Algorithms for propagating resource constraints in AI planning and scheduling: Existing approaches and new results. *Artificial Intelligence, 143*(2), 151–188.
36. Langley, P., & Zytkow, J. M., (1989). Data-driven approaches to empirical discovery. *Artificial Intelligence, 40*(1–3), 283–312.
37. Latah, M., & Toker, L., (2019). Artificial intelligence enabled software-defined networking: A comprehensive overview. *IET Networks, 8*(2), 79–99.
38. Lungarella, M., Iida, F., Bongard, J. C., & Pfeifer, R., (2007). AI in the 21st century–with historical reflections. In: *50 Years of Artificial Intelligence* (pp. 1–8). Springer, Berlin, Heidelberg.
39. Malandraki-Miller, S., & Riley, P. R., (2021). Use of artificial intelligence to enhance phenotypic drug discovery. *Drug Discovery Today, 26*(4), 887–901.

40. McKinion, J. M., & Lemmon, H. E., (1985). Expert systems for agriculture. *Computers and Electronics in Agriculture, 1*(1), 31–40.
41. Mintz, Y., & Brodie, R., (2019). Introduction to artificial intelligence in medicine. *Minimally Invasive Therapy & Allied Technologies, 28*(2), 73–81.
42. Mumford, E., & MacDonald, W. B., (1989). *XSEL's Progress: The Continuing Journey of an Expert System*. John Wiley & Sons, Inc.
43. Nagarajan, N., Yapp, E. K., Le, N. Q. K., Kamaraj, B., Al-Subaie, A. M., & Yeh, H. Y., (2019). Application of computational biology and artificial intelligence technologies in cancer precision drug discovery. *BioMed Research International, 2019*.
44. O'leary, D. E., (1995). On the history of AI applications. II. IEEE conference on artificial intelligence applications. *IEEE Expert, 10*(1), 61–65.
45. Perez, C. L., & Treisman, D., (2018). AI turning points and the road ahead. In: *International Joint Conference on Computational Intelligence* (pp. 89–107). Springer, Cham.
46. Ranschaert, E., (2018). Artificial intelligence in radiology: Hype or hope? *Journal of the Belgian Society of Radiology, 102*(S1), 20.
47. Sahoo, D., Swanson, L., Sayed, I. M., Katkar, G. D., Ibeawuchi, S. R., Mittal, Y., & Ghosh, P., (2021). Artificial intelligence guided discovery of a barrier-protective therapy in inflammatory bowel disease. *Nature Communications, 12*(1), 1–14.
48. Sandkuhl, K., (2019). Putting AI into context-method support for the introduction of artificial intelligence into organizations. In: *2019 IEEE 21st Conference on Business Informatics (CBI)* (Vol. 1, pp. 157–164). IEEE.
49. Sasu, B. J., Cooke, K. S., Arvedson, T. L., Plewa, C., Ellison, A. R., Sheng, J., & Molineux, G., (2010). Antihepcidin antibody treatment modulates iron metabolism and is effective in a mouse model of inflammation-induced anemia. *Blood, The Journal of the American Society of Hematology, 115*(17), 3616–3624.
50. Schmidt, A., (2020). Interactive human centered artificial intelligence: A definition and research challenges. In: *Proceedings of the International Conference on Advanced Visual Interfaces* (pp. 1–4).
51. Schuurman, D. C., (2018). Artificial intelligence: Discerning a Christian response. *Perspect. Sci. Christ. Faith, 70*(1), 72, 73.
52. Schuurman, D. C., (2019). Artificial intelligence: Discerning a Christian response. *Perspectives on Science & Christian Faith, 71*(2).
53. Simmons, A. B., & Chappell, S. G., (1988). Artificial intelligence-definition and practice. *IEEE Journal of Oceanic Engineering, 13*(2), 14–42.
54. Steels, L., (1993). The artificial life roots of artificial intelligence. *Artificial Life, 1*(1, 2), 75–110.
55. Strachna, O., & Asan, O., (2021). Systems thinking approach to an artificial intelligence reality within healthcare: From hype to value. In: *2021 IEEE International Symposium on Systems Engineering (ISSE)* (pp. 1–8). IEEE.

56. Tandon, N., & Tandon, R., (2019). Using machine learning to explain the heterogeneity of schizophrenia. Realizing the promise and avoiding the hype. *Schizophrenia Research, 214*, 70–75.

57. Toosi, A., Bottino, A. G., Saboury, B., Siegel, E., & Rahmim, A., (2021). A brief history of AI: How to prevent another winter (a critical review). *PET Clinics, 16*(4), 449–469.

58. Wang, P., (2019). On defining artificial intelligence. *Journal of Artificial General Intelligence, 10*(2), 1–37.

59. Weiss, S. M., & Kulikowski, C. A., (1983). A practical guide to designing expert systems. In: *A Practical Guide to Designing Expert Systems.* Chapman & Hall.

60. Weitz, K., Schiller, D., Schlagowski, R., Huber, T., & André, E., (2021). "Let me explain!": Exploring the potential of virtual agents in explainable AI interaction design. *Journal on Multimodal User Interfaces, 15*(2), 87–98.

61. Zysman, J., & Nitzberg, M., (2020). *Governing AI: Understanding the Limits, Possibility, and Risks of AI in an Era of Intelligent Tools and Systems, 574, 1-29.*

CHAPTER 6

DATABASE SYSTEMS

UNIT INTRODUCTION

In today's digital age, we generate and consume vast amounts of data on a daily basis, ranging from personal information to financial transactions, to social media interactions, and more. Database systems play a critical role in the management and storage of this data, making it easily accessible and organized for efficient retrieval and processing. Database systems can be defined as software systems that manage and store large amounts of data, allowing users to retrieve, add, update, and delete data as needed (Hellerstein & Stonebraker, 2005). They are used in a variety of industries, including e-commerce, healthcare, finance, education, logistics, and many more.

The concept of database systems has been around for several decades, with the first database management system (DBMS) developed in the 1960s. The early DBMSs were hierarchical and network models, which were eventually replaced by the relational model in the 1980s. The relational model is still widely used today and is considered the foundation of modern database systems. Database systems consist of several key components, including Data Definition Language (DDL), Data Manipulation Language (DML), Data Query Language (DQL), Data Control Language (DCL), and Database Management System (DBMS) (Yeung & Hall, 2007). DDL is used to define the structure of the database, including tables, relationships, and constraints. DML is used to manipulate the data in the database, including adding, updating, and deleting data. DQL is used to retrieve data from the database, and DCL is used to control access to the data in the database. DBMS is the software system that manages the database, providing tools for data storage, retrieval, and processing. DBMSs can be classified into several types, including relational, NoSQL, object-oriented, and others (Jukic et al., 2014). Data storage and retrieval is a critical component of database systems. Primary storage refers to the use of main memory, which provides fast access to data but has limited storage capacity. Secondary storage refers to the use of hard disks or solid-state drives, which provide larger storage capacity but slower access speeds.

Indexing involves creating a data structure that enables swift access to data based on particular conditions, thereby enhancing data retrieval speed. On the other hand, query optimization is employed to boost the efficiency of data retrieval by selecting the most optimal query plan based on the complexity and size of the data. Query execution is the process of executing the selected query plan and returning the results to the user. Database systems have several key characteristics that make them critical for managing large amounts of data. These include data independence, concurrent access, data integrity, security, and scalability. Data independence refers to the ability to change the structure of the database without affecting the applications that use the data (Widom & Ceri, 1995). Concurrent access refers to the ability to allow multiple users to access the data at the same time. Data integrity refers to the ability to maintain the accuracy and consistency of the data in the database (Elmasri & Navathe, 2006). Security refers to the ability to control access to the data in the database to prevent unauthorized access. Scalability refers to the ability to handle increasing amounts of data without compromising performance.

The architecture of database systems can be classified into several types, including client-server architecture, tiered architecture, and distributed architecture. Client-server architecture involves a client that sends requests to a server, which processes the requests and returns the results to the client (Coronel & Morris, 2016). Tiered architecture involves multiple layers of servers, with each layer responsible for specific functions such as web serving, application serving, and database serving. Distributed architecture involves multiple servers distributed across different locations, with each server responsible for a subset of the data. Query processing and optimization are critical components of database systems. Query processing involves several phases, including parsing, translation, optimization, and execution.

Learning Objectives

At the end of this chapter, the readers will be able to:

- Understand the definition of database systems.
- Recognize the importance of database systems in the modern world.
- Trace the brief history of database systems.
- Identify the key components of database systems, including DDL, DML, DQL, DCL, and DBMS.

- Describe the process of data storage and retrieval, including primary storage, secondary storage, indexing, query optimization, and query execution.
- Explain the characteristics of database systems, such as data independence, concurrent access, data integrity, security, and scalability.
- Compare and contrast the different types of architecture in database systems, including client-server, tiered, and distributed architectures.
- Understand the process of query processing and optimization, including query processing phases, query optimization techniques, and query execution plans.
- Appreciate the importance of database systems in modern society and how they contribute to the management and processing of large amounts of data.

Key Terms

- Data
- Database
- Database
- Data Definition Language (DDL)
- Database Management System (DBMS)
- Query Optimization
- Data Independence
- Scalability
- Client-Server Architecture

6.1. BASICS OF DATABASE SYSTEMS

Following are the basics of database systems.

6.1.1. Data

Data is any distinct piece of information that is recorded or stored in a computer or other electronic device. It is a collection of unorganized facts, figures, and statistics that are meaningless until they are processed and turned into useful information. Data can be in different forms, including text, numbers, images, audio, and video. In computing, data is the foundation of any computer program, software, or system (Sokolinsky, 2004). It is the input that the computer uses to perform calculations, process instructions, or produce output. Data is stored in a variety of ways, such as databases, spreadsheets, text files, binary files, and multimedia files. The way in which data is stored and organized can affect its usefulness and accessibility.

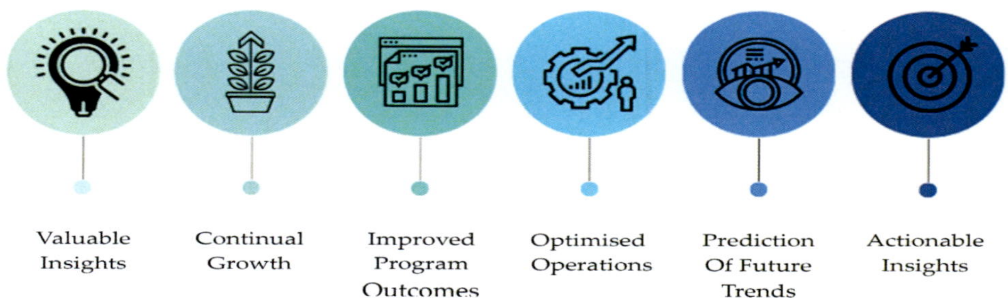

Figure 6.1. Illustration of the Data-Driven Decision Making (Source: Jason Williams, Creative Commons License).

Data is essential for decision-making, research, analysis, and problem-solving in many fields, including business, science, medicine, education, and government. For example, in business, data is used to monitor sales, track inventory, analyze customer behavior, and make strategic decisions. In medicine, data is used to study diseases, monitor patient health, and develop new treatments. In science, data is used to test hypotheses, make predictions, and create models. There are two types of data: structured and unstructured. Structured data is organized in a specific format, such as a spreadsheet or database, and can be easily processed and analyzed. Unstructured data, on the other hand, is not organized in a specific format and may include text, images, or multimedia (Maryanski et al., 1986). It is more difficult to process and analyze unstructured data, but it can provide valuable insights and information (Figure 6.1).

Data can also be classified based on its quality. High-quality data is accurate, complete, relevant, and timely (Chaudhri et al., 2003). It is free from errors, inconsistencies, and duplications. Low-quality data, on the other hand, may be incomplete, outdated, or contain errors, which can lead to incorrect conclusions or decisions. In recent years, the amount of data generated has increased exponentially due to the widespread use of technology and the internet. This has led to the development of big data, which refers to large datasets that are too complex or unstructured to be processed using traditional methods. Big data requires specialized tools and techniques, such as data mining, machine learning, and artificial intelligence, to extract insights and patterns.

6.1.2. Database

A database is an organized collection of structured data that is stored and managed in a computer or other electronic device. It is designed to store and retrieve information efficiently and accurately. Databases can be used for a wide range of applications, from small personal projects to large enterprise systems (Elmasri & Navathe, 2006). A database typically consists of one or more tables that are related to each other. Each table contains a set of records, and each record represents a specific instance of the data that is being stored. The columns in a table represent different attributes of the data, such as name, age, or address. Each column is given a data type that specifies the type of data that can be stored in it, such as text, number, or date (Figure 6.2).

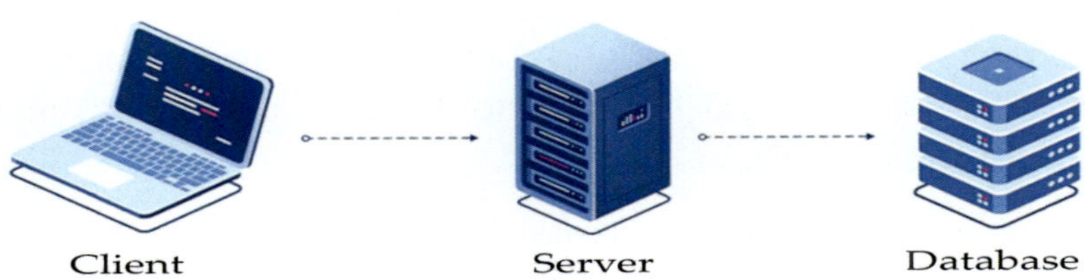

Figure 6.2. Schematic of a database (Source: Night Born, Creative Commons License).

The relationships between tables in a database are defined by a set of rules called database constraints. These constraints ensure that the data is accurate and consistent by enforcing rules such as unique values, data type restrictions, and referential integrity. Referential integrity ensures that the data in one table is consistent with the data in another table by enforcing a set of rules that dictate how data can be entered, updated, or deleted (Connolly & Begg, 2005). Databases can be categorized based on their organization and management approach. The most common types of databases are relational databases, which organize data into tables with predefined relationships between them, and non-relational databases, which organize data in other ways such as key-value pairs or documents. Relational databases use a standardized language called Structured Query Language (SQL) to manipulate data (Bernstein & Goodman, 1981). SQL is a powerful language that allows users to create, modify, and query databases. It can be used to perform a wide range of operations, from simple queries to complex data transformations.

Non-relational databases, on the other hand, use a variety of languages and data models to manage data. Some of the most popular non-relational databases include MongoDB, Cassandra, and Redis (Ulusoy, 1995). Databases are used in a wide range of applications, from small-scale personal projects to large-scale enterprise systems. Some common applications of databases include e-commerce websites, inventory management systems, banking systems, healthcare systems, and social media platforms.

6.2. HISTORY OF DATABASE SYSTEMS

Did you Know?

According to a survey conducted by Forbes, over 90% of organizations rely on data-driven insights to make strategic business decisions, highlighting the critical role that databases play in decision making.

The history of database systems dates back to the 1960s, when the first electronic computers were developed. During this time, data was primarily stored on magnetic tapes and punched cards, and the processing of data was time-consuming and error-prone. In the 1970s, Edgar F. Codd, a researcher at IBM, introduced the concept of relational databases. Codd proposed that data should be organized into tables with a fixed number of columns, each with a defined data type, and that relationships between tables should be established using primary and foreign keys. This approach was designed to simplify data management and improve data integrity (Grad & Bergin, 2009).

The first commercially available relational database management system (RDBMS) was developed by IBM in the late 1970s. This system, called System R, was based on Codd's relational model and was used internally by IBM for several years before being released to the public (Miklau et al., 2007). In the 1980s and 1990s, the use of database systems became more widespread as the cost of computing hardware decreased and the need for efficient data management increased. During this time, several new RDBMSs were developed, including Oracle, Sybase, and Microsoft SQL Server. In the late 1990s and early 2000s, the emergence of the internet and the growth of e-commerce led to the development of new database systems designed to handle large volumes of web-based data. These systems, known as NoSQL databases, were based on non-relational data models and were designed to be more flexible and scalable than traditional RDBMSs (Abadi et al., 2013). Today, database systems continue to evolve and improve, with new technologies such as cloud computing, big data analytics, and machine learning playing an increasingly important role. The use of databases has become ubiquitous, with virtually every organization relying on some form of database system to manage their data.

6.3. IMPORTANCE OF DATABASE SYSTEMS

Database systems play a critical role in modern organizations by providing a centralized and efficient way to store, manage, and access large amounts of data. The importance of database systems can be understood from the following perspectives.

6.3.1. Data Integration and Data Quality

Database systems allow organizations to integrate data from multiple sources, ensuring data consistency and accuracy (Cai & Zhu, 2015). By eliminating data redundancy, database systems help to maintain data integrity and enhance data quality.

KEYWORD

Database Systems or DBMS is software that caters to the collection of electronic and digital records to extract useful information and store that information is known as Database Systems/ Database Management Systems or DBMS.

6.3.2. Decision Making

Database systems provide users with the ability to access and analyze data quickly and easily, allowing organizations to make informed decisions based on accurate and up-to-date information (Azeroual et al., 2018). This is particularly important for organizations operating in dynamic environments where quick decisions can make a significant difference.

6.3.3. Efficient Data Management

Database systems provide an efficient way to manage data, including indexing, searching, and updating data. This helps to reduce data entry errors, increase data consistency, and improve data security (Figure 6.3).

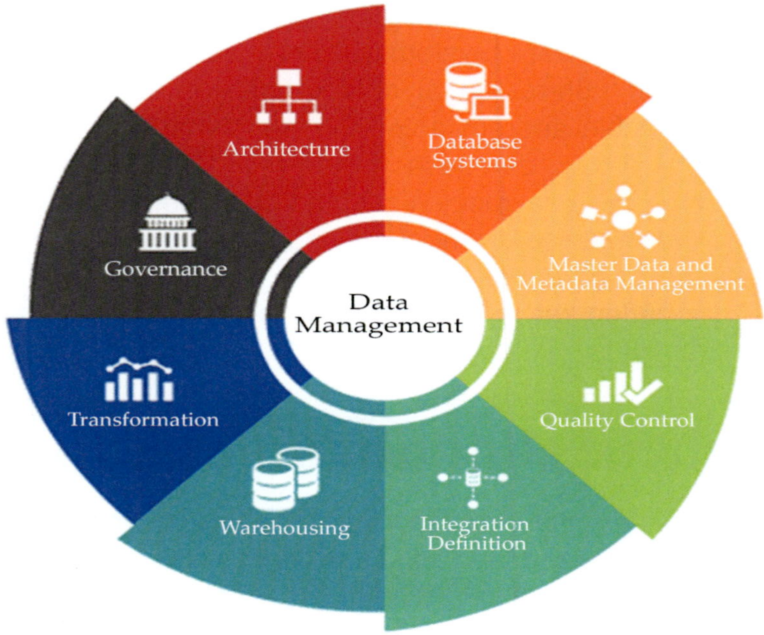

Figure 6.3. Schematic of the data management (Source: Virtual Staffing, Creative Commons License).

6.3.4. Cost Savings

By centralizing data storage and management, database systems can reduce hardware and software costs, as well as administrative costs associated with maintaining and updating data (Wang & Strong, 1996).

6.3.5. Scalability

Database systems can be designed to scale up or down based on the needs of an organization, allowing them to handle large volumes of data without sacrificing performance.

6.3.6. Regulatory Compliance

Many organizations are subject to regulatory requirements that mandate the secure storage and management of sensitive data (DeFazio et al., 2001). Database systems provide the necessary features and controls to ensure compliance with these regulations.

6.3.7. Improved Customer Experience

Database systems can be used to store and manage customer data, allowing organizations to personalize their interactions with customers and provide a better overall customer experience (Sawyer & Mariani, 1995) (Figure 6.4).

Figure 6.4. Illustration of the Importance of Customer Database (Source: MBA Skool, Creative Commons License).

In conclusion, the importance of database systems in modern organizations cannot be overstated. By providing a centralized and efficient way to store, manage, and access data, database systems help organizations to make informed decisions, improve data quality, and reduce costs.

6.4. COMPONENTS OF DATABASE SYSTEMS

Database systems are complex software systems that include various components that work together to manage and store large amounts of data. The main components of a database system are discussed below (Figure 6.5).

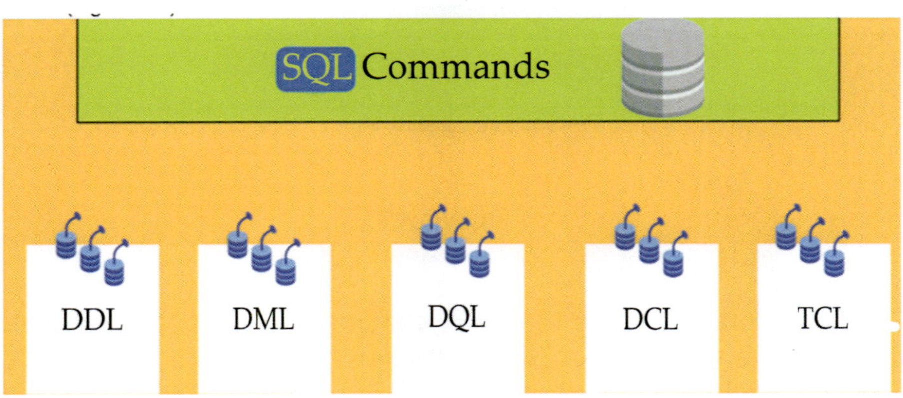

Figure 6.5. Components of the Database components (Source: Testing Docs, Creative Commons License).

6.4.1. Data Definition Language (DDL)

Data Definition Language (DDL) is a set of SQL commands used to create and modify the structure of database objects, such as tables, indexes, and views. DDL is one of the core components of database management systems (DBMS) and is used to define and manage the database schema (Wells, 2001).

Some common DDL statements include:

1. CREATE: This statement is used to create a new database object, such as a table or index. The syntax of the CREATE statement varies depending on the type of object being created.
2. ALTER: This statement is used to modify the structure of an existing database object, such as adding a new column to a table or modifying an index (Anwar, 2018).
3. DROP: This statement is used to delete an existing database object, such as a table or view. The DROP statement is a destructive operation and should be used with caution.
4. TRUNCATE: This statement is used to remove all the data from a table while keeping the table structure intact. The TRUNCATE statement is faster than using the DELETE statement to remove data (Wu, 2018).
5. RENAME: This statement is used to rename an existing database object, such as a table or column name. The RENAME statement is often used to improve the readability and maintainability of database objects (Figure 6.6).

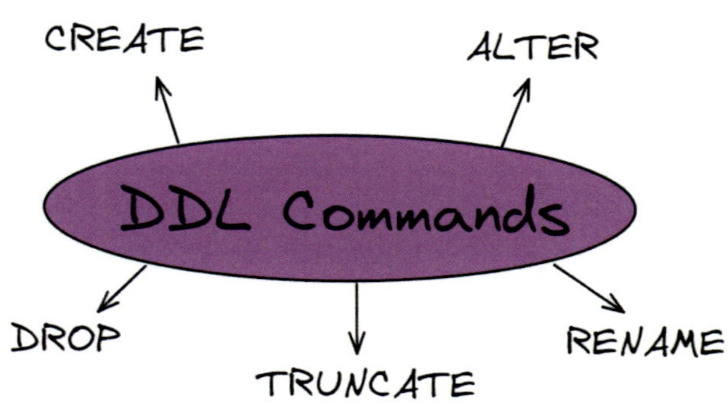

Figure 6.6. Schematic of the DDL Commands (Source: Algo Daily, Creative Commons License).

It is important to note that DDL statements are not transactional, which means that once a DDL statement is executed, it cannot be rolled back like a transaction. Therefore, it is important to carefully review and test DDL statements before executing them to ensure that they do not cause any unintended consequences.

6.4.2. Data Manipulation Language (DML)

Data Manipulation Language (DML) is a set of SQL commands used to retrieve, insert, update, and delete data in a database. DML is an important component of database management systems (DBMS) and is used to manage the data stored in the database (Ghali & Abu-Naser, 2019) (Figure 6.7).

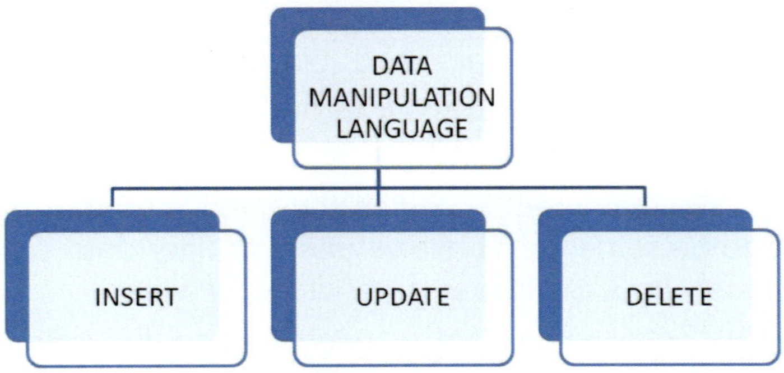

Figure 6.7. Illustration of the Data Manipulation Language (DML) (Source: Anushree Goswami, Creative Commons License)

Some common DML statements include:

1. INSERT: This statement is used to insert new data into a table. The INSERT statement specifies the values to be inserted into each column of the table (Shaw et al., 2016).
2. UPDATE: This statement is used to modify existing data in a table. The UPDATE statement specifies the new values for each column that is being modified.
3. DELETE: This statement is used to delete data from a table. The DELETE statement specifies the rows to be deleted from the table (Litwin & Abdellatif, 1987).

It is important to note that DML statements are transactional, which means that they can be rolled back if an error occurs during execution. This allows for data consistency and helps ensure that the database remains in a valid state. ML is an important component of database management systems that is used to manipulate the data stored in the database. DML statements are used to retrieve, insert, update, and delete data from tables, and are executed by applications or users who need to manage the data in the database. DML statements are transactional and can be rolled back if an error occurs during execution.

6.4.3. Data Query Language (DQL)

Data Query Language (DQL) is a subset of Structured Query Language (SQL) used to retrieve data from a database (Brodsky et al., 2009). DQL statements are designed to extract information from one or more database tables based on specific criteria, and are used extensively in database management systems (DBMS) to retrieve data required by users or applications. There are several DQL statements used to retrieve data from a database, including:

1. SELECT: This is the most commonly used DQL statement. It allows the user to retrieve specific data from one or more tables in the database based on certain criteria. The SELECT statement can also be used to calculate values, group data, and join multiple tables.
2. FROM: This statement specifies the name of the table or tables from which data is to be retrieved.
3. WHERE: This statement specifies the conditions that must be met for the data to be retrieved. It allows users to filter data based on specific criteria, such as a particular date range or value.
4. ORDER BY: This statement is used to sort the retrieved data in a specific order, such as ascending or descending order (Jäkel et al., 2014).
5. GROUP BY: This statement is used to group data based on a specific column in the table. It is often used with aggregate functions such as SUM, AVG, and COUNT.
6. HAVING: This statement is used in conjunction with GROUP BY to filter the results of the group by statement based on a specific condition (Fikes et al., 2002).

In summary, DQL is a subset of SQL used to retrieve data from a database. DQL statements are used to extract information from one or more tables based on specific criteria, and are executed by the DBMS to extract the requested data. Common DQL statements include SELECT, FROM, WHERE, ORDER BY, GROUP BY, and HAVING. DQL is an essential component of DBMS and is used by application developers and database administrators to retrieve data for a variety of purposes.

6.4.4. Data Control Language (DCL)

Data Control Language (DCL) is a subset of Structured Query Language (SQL) used to manage the security and access control of a database (Rao et al., 2019). It allows database administrators (DBAs) to grant or revoke access to the database for users and to control the actions that users can perform on the database (Figure 6.8).

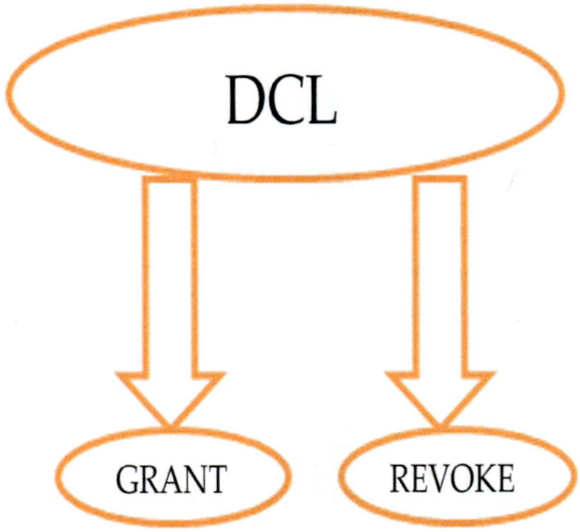

Figure 6.8. Schematic of the DCL statements (Source: Developers Tutorials, Creative Commons License).

There are several DCL statements used to control access to a database, including:

1. GRANT: This statement is used to give specific privileges to a user, such as the ability to read, write or execute database objects like tables, views, or procedures (Wyatt, 1994).
2. REVOKE: This statement is used to remove the previously granted privileges from the user.
3. DENY: This statement is used to explicitly deny a user access to a specific database object or system resource (El-Mehalawi & Miller, 2003).

Database administrators use DCL statements to create security policies and enforce them in the database system. They can specify which users or groups of users have access to the database and which actions they are allowed to perform. This helps to ensure that data is only accessed and manipulated by authorized personnel. DCL is a subset of SQL used to manage the security and access control of a database. DCL statements such as GRANT, REVOKE, and DENY are used to grant or revoke access to specific database objects or system resources. DCL statements help to enforce security policies in a database system and protect data from unauthorized access (Yu & Zhou, 2019). Database administrators use DCL statements to control access to the database and to ensure that data is only accessed and manipulated by authorized personnel.

6.4.5. Database Management System (DBMS)

A Database Management System (DBMS) is software that manages the storage, retrieval, and updating of data in a computer system.

It is a collection of programs that enable users to create and maintain a database, and to access and manipulate data stored in the database. A DBMS provides an interface for users to interact with the database, and it acts as an intermediary between the user and the database (Rawat & Purnama, 2021). Users can use commands or queries to retrieve and manipulate data stored in the database. The DBMS is responsible for managing the storage of data, ensuring data integrity, and controlling access to the database (Figure 6.9).

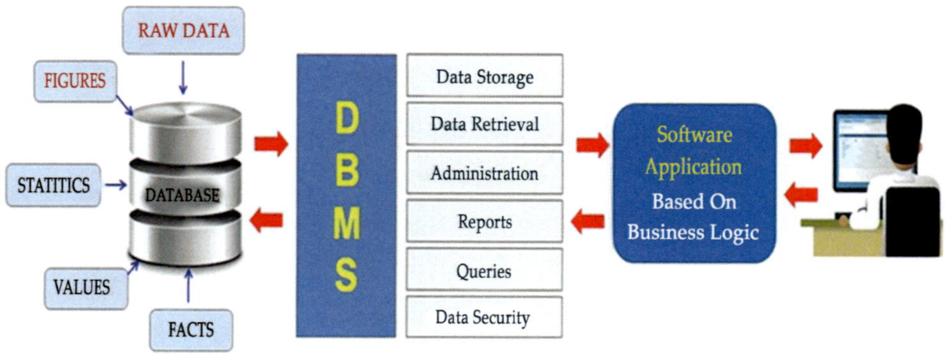

Figure 6.9. Illustration of the DBMS (Source: Learn Computer Science, Creative Commons License).

There are several types of DBMS, including:

1. Relational DBMS: A type of DBMS that stores data in tables, with each table consisting of rows and columns. Relational DBMSs use SQL (Structured Query Language) to access and manipulate data (Dittrich et al., 1995).
2. Object-oriented DBMS: A type of DBMS that stores data in objects, which can include data and the methods used to manipulate the data.
3. Hierarchical DBMS: A type of DBMS that organizes data in a hierarchical structure, with each record having a parent record and zero or more child records.
4. Network DBMS: A type of DBMS that stores data in a network structure, with each record having multiple parent and child records (Olle, 2003).

A DBMS is essential for managing large amounts of data in an organized and efficient manner. It allows multiple users to access and manipulate the same data simultaneously, while maintaining data integrity and security. A DBMS also enables users to retrieve and manipulate data easily, using a variety of tools and interfaces. DBMS is software that manages the storage, retrieval, and updating of data in a computer system. It provides an interface for users to interact with the database, and it is responsible for managing the storage of data, ensuring data integrity, and controlling access to the database (Anjard, 1994). There are several types of DBMS, including relational, object-oriented, hierarchical, and network DBMS. A DBMS is essential for managing large amounts of data in an organized and efficient manner.

6.5. DATA STORAGE AND RETRIEVAL

Data storage and retrieval are two essential aspects of database management systems. A DBMS must efficiently store and retrieve data to support the application's requirements (Levine, 1985). We will discuss the various techniques and methods used for data storage and retrieval in DBMS.

6.5.1. Primary Storage

Primary storage, also known as main memory or RAM, is the memory used to store the currently executing application and its data. Primary storage is volatile, meaning its contents are lost when the power is turned off. DBMS uses primary storage to cache frequently accessed data and improve query response time (Chessa & Maestrini, 2003).

Remember

A DBMS is a software system designed to manage and control access to a database, ensuring data integrity, security, and efficient data retrieval and manipulation.

6.5.2. Secondary Storage

Secondary storage is the non-volatile memory used to store data persistently. Secondary storage devices include hard disk drives, solid-state drives, and magnetic tapes. Secondary storage is used for long-term storage of the database, transaction logs, and backups.

6.5.3. Indexing

Indexing is a technique used to improve the performance of data retrieval operations (Xue et al., 2019). It involves creating an index, which is a data structure that contains the values of one or more columns of a table, along with a pointer to the location of the corresponding record in the table. When a query is executed, the index is searched instead of the table, resulting in faster data retrieval.

6.5.4. Query Optimization

Query optimization is the process of selecting the most efficient query execution plan to retrieve data from the database (Heanue et al., 1994). The query optimizer analyzes the query and the database's schema to generate an execution plan that minimizes the amount of disk I/O and CPU processing required to retrieve the data.

TIPS

Ensure data reliability and accessibility by storing primary data in multiple locations with data backups.

6.5.5. Query Execution

Query execution is the process of retrieving data from the database based on the execution plan generated by the query optimizer. The DBMS retrieves data from the storage devices, applies any necessary sorting or aggregation operations, and returns the results to the application (Barrett, & Edgar, 2006). Query execution performance is critical for applications that require fast and efficient data retrieval.

In conclusion, data storage and retrieval are crucial components of a DBMS. Efficient data storage and retrieval techniques are essential for supporting fast and reliable application performance. Primary and secondary storage, indexing, query optimization, and query execution are some of the critical techniques used for efficient data storage and retrieval in a DBMS.

6.6. CHARACTERISTICS OF DATABASE SYSTEMS

A database system must possess certain characteristics to be considered efficient and reliable. In this section, we will discuss some of the key characteristics of a database system.

6.6.1. Data Independence

One of the most important characteristics of a database system is data independence. It means that the application programs should be independent of the physical storage structure of the data (Naughton, 1985). It allows changes to be made to the database structure without affecting the application programs. There are two types of data independence: logical and physical.

6.6.2. Concurrent Access

Database systems must be designed to support multiple users accessing the database at the same time. This is known as concurrent access. The DBMS must ensure that each user sees a consistent view of the database, even if other users are modifying the data at the same time (Bernstein & Goodman, 1981). This is achieved through concurrency control mechanisms that allow multiple transactions to execute concurrently while ensuring the consistency of the database.

6.6.3. Data Integrity

Data integrity is the assurance of the accuracy and consistency of the data stored in the database. The DBMS must ensure that data is stored correctly and is consistent with other data in the database. The database system must enforce the integrity constraints that are specified in the database schema to ensure the data is accurate and consistent (Yesin et al., 2021) (Figure 6.10).

Figure 6.10. Data Integrity and its components (Source: CFI Team, Creative Commons License).

6.6.4. Security

Database systems must provide security mechanisms to protect the database from unauthorized access and ensure the confidentiality, integrity, and availability of the data (Bertino & Sandhu, 2005). This includes authentication, authorization, and encryption mechanisms to protect the data from unauthorized access.

6.6.5. Scalability

Database systems must be designed to scale up or down to meet the changing demands of the application (Kuhlenkamp et al., 2014). The system must be able to handle increasing amounts of data and users without compromising performance or availability. This can be achieved through techniques such as partitioning, replication, and clustering. The characteristics of a database system include data independence, concurrent access, data integrity, security, and scalability. These characteristics ensure that the database system is efficient, reliable, and able to handle the demands of modern applications.

6.7. ARCHITECTURE OF DATABASE SYSTEMS

Database systems can have different architectures, depending on the specific requirements of the application. The architecture of a database system determines how the different components of the system are organized, how they interact with each other, and how the data is processed and stored. There are three main types of database architectures.

6.7.1. Client-Server Architecture

The client-server architecture is a common architecture for database systems. In this architecture, the system is divided into two parts: the client and the server (McLeod & Heimbigner, 1980). The client is the user interface that interacts with the user, while the server is responsible for storing and managing the data. The client sends requests to the server, which processes the request and sends back the results.

6.7.2. Tiered Architecture

The tiered architecture is a multi-layered architecture that separates the presentation layer, application logic layer, and data storage layer. In this architecture, the application is divided into three tiers: the user interface, the business logic layer, and the data storage layer (Hurson et al., 1989). The user interface communicates with the business logic layer, which in turn communicates with the data storage layer. This architecture provides scalability and flexibility to the system.

6.7.3. Distributed Architecture

The distributed architecture is a distributed database system that is spread across multiple locations or sites. In this architecture, the data is distributed across multiple servers, and each server is responsible for a specific set of data. The servers are connected through a network, and they work together to process user requests. This architecture provides scalability and fault tolerance to the system (Lam & Kuo, 2000).

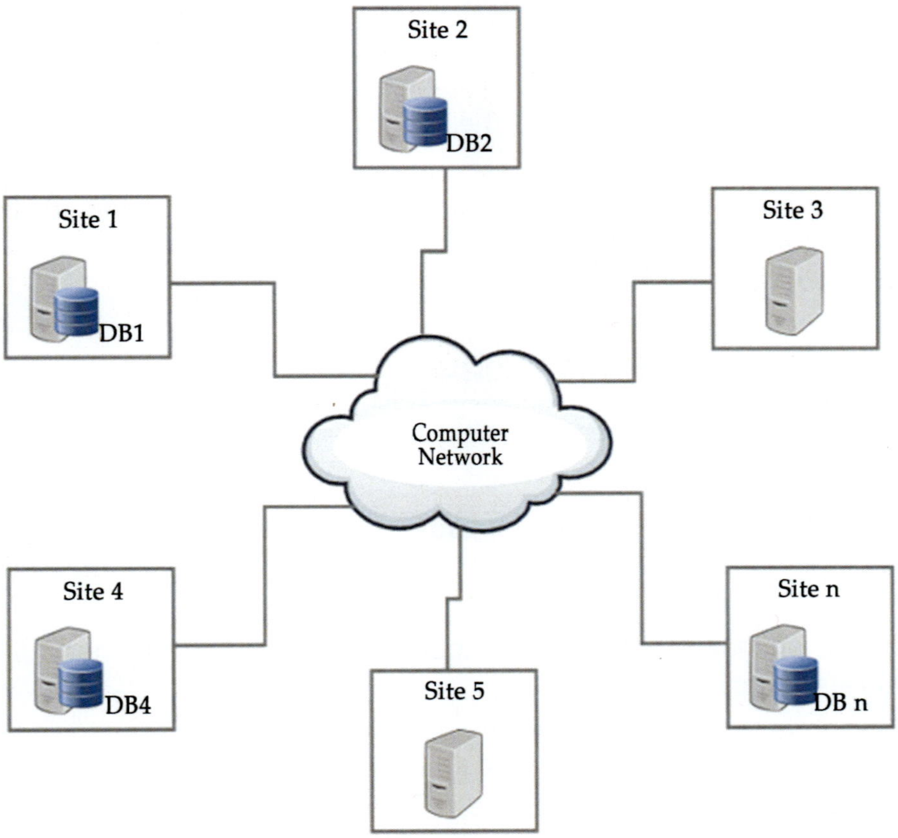

Figure 6.11. Illustration of the Distributed Architecture (Source: Katembo Kituta Ezéchiel et al. Creative Commons License).

Each of these architectures has its own advantages and disadvantages, and the choice of architecture depends on the specific requirements of the application (Figure 6.11).

6.8. QUERY PROCESSING AND OPTIMIZATION

Query processing and optimization are essential components of database systems that ensure efficient and fast retrieval of data. Query processing refers to the translation of a user's query into an efficient form that can be executed by the system. Query optimization, on the other hand, involves selecting the most efficient execution plan for a given query.

6.8.1. Query Processing Phases

The query processing phases are as follows:

i. Parsing: This is the first phase of query processing, where the system checks the syntax of the query and creates a parse tree (Park et al., 2013).
ii. Optimization: In this phase, the system generates different execution plans for the query and selects the most efficient one based on the query cost model.
iii. Code generation: Once the optimized execution plan is selected, the system generates the code to execute the query (Antoshenkov & Ziauddin, 1996).

6.8.2. Query Optimization Techniques

There are several query optimization techniques used in database systems, including:

i. Cost-based optimization: This technique uses a cost model to estimate the execution time and selects the plan with the lowest estimated cost (Alom et al., 2009).
ii. Rule-based optimization: This technique uses a set of predefined rules to generate execution plans.
iii. Dynamic programming: This technique solves the query optimization problem by breaking it down into smaller sub-problems (Ouzzani & Bouguettaya, 2004).

6.8.3. Query Execution Plans

The execution plan describes how the system will execute the query. It includes information on how the system will access the data, the order in which the operations will be performed, and how the results will be returned. The query execution plan is generated during the query optimization phase and is critical to the performance of the system. The system will execute the query according to the plan, and any inefficiencies in the plan can lead to slow performance and decreased efficiency.

In conclusion, query processing and optimization are critical components of a database system. They ensure efficient and fast retrieval of data, and the performance of the system depends on their proper implementation. A well-designed query processing and optimization system can make a significant difference in the overall performance and efficiency of a database system.

6.9. IMPORTANCE OF DATABASE SYSTEMS IN MODERN WORLD

Database systems play a crucial role in the modern world where data has become an essential part of businesses, organizations, and individuals. Here are some of the key reasons why database systems are important in the modern world.

6.9.1. Data Management

Database systems help organizations manage large volumes of data efficiently (Chaudhri et al., 2003). It provides a structured way to store, manage, and retrieve data, ensuring data accuracy and consistency.

6.9.2. Decision Making

Database systems provide a platform to analyze and process data, which can help in making informed decisions (Wang et al., 2016). For instance, businesses can analyze sales data to determine which products are selling well and which ones need improvement.

KEYWORD

Decision making is the process of making choices by identifying a decision, gathering information, and assessing alternative resolutions.

6.9.3. Improved Efficiency

With a database system, data can be accessed and processed faster, reducing the time required to perform routine tasks. This improved efficiency can help organizations to be more productive and profitable.

6.9.4. Cost Savings

Database systems can help businesses save money by reducing the need for physical storage space, paper records, and manual data entry. It can also reduce the likelihood of errors and inconsistencies, which can be costly to correct.

6.9.5. Data Security

Database systems can help organizations secure sensitive data and prevent unauthorized access. By implementing user authentication and access control mechanisms, businesses can protect data from internal and external threats (Malik & Patel, 2016).

6.9.6. Compliance

Many organizations are required to comply with regulatory requirements such as GDPR, HIPAA, and PCI DSS. Database systems can help ensure compliance by providing features such as auditing, logging, and encryption (Wang, 2022).

6.9.7. Innovation

Database systems provide a foundation for innovation in areas such as machine learning, artificial intelligence, and the Internet of Things (Bradley et al., 2019). By leveraging data stored in a database, businesses can gain insights into new opportunities, products, and services.

Overall, the importance of database systems in the modern world cannot be overstated. They provide a structured way to manage and analyze data, enabling businesses and organizations to make informed decisions and stay competitive in a data-driven world.

ACTIVITY 6.1.

You are tasked with explaining the basic components of a database system to a group of stakeholders. Describe the various components, such as the data model, database schema, query language, and database management system, and explain how they work together to store, manage, and retrieve data.

SUMMARY

The chapter on Introduction to Database Systems provides an overview of the fundamentals of database systems. It starts by defining what database systems are and their importance in the modern world. The chapter then delves into the history of database systems, highlighting the major milestones that have led to the development of modern database systems. The chapter also discusses the different components of database systems, including Data Definition Language (DDL), Data Manipulation Language (DML), Data Query Language (DQL), Data Control Language (DCL), and Database Management System (DBMS). The discussion on each component provides a detailed explanation of what it does and its role in the database system.

The chapter also covers data storage and retrieval, with a focus on primary storage, secondary storage, indexing, query optimization, and query execution. Additionally, the chapter highlights the key characteristics of database systems, such as data independence, concurrent access, data integrity, security, and scalability. The architecture of database systems is also discussed in detail, with an emphasis on the client-server architecture, tiered architecture, and distributed architecture. Finally, the chapter provides an overview of query processing and optimization, covering query processing phases, query optimization techniques, and query execution plans.

REVIEW QUESTIONS

1. Define database systems and explain their importance.
2. Describe the components of database systems and their roles.
3. Explain the different types of data storage in database systems.
4. Discuss the characteristics of database systems and their significance.
5. Compare and contrast the different types of database architecture.
6. Describe the phases of query processing and explain their importance.
7. Explain the techniques used for query optimization.
8. Discuss the role of query execution plans in database systems.

MULTIPLE CHOICE QUESTIONS

1. Which of the following is not a component of database systems?

a. Data Definition Language
b. Data Control Language
c. Data Access Language
d. Database Management System

2. **Which of the following is a characteristic of database systems?**
   a. Scalability
   b. Flexibility
   c. Reliability
   d. Speed
3. **Which of the following is a type of database architecture?**
   a. Centralized architecture
   b. Decentralized architecture
   c. Distributed architecture
   d. All of the above
4. **Which of the following is used to define the structure of a database?**
   a. Data Definition Language
   b. Data Manipulation Language
   c. Data Query Language
   d. Data Control Language
5. **Which type of storage is volatile in nature?**
   a. Primary storage
   b. Secondary storage
   c. Both A and B
   d. None of the above
6. **Which of the following is not a phase of query processing?**
   a. Parsing
   b. Optimization
   c. Execution
   d. Storage
7. **Which type of architecture allows for scalability in database systems?**
   a. Client-Server Architecture
   b. Tiered Architecture
   c. Distributed Architecture
   d. All of the above
8. **Which of the following is not a characteristic of database systems?**
   a. Scalability
   b. Reliability
   c. Compatibility
   d. Security

Answers to Multiple Choice Questions

1. (a) 2. (d) 3. (b) 4. (c) 5. (a)

6 (b) 7. (c) 8. (d)

REFERENCES

1. Abadi, D., Boncz, P., Harizopoulos, S., Idreos, S., & Madden, S., (2013). The design and implementation of modern column-oriented database systems. *Foundations and Trends® in Databases, 5*(3), 197–280.
2. Alom, B. M., Henskens, F., & Hannaford, M., (2009). Query processing and optimization in distributed database systems. *IJCSNS, 9*(9), 143.
3. Anjard, R. P., (1994). The basics of database management systems (DBMS). *Industrial Management & Data Systems, 94*(5), 11–15.
4. Antoshenkov, G., & Ziauddin, M., (1996). Query processing and optimization in oracle Rdb. *The VLDB Journal, 5*, 229–237.
5. Anwar, I., (2018). *Penerjemahan Teks Bahasa Indonesia Menjadi Data Definition Language (Ddl) Dengan Penanganan Kalimat Majemuk* (2nd edn, pp. 4–10). Doctoral dissertation, Universitas Komputer Indonesia.
6. Azeroual, O., Saake, G., & Schallehn, E., (2018). Analyzing data quality issues in research information systems via data profiling. *International Journal of Information Management, 41*, 50–56.
7. Barrett, T., & Edgar, R., (2006). [19] Gene expression omnibus: Microarray data storage, submission, retrieval, and analysis. *Methods in Enzymology, 411*, 352–369.
8. Bernstein, P. A., & Goodman, N., (1981). Concurrency control in distributed database systems. *ACM Computing Surveys (CSUR), 13*(2), 185–221.
9. Bertino, E., & Sandhu, R., (2005). Database security-concepts, approaches, and challenges. *IEEE Transactions on Dependable and Secure Computing, 2*(1), 2–19.
10. Bradley, D., Merrifield, M., Miller, K. M., Lomonico, S., Wilson, J. R., & Gleason, M. G., (2019). Opportunities to improve fisheries management through innovative technology and advanced data systems. *Fish and Fisheries, 20*(3), 564–583.
11. Brodsky, A., Bhot, M. M., Chandrashekar, M., Egge, N. E., & Wang, X. S., (2009). A decisions query language (DQL) high-level abstraction for mathematical programming over databases. In: *Proceedings of the 2009 ACM SIGMOD International Conference on Management of Data* (Vol. 1, pp. 1059–1062).
12. Cai, L., & Zhu, Y., (2015). The challenges of data quality and data quality assessment in the big data era. *Data Science Journal, 14*(1), 4–10.
13. Chaudhri, A. B., Rashid, A., & Zicari, R., (2003). *XML Data Management: Native XML and XML-Enabled Database Systems* (Vol. 4, No. 1, pp. 2–9). Addison-Wesley Professional.

14. Chessa, S., & Maestrini, P., (2003). Dependable and secure data storage and retrieval in mobile, wireless networks. In: *DSN* (Vol. 2003, pp. 207–216).
15. Connolly, T. M., & Begg, C. E., (2005). *Database Systems: A Practical Approach to Design, Implementation, and Management* (2nd edn., pp. 1–15). Pearson Education.
16. Coronel, C., & Morris, S., (2016). *Database Systems: Design, Implementation, & Management* (Vol. 3, No. 2, pp. 2–8). Cengage Learning.
17. DeFazio, S., Krishnan, R., Srinivasan, J., & Zeldin, S., (2001). The importance of extensible database systems for e-commerce. In: *Proceedings 17th International Conference on Data Engineering* (Vol. 1, pp. 63–70). IEEE.
18. DeWitt, D., & Gray, J., (1992). Parallel database systems: The future of high performance database systems. *Communications of the ACM, 35*(6), 85–98.
19. Dittrich, K. R., Gatziu, S., & Geppert, A., (1995). The active database management system manifesto: A rule base of ADBMS features. In: *Rules in Database Systems: Second International Workshop, RIDS'95 Glyfada, Athens, Greece, September 25–27, 1995 Proceedings 2* (Vol. 1, pp. 1–17). Springer Berlin Heidelberg.
20. Elmasri, R., & Navathe, S. B., (2006). *Database Systems: Models, Languages, Design, and Application Programming* (Vol. 4, No. 1, pp. 7–9). Pearson Education India.
21. El-Mehalawi, M., & Miller, R. A., (2003). A database system of mechanical components based on geometric and topological similarity. Part I: Representation. *Computer-Aided Design, 35*(1), 83–94.
22. Fikes, R., Hayes, P., & Horrocks, I., (2002). *DQL-a Query Language for the Semantic Web* (2nd edn., pp. 4–9). Knowledge Systems Laboratory.
23. Ghali, M. J. A., & Abu-Naser, S. S., (2019). *ITS for Data Manipulation Language (DML) Commands Using SQlite* (3rd edn., pp. 6–9).
24. Grad, B., & Bergin, T. J., (2009). Guest editors' introduction: History of database management systems. *IEEE Annals of the History of Computing, 31*(4), 3–5.
25. Heanue, J. F., Bashaw, M. C., & Hesselink, L., (1994). Volume holographic storage and retrieval of digital data. *Science, 265*(5173), 749–752.
26. Hellerstein, J. M., & Stonebraker, M., (2005). *Readings in Database Systems* (Vol. 1, pp. 2–5). MIT press.
27. Hurson, A. R., Miller, L. L., Pakzad, S. H., Eich, M. H., & Shirazi, B., (1989). Parallel architectures for database systems. In: *Advances in Computers* (Vol. 28, pp. 107–151). Elsevier.
28. Jäkel, T., Kühn, T., Voigt, H., & Lehner, W., (2014). RSQL-a query language for dynamic data types. In: *Proceedings of the 18th International Database Engineering & Applications Symposium* (Vol. 1, pp. 185–194).
29. Jukic, N., Vrbsky, S., Nestorov, S., & Sharma, A., (2014). *Database Systems: Introduction to Databases and Data Warehouses* (Vol. 1, p. 400). Pearson.
30. Kuhlenkamp, J., Klems, M., & Röss, O., (2014). Benchmarking scalability and

elasticity of distributed database systems. *Proceedings of the VLDB Endowment, 7*(12), 1219–1230.

31. Lam, K. Y., & Kuo, T. W., (2000). *Real-Time Database Systems: Architecture and Techniques* (2nd edn., Vol. 593, pp. 4–10). Springer Science & Business Media.
32. Levine, H. G., (1985). Principles of data storage and retrieval for use in qualitative evaluations. *Educational Evaluation and Policy Analysis, 7*(2), 169–186.
33. Litwin, W., & Abdellatif, A., (1987). An overview of the multi-database manipulation language MDSL. *Proceedings of the IEEE, 75*(5), 621–632.
34. Malik, M., & Patel, T., (2016). Database security-attacks and control methods. *International Journal of Information, 6*(1, 2), 175–183.
35. Maryanski, F., Bedell, J., Hoelscher, S., Hong, S., McDonald, L., Peckham, J., & Stock, D., (1986). The data model compiler: A tool for generating object-oriented database systems. In: *Proceedings on the 1986 International Workshop on Object-Oriented Database Systems* (Vol. 1, pp. 73–84).
36. McLeod, D., & Heimbigner, D., (1980). A federated architecture for database systems. In: *Proceedings of the May 19–22, 1980, National Computer Conference* (Vol. 1, pp. 283–289).
37. Miklau, G., Levine, B. N., & Stahlberg, P., (2007). Securing history: Privacy and accountability in database systems. In: *CIDR* (2nd edn, pp. 387–396).
38. Naughton, J., (1985). Data independent recursion in deductive databases. In: *Proceedings of the Fifth ACM SIGACT-SIGMOD Symposium on Principles of Database Systems* (2nd edn., pp. 267–279).
39. Olle, T. W., (2003). Database management system (DBMS). In: *Encyclopedia of Computer Science* (Vol. 1, pp. 517–520).
40. Ouzzani, M., & Bouguettaya, A., (2004). Query processing and optimization on the web. *Distributed and Parallel Databases, 15*(1), 187–218.
41. Park, H., Pang, R., Parameswaran, A., Garcia-Molina, H., Polyzotis, N., & Widom, J., (2013). An overview of the deco system: Data model and query language; query processing and optimization. *ACM SIGMOD Record, 41*(4), 22–27.
42. Rao, T. R., Mitra, P., Bhatt, R., & Goswami, A., (2019). The big data system, components, tools, and technologies: A survey. *Knowledge and Information Systems, 60*(1), 1165–1245.
43. Rawat, B., & Purnama, S., (2021). MySQL database management system (DBMS) on FTP site LAPAN Bandung. *International Journal of Cyber and IT Service Management, 1*(2), 173–179.
44. Sawyer, P., & Mariani, J. A., (1995). Database systems: Challenges and opportunities for graphical HCI. *Interacting with Computers, 7*(3), 273–303.
45. Shaw, S., Vermeulen, A. F., Gupta, A., Kjerrumgaard, D., Shaw, S., Vermeulen, A. F., & Kjerrumgaard, D., (2016). Data manipulation language (DML). *Practical Hive: A Guide to Hadoop's Data Warehouse System, 1*, 77–98.

46. Sheth, A. P., & Larson, J. A., (1990). Federated database systems for managing distributed, heterogeneous, and autonomous databases. *ACM Computing Surveys (CSUR), 22*(3), 183–236.
47. Sokolinsky, L. B., (2004). Survey of architectures of parallel database systems. *Programming and Computer Software, 30*, 337–346.
48. Ulusoy, Ö., (1995). Research issues in real-time database systems: Survey paper. *Information Sciences, 87*(1–3), 123–151.
49. Wang, H., Xu, Z., Fujita, H., & Liu, S., (2016). Towards felicitous decision making: An overview on challenges and trends of big data. *Information Sciences, 367*, 747–765.
50. Wang, L., (2022). Providing compliance in critical computing systems. In: *System Dependability and Analytics: Approaching System Dependability from Data, System and Analytics Perspectives* (Vol. 1, pp. 191–206). Cham: Springer International Publishing.
51. Wang, R. Y., & Strong, D. M., (1996). Beyond accuracy: What data quality means to data consumers. *Journal of Management Information Systems, 12*(4), 5–33.
52. Wells, G., (2001). Data definition language. In: *Code Centric: T-SQL Programming with Stored Procedures and Triggers* (Vol. 1, pp. 35–70). Berkeley, CA: A Press.
53. Widom, J., & Ceri, S., (1995). *Active Database Systems: Triggers and Rules for Advanced Database Processing* (Vol. 2, No. 1, pp. 5–10). Morgan Kaufmann.
54. Wu, M., (2018). *Property Graph Type System and Data Definition Language* (2nd edn, pp. 5–9). arXiv preprint arXiv:1810.08755.
55. Wyatt, J. C., (1994). Clinical data systems, part 2: Components and techniques. *The Lancet, 344*(8937), 1609–1614.
56. Xue, J., Xu, C., & Bai, L., (2019). DStore: A distributed system for outsourced data storage and retrieval. *Future Generation Computer Systems, 99*(1), 106–114.
57. Yesin, V., Karpinski, M., Yesina, M., Vilihura, V., & Warwas, K., (2021). Ensuring data integrity in databases with the universal basis of relations. *Applied Sciences, 11*(18), 8781.
58. Yeung, A. K., & Hall, G. B., (2007). *Spatial Database Systems: Design, Implementation and Project Management* (Vol. 87, pp. 4–8). Springer Science & Business Media.
59. Yu, J. H., & Zhou, Z. M., (2019). Components and development in big data system: A survey. *Journal of Electronic Science and Technology, 17*(1), 51–72.

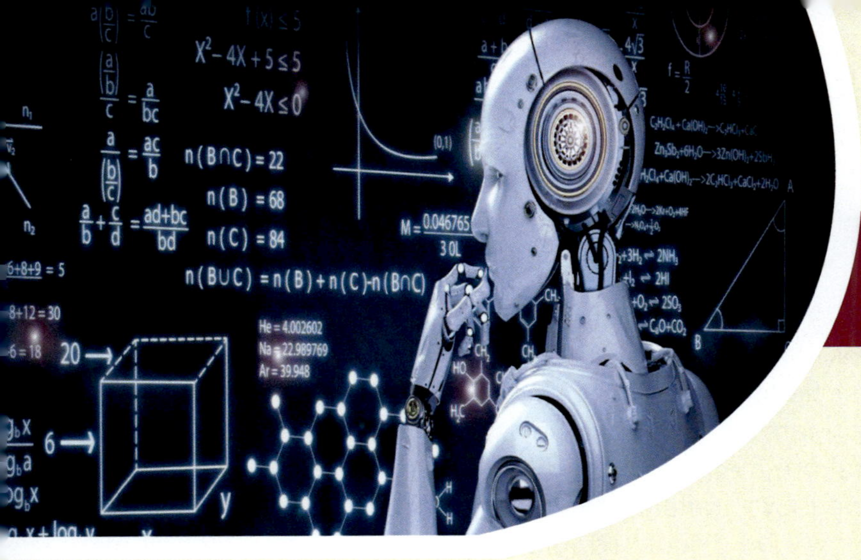

CHAPTER 7

MACHINE LEARNING

UNIT INTRODUCTION

Artificial intelligence (AI) has a subdivision known as machine learning. To comprehend the system of data and conjugate that data into models that can be recognized and employed by people is the general aim of machine learning (Du & Swamy, 2014; Kelleher et al., 2015).

Machine learning differs from conventional computational processes even though it is a discipline within computer science. In customary computing, calculating and deciphering problems are done by computers which are collections of explicitly automated directions called algorithms. Machine learning processes instead use arithmetic analysis to yield values that fall within a distinct range and permit for computers to train on information inputs. Consequently, to develop decision-making programs based on statistical inputs, the computer is helped by machines to construct models from test data (DasGupta, 2011; Kelleher, 2016).

Machine study has serviced anyone who uses technology today. Social media forums help users to connect and share images of friends due to facial identification technology. Images of words into a mobile type can be transformed by Optical character recognition (OCR). Based on user inclination, the suggestion engines, fueled by machine learning, propose what television dramas or movies to watch. The public may soon have access to self-driving automobiles that depend on machine learning to steer (Schmid et al.,

2014; Buduma & Locascio, 2017). Machine learning is a constantly advancing field. Thus, as you deconstruct the magnitude of machine learning procedures and work with machine learning techniques, there are some factors to keep in view (Price et al., 2019; Yoganarasimhan, 2020).

In the following tutorial, we'll look into ordinary algorithmic methodologies in machine learning, in addition to the k-nearest neighbor algorithm, in-depth learning, decision tree learning, and the standard machine learning processes of supervised and unsupervised learning. Programming languages that are most used in machine learning will be evaluated, including some of the positive and negative traits of each. Furthermore, machine learning algorithms that project certain biases will be discussed, plus when constructing algorithms that can be kept in mind to avoid these biases (Michie et al., 1994; Rasmussen, 2003).

Currently, one of the most prominent and powerful technologies is undoubtedly Machine Learning. More noticeably, its full intent is still far from view. Without a doubt, soon it will keep on making headlines. A preface to the Machine Learning concepts, explaining all the basic ideas without being too high level is covered in this chapter (Holmes et al., 1994; Pedregosa et al., 2011) (Figure 7.1).

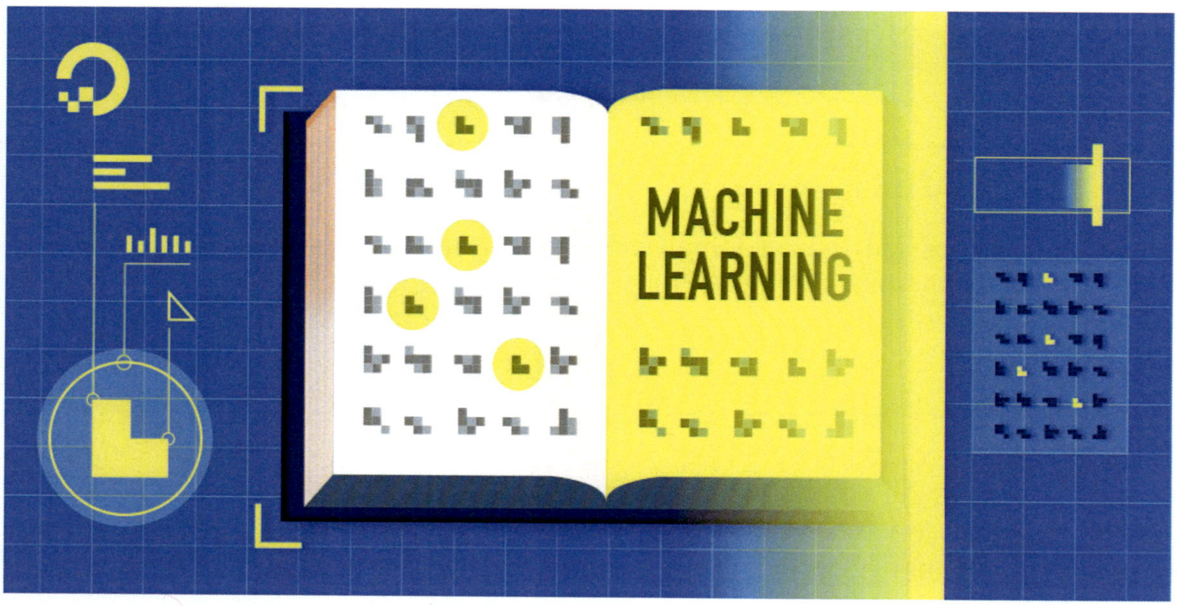

Figure 7.1. Chart for Machine Learning (Source: Digital Ocean, Creative Commons License).

Information can be changed into knowledge by a medium known as Machine Learning. There has been an outburst of data in the previous 50 years. Unless a load of data is broken down and the patterns concealed within it are found, it is futile. Invaluable underlying arrangements that we would otherwise find hard to obtain can be automatically found by Machine Learning means (Jordan & Mitchell, 2015). To execute all kinds of difficult decision making and foretell future events, the veiled patterns and knowledge about a dilemma can be used (Vartak et al., 2016; Herbrich, 2017).

We are drowning in information and starving for knowledge—John Naisbitt

Machine Learning is being communicated with everyday yet most of us are ignorant of that. It is continuously learning and enhancing from every interaction by becoming a bit of the engine behind each image we take, listen to music, or google something. Creating new antidotes, determine cancer and self-driving cars are also backed up by Machine Learning (Sebastiani, 2002; King, 2009).

It is merely an inch away from all our prior rule-based systems which make Machine Learning all the more entertaining:

if(x = y): do z

Customarily, to produce answers to an issue, data were joined with human forged rules by software engineering. Machine Learning, on the other hand, ascertains the rules behind a dilemma by using data and answers (Chollet, 2017) (Figure 7.2).

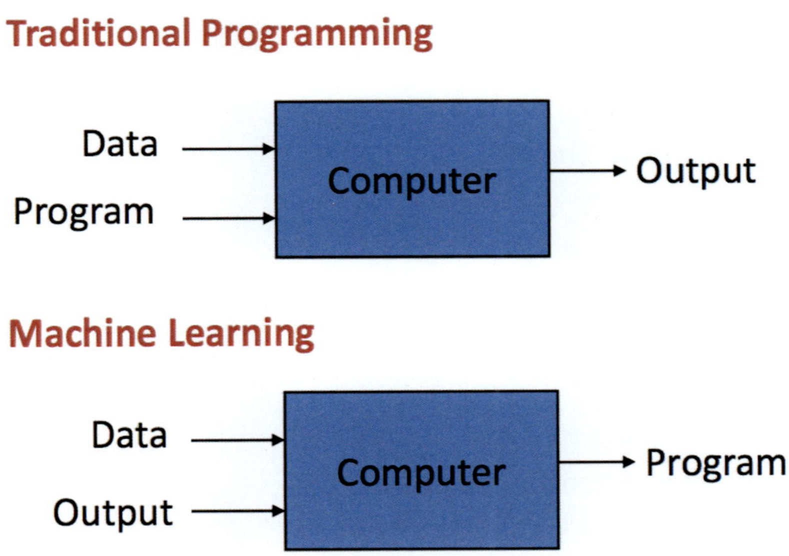

Figure 7.2. Machine Learning vs. Traditional Programming (Source: Ravindra Lokhande, Creative Commons License).

Machines have to undergo a learning process to grasp from how well they execute and try distinct rules so that they can learn the directives regulating a phenomenon.

Semi-supervised, supervised, unsupervised, and reinforcement learning are several forms of Machine Learning. Although they all pursue the same fundamental theory and process, all kinds of Machine Learning have, unlike approaches. The scrutiny on each approach and the overall Machine Learning concept is included in this explanation (Dietterich, 2000; Biamonte et al., 2017).

Learning Objectives

At the end of this chapter, readers will be able to:

- Understand the fundamentals of machine learning and its brief history.
- Familiarize with the terminology used in machine learning.
- Gain knowledge about the machine learning process and its background theory.
- Recognize different approaches, methods, and algorithms used in machine learning.
- Identify programming languages used in machine learning.
- Comprehend the concept of human biases in machine learning.

Key Terms

- Machine Learning
- Artificial Intelligence
- Data Mining
- Probability Theory
- K-nearest Neighbor
- Decision Tree Learning
- Deep Learning
- Supervised Learning
- Unsupervised Learning
- Semi-supervised learning
- Reinforcement Learning
- Linear Classifiers
- K-Means Clustering
- Neural Network
- Self-Organized Map

7.1 MACHINE LEARNING: A BRIEF HISTORY

ENIAC (Electronic Numerical Integrator and Computer), the initial manually run computer system was designed in the 1940s. ENIAC was named a numerical computing machine because, at the time, a human with vigorous numerical computation potentials was called the word "computer." You are wrong if you say that it has nothing to do with learning. To make a machine able to mimic human learning and reasoning was the concept from the start (Kononenko, 2001; Zhang et al., 2017) (Figure 7.3).

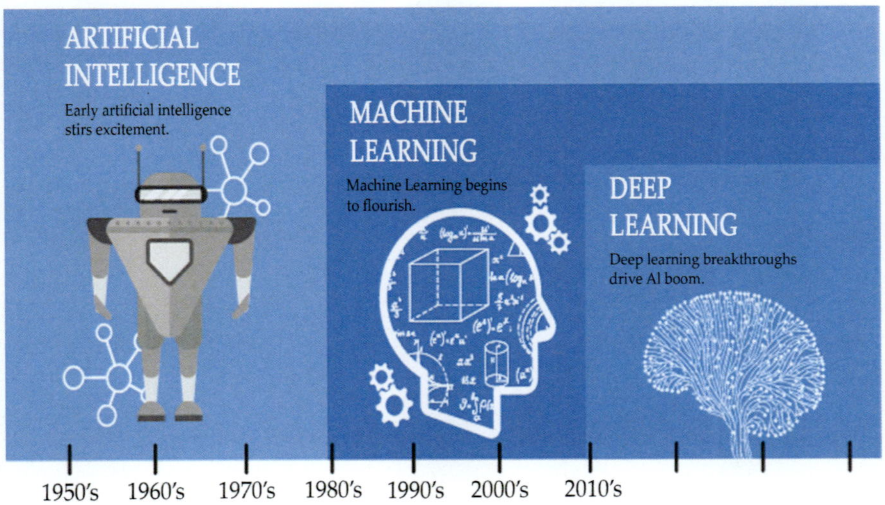

Figure 7.3. Progression of Machine Learning, Deep Learning, and Artificial Intelligence (Source: Natarajan Siva, Creative Commons License).

Allegations to be able to defeat the checker's world champion were carried out by the primal computer game program in the 1950s. This application aided checkers players a lot in bettering their abilities. The (Source: Ayush Pant, Creative Commons License) Perceptron which when integrated into grand numbers, in a matrix, became a mighty monster, but otherwise was a plain classifier that was manufactured around the same period by Frank Rosenblatt. It was a real milestone at the time as it was respective to that time. Due to its intricacy in solving particular problems, various years of inactivity of the neutral network domain were seen after that (Rouet-Leduc et al., 2017; Akbulut et al., 2018) (Figure 7.4).

In the 1990s, machine learning became incredibly renowned thanks to statistics. The possible approaches in AI were given life to by the convergence of statistics and computer science. This deviated the field ahead toward data-driven approaches. Intelligence systems that we're able to assimilate from large amounts of information and analyze it were starting to be built by scientists due to the large-scale data available. As a headliner, the world champion of chess, the grand-master Garry Kasparov was beaten by IBM's Deep Blue system. Presently, Deep Blue is resting undisturbed in a museum following Kasparov accusing IBM of cheating but that is the past (Goswami et al., 2016; Wilson et al., 2017).

Figure 7.4. EIMC—Electronic Numerical Integrator and Computer (Source: Ayush Pant, Creative Commons License).

7.2 TERMINOLOGY

Below are the principal terms of Machine Learning (Navigli et al., 2003; Claveau & L'Homme, 2005; Mooney & Pejaver, 2018).

7.2.1 Dataset

To work out a question, an array of data examples is provided that contain significant features (Witschel, 2005; Sclano & Velardi, 2007).

7.2.2 Features

Machine Learning system is fed essential bits of data that teach and aids us in comprehending a problem (Song et al., 2011).

7.2.3 Model

When a Machine Learning algorithm has perceived a fact, this is a demonstration (internal model) of it. The figures that are shown to it at the time of preparation teaches it this. After the tutoring of an algorithm, this replica is the output you receive. For instance, a decision tree clone would be the production after the training of a decision tree process (Kenett & Shmueli, 2015).

7.3 MACHINE LEARNING PROCESS

Provided below is the method of the Machine Learning procedure (Doan et al., 2004; Cho et al., 2005; Ge et al., 2017).

7.3.1 Data Collection

Gather the facts that the algorithm will gain an understanding from.

7.3.2 Data Preparation

Carry out dimensionality decrement and remove important properties from the data which should be configured and set up into the optical model (Snelson, 2007).

7.3.3 Training

The data that has been gathered and assembled is displayed to the Machine Learning program so it learns from it and this is called the fitting stage (Vellido et al., 2012).

7.3.4 Evaluation

To see how finely it performs, evaluate the model.

7.3.5 Tuning

Optimize its efficiency by fine-tuning the design.

7.4 BACKGROUND THEORY

7.4.1 Origins

Anything in the universe could be explained with math was a conception by maybe the first computer analyst and one of the originators of processing,

Ada Lovelace (Camastra & Vinciarelli, 2015; Sammut & Webb, 2017). More essentially, the bond representing any occurrence can be obtained by generating a mathematical formula. Human cooperation was not required and machines had the aptitude to discern the world without them was discovered by Ada Lovelace (Balasubramanian et al., 2014).

The Analytical Engine weaves algebraic patterns just as the Jacquard weaves flowers and leaves—Ada Lovelace

These foundational ideas are pivotal in Machine Learning around 200 years after. Data can be marked as data spots onto a grid no matter what the issue is. The correlation and mathematical arrangements within the prime information are tried to be found by Machine Learning (Zuccala et al., 2014).

7.4.2 Probability Theory

The probability theory which is exhibited into Machine Learning has notions that are important to it which were identified by another mathematician, Thomas Bayes (Muggleton & De Raedt, 1994).

Probability is orderly opinion… inference from data is nothing other than the revision of such opinion in the light of relevant new information—Thomas Bayes

We exist in a probabilistic society. Apprehension is bound to all that happens. Machine Learning is structured upon the Bayesian expression of probability. We imagine probability as assessing the ambiguity of an affair is the definition of Bayesian probability (Figure 7.5).

Figure 7.5. The figure of Probability Theory (Source: Gavin Edwards, Creative Commons License).

Due to this, instead of calculating the number of recurrent trails, we have to ground our probabilities on the knowledge available about an occasion. Such as a Bayesian method would use pertinent information such as the opening team, present form, and league placing while guessing a football game instead of gauging the total number of times Manchester United has triumphed against Liverpool (Bowers et al., 1997).

As the decision-making scheme is resting on logic and relevant characteristics, probabilities can still be delegated to infrequent events which are an advantage.

7.5 MACHINE LEARNING APPROACHES

It is helpful to have previous knowledge in statistics to apprehend and leverage system learning algorithms as machine learning as an area of study is heavily linked to computational statistics (Srinivasan & Fisher, 1995; Ng & Cardie, 2002).

To study the relationship between quantitative factors, usually used practices are correlation and regression whose meaning can prove to be useful for those who may not have learned statistics (Monostori et al., 1996; Shrestha & Solomatine, 2006). Two components that are not structured as either independent or dependent, hence the degree of relationship between them is called Correlation. The affiliation among one dependent and one independent element is inspected by using Regression at an initial level. Regression allows prediction potential because when the independent factor is known, regression statistics can be utilized to estimate the dependent variable (Guzella & Caminhas, 2009; Ye et al., 2009).

Advancements are continuous for approaches to machine knowledge. Some of the famous approaches that are being applied in machine learning at the point of writing will be examined for our benefit (Nielsen et al., 1999; Lavecchia, 2015).

7.5.1 K-Nearest Neighbor

A model that can be utilized for regression, as well as categorization, is the k-nearest neighbor program which is a pattern recognition archetype. The '*k*' in the k-nearest neighbor is generally small and is a positive number, regularly abbreviated as k-NN. The k closest training samples within an area will be in the submission in any of the two; classification or regression (Dudani, 1976; Keller et al., 1985).(Figure 7.6).

The class association is the output in this procedure. The genus most standard amidst its k nearest neighbors will be appointed a new object. The class of the sole closest neighbor will be designated the object in the instance of k = 1(Denoeux, 2008; Garcia et al., 2008). As inference beyond the training information does not take place until a question is made to the network, the k-nearest neighbor is said to be a kind of "lazy learning" amongst the most principal of machine learning algorithms (Tan, 2005; Yu et al., 2005).

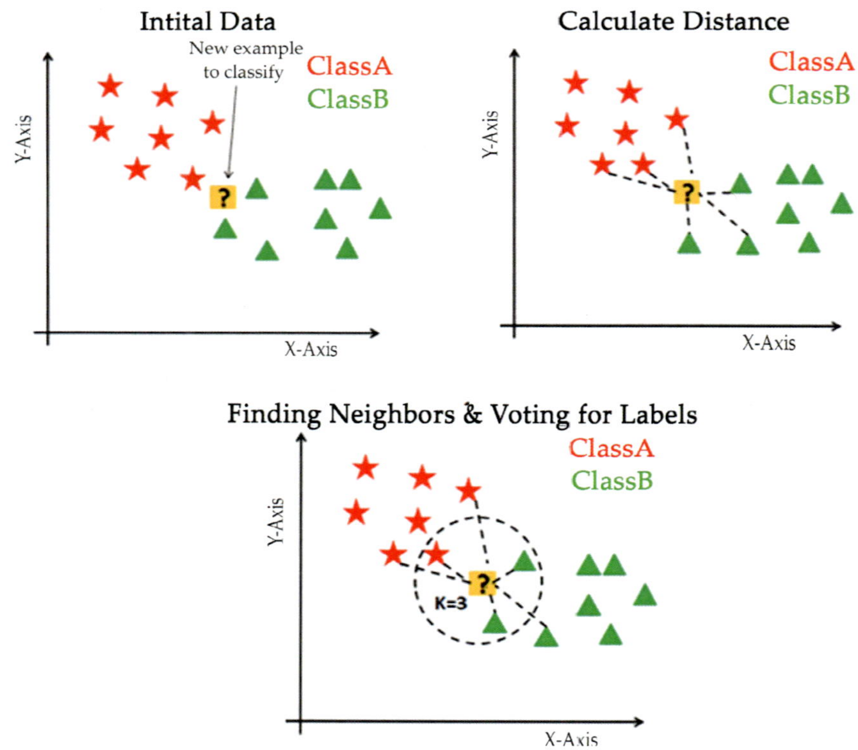

Figure 7.6. Image of K-nearest Neighbor approach (Source: Adam Shafi, Creative Commons License).

7.5.2 Decision Tree Learning

To show or promote decision making and to viably represent preferences, decision trees are typically employed. Decision trees are applicable as a predictive template when engaging with data mining and machine learning. The data's intended value is deduced from inspections about data by these models' outline (Freund & Mason, 1999; Kamiran et al., 2010).

To make a model that will foretell the worth of a target grounded on input components is the aim of decision tree learning (Kearns & Mansour, 1999).

The outcomes about the data's desired value are presented in the leaves while the data's aspects that are specified through monitoring are represented by the sections in the predictive model. An attribute value assessment is replicated on each of the procured subsets periodically which comprise the divided root data when "learning" a tree. The recursion procedure will be finished once the subset at a joint has a similar value as its aimed value has (Liu et al., 2008). Whether or not one should go casting can be resolved by looking at a case of various conditions. Barometric pressure states as well as weather statuses are included in this (Figure 7.7).

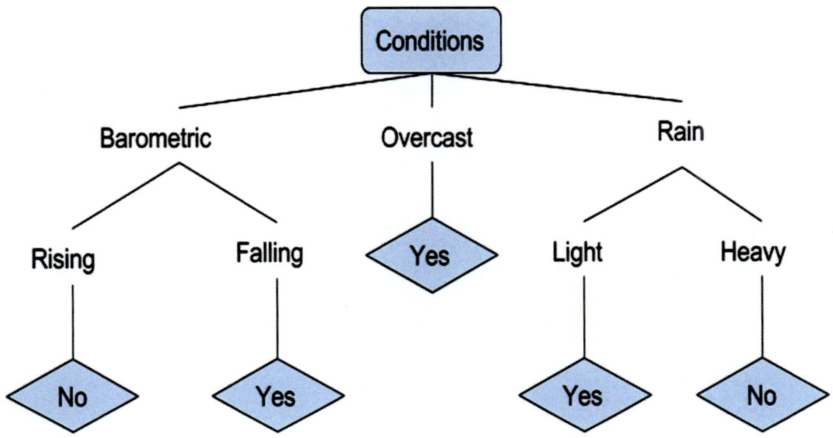

Figure 7.7. Flowchart of decision tree learning (Source: Gavin Edwards, Creative Commons License).

An example is codified by grouping it through the tree to the suitable leaf node in the clarified decision tree above. The outcome which is either a Yes or a No is then sent back the classification connected with the specific leaf. Whether a day's temperature is appropriate or not for going fishing is classified by the tree.

The interconnection should be direct to determine, however; a genuine classification tree data group would have many more qualities than what is summarized above. Comprehending when the decision tree has come to an evident ending, what conditions to utilize for splitting, and what characteristics to choose are various determinations that need to be made when working along with decision tree learning (Gaddam et al., 2007).

7.5.3 Deep Learning

How the human mind deals with light and auditory stimuli into sight and hearing is an endeavor at duplication by deep learning. Biological neural webbing which consists of numerous layers in a synthetic neural network built of hardware and GPUs is the influence behind deep learning architecture (Deng & Yu, 2014); LeCun et al., 2015).

To take out or convert properties (or representations) of the information, a flow of nonlinear processing unit tiers is used by deep learning. The input of a single layer acts as the output of the prior layer. Algorithms can be either unsupervised and carry out pattern evaluation or supervised and work to categorize data in deep learning (Figure 7.8).

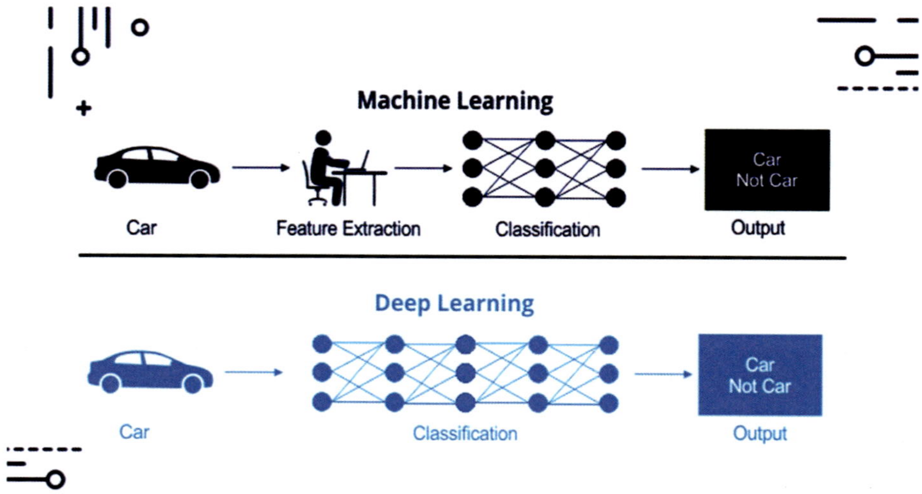

Figure 7.8. Flowchart showing Deep Learning vs. Machine learning process (Source: Sumeet Bansal, Creative Commons License).

Deep learning has proved capable to defeat humans in some intellectual tasks and digests the most data between the machine learning algorithms that are presently being used and enhanced. In the artificial surveillance space, deep learning has come to be the approach with considerable potential due to these qualities.

Deep learning methods have proved to realize notable breakthroughs for computer vision and dialog recognition. A prominent example of a network that exploits deep learning is IBM Watson (Chetlur et al., 2014; Schmidhuber, 2015).

7.6 MACHINE LEARNING METHODS

Functions are commonly divided into vast categories in machine learning. How response on the learning is provided to the system advanced or how learning is obtained is the footing of these categories.

Unsupervised learning which supplies the algorithm with no assigned data to enable it to search structure within its input information and, supervised learning which teaches algorithms based on sample input and output data which is tagged by humans are two of the most vastly adopted machine learning processes. These procedures will be analyzed with more scrutiny (Olden et al., 2008; Parmar et al., 2015).

While managing Machine Learning, many methods can be taken. Listed below are the zones they are generally classified into. The most frequently used and deep-rooted approaches are Supervised and unsupervised. The Learnings which have shown striking results and are fresher and more intricate are Semi-supervised and Reinforcement Learning.

The *No Free Lunch theorem* is popular in Machine Learning. Every task that you attempt to decipher has its idiosyncrasies. There is no sole algorithm that will work nicely for all processes is its statement. Hence, to fit each issue's traits, there are many algorithms and methods. Patterns that best suit various problems will keep being created of Machine Learning and AI. Below are 4 processes of machine learning (Buczak & Guven, 2015; Voyant et al., 2017):

1. semi-supervised learning;
2. supervised learning;
3. reinforcement learning; and
4. unsupervised learning.

7.6.1 Supervised Learning

Sample inputs that are denoted with their required outputs are given to the computer in supervised learning. By contrasting its real output with the "learned" outputs to find mistakes, and transform the model appropriately, the algorithm can "ascertain" and that is the aim of this approach. Accordingly, patterns are used to foresee label factors on further unlabeled figures by supervised learning (Caruana & Niculescu-Mizil, 2006; Zhu & Goldberg, 2009).

For instance, information with pictures of oceans tagged as water and shots of sharks marked as fish may be provided to the system with supervised learning. Unlabeled ocean photos as water and label-less shark images as fish should be identifiable to the supervised learning algorithm after being educated on this data.

Employing historical facts to predict statistically probably future events is a normal use type of supervised learning. Historical stock exchange information may be utilized by it to expect future fluctuations or be used to clear out spam emails. Unlabeled images of dogs can be categorized by using tagged images of dogs in supervised learning (Zhu et al., 2003; Kingma et al., 2014).

Amidst a group of *inputs* and *outputs*, the aim is to attain the *mapping* (the *rules*) in supervised learning. For instance, the results would be the guests to the seaside and the inputs could be the weather prediction. To *comprehend the mapping that explains the link* between the number of beach guests and temperature is the aim of supervised learning.

The name "supervised" learning suggests that to educate the model how it should act, sample *labeled* data is given of past *input and output couplets* during the learning procedure. An example would be that the machine learning system will *output a future forecast* for the number of visitors when fresh inputs are offered in future temperatures.

The critical *generalization* portion of machine learning is being able to adjust to new inputs and make forecasts. The supervised model explains the authentic 'general' basic relationship because we want to increase generalization during training. The figure would be *unable to conform* to new, formerly unseen inputs if the model is over-educated because it ends in *over-fitting* to the examples used. The guidance we supply presents bias to the learning and is a consequence to be conscious of in supervised learning. It is very essential to show it *trusty, unbiased samples* as the design can only be *echoing* exactly what it was portrayed. While it comprehends, supervised learning needs a lot of information. The toughest and the costliest part of using supervised learning is oftentimes gaining enough *reliably labeled data*. (Hence the reason why new oil is the name data is called)

For the extent of visitors to the seaside for example [high, medium, low], a *section* from a finite collection could be the result from a supervised Machine Learning pattern:

Input [temperature=**20**] -> *Model* -> Output = [visitors=**high**]

This is called *classification* as it is determining how to *categorize the input* in this condition.

As an alternative, a *real-world scalar* could be the product (output a value):

Input [temperature=**20**] -> *Model* -> Output = [visitors=300]

It is called regression when such is the condition (Figure 7.9).

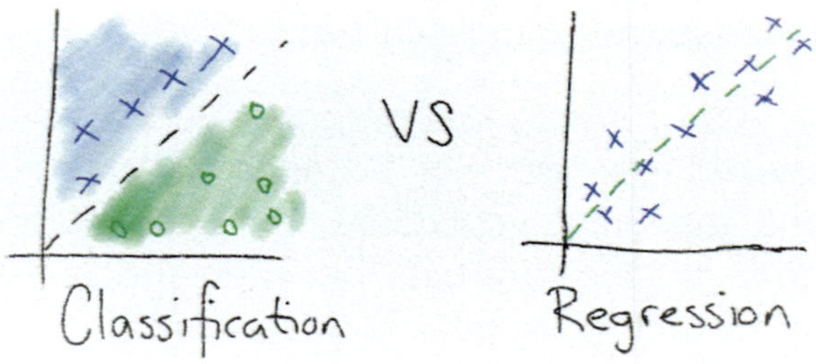

Figure 7.9. Graph for classification vs regression in supervised learning (Source: Gavin Edwards, Creative Commons License).

7.6.2 Classification

To categorize, the comparable data records are combined into distinct sections by something called Classification. *The rules* that describe how to detach the different information points are found through the use of Machine Learning.

However, how does the formation of the magical rules happen? To find the rules, various methods are available. To *use information and answers to acquire rules* that *linearly detach* data points is focused on by them (Kotsiantis et al., 2007; Ye et al., 2009).

A chief concept in machine learning is linear separability. "Can the distinctive data points be disjointed by a line?" is all that linear separability signifies. Simply put, the finest way to segregate data records with a line is tried to be found by classification approaches.

Decision boundaries is the name given to the lines depicted between classes. *The decision surface* is the whole area that is appointed to describe a class. A particular class will be designated to a figure point if it stands within its perimeter is what decision surface explains (Shami & Verhelst, 2007; Jain et al., 2009) (Figure 7.10).

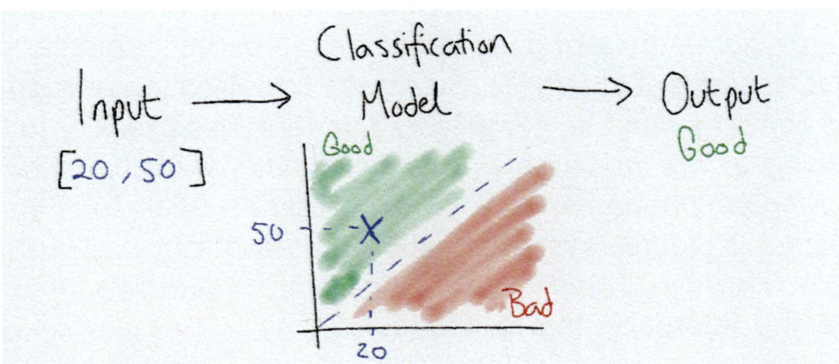

Figure 7.10. Classical model representation (Source: Gavin Edwards, Creative Commons License).

7.6.2.1 Regression

Another type of supervised learning is regression. Regression *produces a number* rather than a category is the distinction amidst classification and regression. Hence, when foretelling the probability of an occasion, the climate for a given day, or value-based issues like stock market costs, regression proves to be convenient (Briggs et al., 2010; Criminisi et al., 2012) (Figure 7.11).

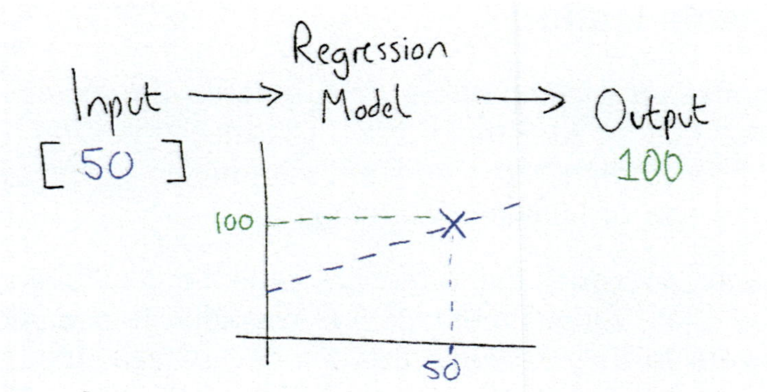

Figure 7.11. Regression Model Representation (Source: Gavin Edwards, Creative Commons License).

7.6.2.2 Examples

To choose when to purchase/sell and make a profit, regression is used in fiscal trading to search the designs in stocks and other goods. If an email you get is spam, classification is already being utilized to classify it.

Supervised learning methods; regression and classification can be widened towards much more intricate tasks. For instance, oration and sound tasks. Some examples are object spotting, chatbots, and picture classification.

A model educated with supervised learning to practically fake videos of humans talking is used in a present example shown below (Dasgupta et al., 2011). How does classification or regression have a concern with this complicated image-based task, you think? *Everything in the universe is explained with math and numbers, even intricate phenomenon* is what it comes back to. Similar to regression, a neural system is still only producing values in this example. However, *numerical 3d coordinate numbers of a facial net* are the figures in this instance.

7.6.3 Unsupervised Learning

The learning system is left to search similarities among its input information as data is unlabeled in unsupervised learning. Machine learning techniques that help unsupervised learning are especially valuable because unlabeled data are more extensive than labeled data (Figueiredo & Jain, 2002).

Unsupervised learning may have an aim of feature studying through which the outlines that are required to categorize raw information are reflexively obtained by the computational machine, but it may also be as direct as finding hidden designs within a dataset. Transactional figures are what unsupervised learning is generally used for. To work out what alike qualities can be taken out from customer descriptions and their kinds of purchases from a huge dataset of clients and their buying may be improbable for you as a person. A marketing operation associated with pregnancy and baby merchandise can be aimed at the clientele to maximize their amount of purchases after calculating that women of a particular age range who purchase unscented soaps are more probable to be pregnant by entering this information into an unsupervised learning system (Hofmann, 2001).

Difficult data that is wider and unrelated can be structured in potentially coherent ways by unsupervised learning techniques without being informed of a "right" answer. Recommender networks that suggest what goods to purchase next, oddity detection, and for crooked credit card buying is what unsupervised learning is mostly used for. To search similarities and categorize dog images together, untagged pictures of dogs can be utilized as input information for the system in unsupervised learning.

In the examples, **only input statistics** are given in unsupervised learning. There are no labeled instance productions to aim for. Surprisingly, many appealing and labyrinthine designs hidden within the information without any notes are still likely to be found.

Sorting various color coins into distinct piles is a real-life instance of unsupervised learning. You can recognize which color coins are *linked* and *sort* them into their accurate groups by just seeing their attributes such as color even though no one taught you how to segregate them (Figure 7.12).

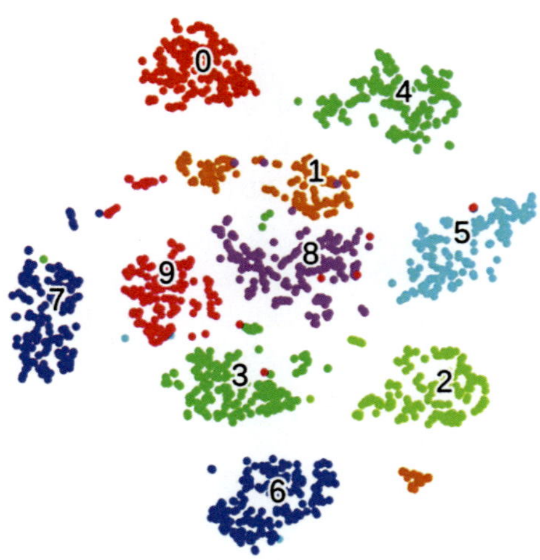

Figure 7.12. Rooted only on their features, handwritten figures are accurately sorted into groups by an unsupervised learning algorithm (t-SNE) (Source: Cyrille Rossant, Creative Commons License).

The issue becomes less defined with the expulsion of supervision; hence, unsupervised learning can be tougher than supervised learning. A concept of what designs to look for is less focused on the system.

Imagine it in your studying. By re-using the supervised information of notes, harmony, and rhythms, you would comprehend how to play guitar faster under the supervision of an instructor. However, you'd find it so much more difficult knowing where to begin if you only taught yourself.

You begin from a clean slate with less partiality and may even find a fresh, better way to decipher an issue by being unsupervised in a laissez-faire educating style. Thus, that is the reason knowledge history is what unsupervised learning is also called. When performing an exploratory information analysis, unsupervised learning is quite necessary.

KEYWORD

Unsupervised learning, also known as unsupervised machine learning, uses machine learning algorithms to analyze and cluster unlabeled datasets.

To find the interesting structures in unlabeled data, we use density estimation. The most common form of which is clustering. Among others, there is also dimensionality reduction, latent variable models, and anomaly detection. More complex unsupervised techniques involve neural networks like Auto-encoders and Deep Belief Networks, but we won't go into them in this introduction blog.

We use density estimation to look for the appealing structures in unlabeled figures. Clustering is the most general form. Dormant variable models, anomaly recognition, and dimensionality reduction amidst others are also within them. Neural systems like Deep Belief Networks and Auto-encoders are engaged in more complicated unsupervised methods, but we won't get into them in this chapter.

7.6.3.1 Clustering

Clustering is what unsupervised learning is applied for. Creating sections with differing features is the act called Clustering. Within a data file, several subgroups are strived to be found by Clustering. We are not limited to any group of labels and are at liberty to pick how many clusters to make as this is unsupervised learning. This is both a burden and a fortune. An empirical design selection procedure is performed after choosing a model that has the appropriate number of clusters (complexity) (Chen et al., 2005; Caron et al., 2018) (Figure 7.13).

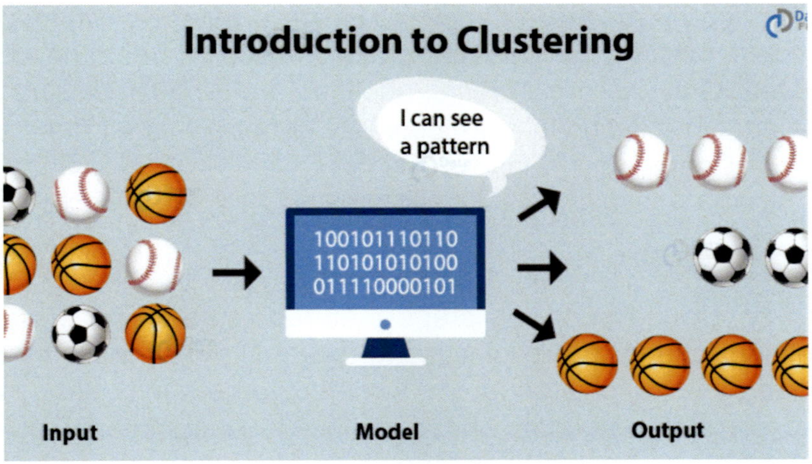

Figure 7.13. Machine Learning's application; Data Clustering (Source: Data Flair, Creative Commons License).

7.6.3.2 Association

You want to reveal the rules that explain your data in Association Learning. If someone watches video A, they will probably watch video B is an instance of it. For examples such as this where you wish to look for related things, association directions are perfect (Cios et al., 2007; Li et al., 2018).

7.6.3.3 Anomaly Detection

The recognition of odd or uncommon items that diverge from the mass of data. For instance, fraudulent movement on your card will be noticed through the application of this by your bank. Within a standard range of attitudes and values is where your standard spending routines will fall into. The attitude will be distinct from your normal habit, however; when anyone attempts to rob you using your card. To detach and recognize these weird happenings, anomaly detection uses unsupervised learning (Schlegl et al., 2017).

7.6.3.4 Dimensionality Reduction

An inferior more systematic set that still encrypts the significant data after the alleviation from the initial feature set down is the most crucial quality aimed to be found by Dimensionality reduction.

For instance, the day of the week, month, the number of occasions arranged for that day, and the weather might be used as inputs while foretelling the number of guests to the seaside. For forecasting the number of guests, however; the month might not be essential (Kumar et al., 2017; 2019).

Less precision and effectiveness are created by unimportant characteristics such as this that make a Machine Learning system confused. Only the most crucial qualities are recognized and used by using dimensionality reduction. A generally used method is Principal Component Analysis (PCA).

7.6.3.5 Examples

In reality, grounded on the star's features, a new kind of star by inspecting what subsets of star automatically manifest has been founded by using clustering. To divide customers into alike groups based on their attitudes and qualities, it is commonly used in marketing. To suggest or look for related things, associating learning is used. Market basket analysis is a general example. Based on what they have put in their cart, association conditions are found to foretell other things a customer is expected to purchase in market basket analysis. Amazon utilizes this. They suggest things like a laptop case through their association rules if you put a new laptop in your cart.

Situations such as fraud recognition and malware recognition, anomaly detection are compatible.

7.6.4 Semi-Supervised Learning

A blend amongst supervised and unsupervised approaches is called semi-supervised learning. Semi-supervised learning takes the central path. We don't let the system do its own thing and give no type of feedback but the learning procedure isn't carefully supervised with example productions for every single input (Zhu et al., 2005; Zhu & Goldberg, 2009) (Figure 7.14).

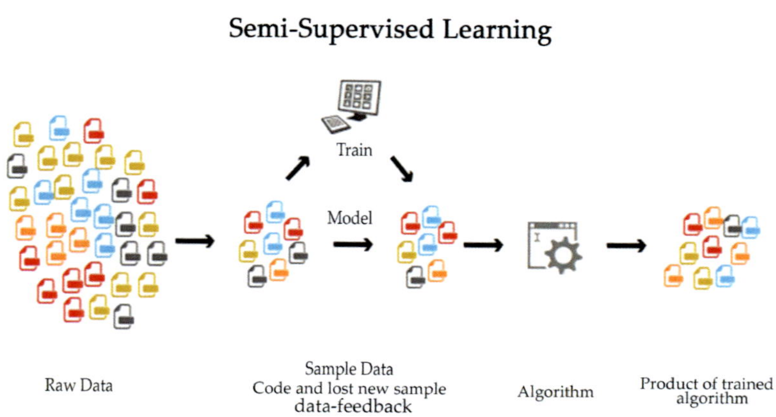

Figure 7.14. Semi-supervised Machine Learning illustration (Source: Simpli learn, Creative Commons License).

To lessen the weight of having adequate labeled information, a much bigger unlabeled dataset is combined with less amount of labeled information. Hence, Machine Learning's capability to resolve many more issues is opened up by it.

7.6.4.1 Generative Adversarial Networks

A current advancement with amazing outputs has been Generative Adversarial Networks (GANs). A discriminator and generator are two neural systems used by GANs. The discriminator reviews the product and the generator creates it. They both become progressively proficient by competing against each other.

It can be categorized as semi-supervised because by utilizing a system to both create input and another one to generate the result, there is no need for us to give obvious labels every single time (Zhang et al., 2019).

7.6.4.2 Examples

Breast cancer examinations are an excellent example of medical tests. It is laborious and very costly and a skilled expert is needed to tag these. The semi-supervised system would be able to mark a larger group of scans if a professional can label just a slight set of breast cancer tests by using the small subset.

The most splendid instances of semi-supervised learning, for me, are GAN's. Unsupervised learning is being utilized to connect aspects from a picture to the other by a Generative Adversarial Network in the video below.

Without using designated training information, a neural system known as a GAN (generative adversarial network) is used to fuse pictures.

7.6.5 Reinforcement Learning

You'll have noted reinforcement learning if you're accustomed to psychology. We study it in daily life so you'll already know the basis if not. To strengthen behaviors in this method, a random positive and negative response is used. Good behaviors are compensated with a present and become more ordinary just like if imagine it as if instructing a dog. Bad behaviors are chastened and become less ordinary. In reinforcement learning, this present-motivated attitude is key (Kaelbling et al., 1996; Mnih et al., 2015) (Figure 7.15).

The style we as humans learn is quite alike to it. We frequently learn by getting positive and negative indications throughout our lives. We get these gestures by the substances in our brain which is one of many methods. We become more probable to redo that particular action which makes us feel pleasant because the neurons in our minds give a boost of positive neurotransmitters such as dopamine when anything nice happens. Like in supervised learning, we don't need frequent supervision to understand. We still learn very successfully by only providing the incidental reinforcement signals.

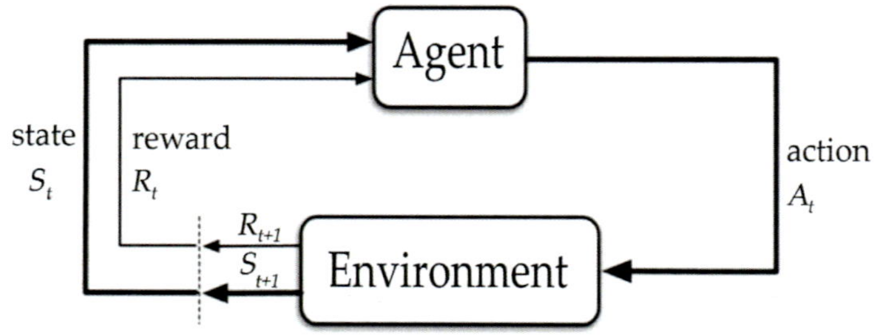

Figure 7.15. Reinforcement Learning being influenced by Cyclic (Source: Shweta Bhatt, Creative Commons License).

It is an initial step away from teaching on static datasets, and rather than being able to employ dynamic, loud data-rich environments is one of the most thrilling parts of Reinforcement Learning. A learning method used by humans is brought nearer to Machine Learning. The Erath is simply our loud, intricate data-rich environment. In Reinforcement Learning investigation, games are very renowned. Classic data-rich surroundings are delivered by them. To teach reward-motivated attitudes, the points in games are fitting reward signals. Plus, to decrease overall teaching time, time can be accelerated in an artificial game environment. By playing the game repeatedly, a Reinforcement Learning system just plans to increase its rewards. It is expected to be fitted to Reinforcement Learning if you can mount an issue with a constant 'score' as a gift. Because of how fresh and complicated it is, reinforcement learning hasn't been employed as much in the actual world. However, to decrease information center running prices by directing the cooling networks more productively, the use of reinforcement learning is an actual-world example. To receive the lowest energy prices, the system learns an optimal strategy of how to act. The more gifts it gets is linked to how low the price is. It is constantly used in games in testing. Imperfect data (where sections of the state are concealed e.g. the actual world) and perfect data (where you can see the whole state of the surrounding) in games have both seen an extraordinary success that eclipse humans.

7.7 MACHINE LEARNING ALGORITHMS

In the extent of supervised learning where which mostly classification is dealt with, following are the types of algorithms:

i. Linear Classifiers
ii. K-Means Clustering
iii. Quadratic Classifiers
iv. Perceptron
v. Random Forest
vi. Boosting
vii. Naïve Bayes Classifier
viii. Logical Regression
ix. Support Vector Machine
x. Decision Tree
xi. Bayesian Networks
xii. Neural networks

A few algorithms are discussed in detail in following sections.

7.7.1 Linear Classifiers

In the process machine learning, classification is used to group objects with comparable feature values, into the groups. Timothy et al. (1998) declared that the linear classifiers accomplish this with the help of a classification decision (Grzymala-Busse & Hu, 2000; Grzymala-Busse et al., 2005). The classification decision is dependent on the input of linear combination. If the real vector $\vec{x}$ is the input to the classifier, then the output is given as:

$$y = f(\vec{w} \cdot \vec{x}) = f(\sum_j w_j x_j)$$

Where, $\vec{w}$ real weights vector,f→ function in which the dot product of two vectors is translated into the preferred output. A set of marked training samples helps to deduce the vector $\vec{w}$. Usually the values above a specific threshold are mapped to first class and the rest of the values to second class by the function f. The probability that a certain item fits in a certain class is given by the complex function f (Li et al., 2004; Honghai et al., 2005; Luengo et al., 2012).

In the two-class classification, the functionality of the linear classifier can be visualized as dividing with hyperplane the high-dimensional input space. The points on the one side of hyperplane are marked as "yes," while the points on the other side are marked as "no." Linear classifiers are frequently used in conditions where the pace of classification is a problem because linear classifiers are the fastest classifiers especially when the real vector $\vec{x}$ is sparse. The decision trees are also capable to be faster (Hornik et al., 1989; Schaffalitzky & Zisserman, 2004). Linear classifiers usually perform very well when in the real vector $\vec{x}$ the number of dimensions is large. In document classification, every element in the real vector $\vec{x}$ is usually the counts of a certain word in the document. The classifier must be well-regularized in these cases (Dempster et al., 1997; Haykin & Network, 2004).

SVM models are closely related to the traditional multilayer (PNN) perceptron neural networks. Using a kernel function, Support vector machine models are the substitute training scheme for the polynomials, radial basis functions and multi-layer perceptron neural networks classifiers. In SVM the weight of the network is found by resolving the quadratic programming problem having linear constraints, instead of resolving a non-convex and unconstrained minimization problem such as used in the standard neural network teaching (Gross et al., 1969; Zoltan-Csaba et al., 2011; Olga et al., 2015).

As indicated by Luis- Gonz (2005), support vector machine executes classification by creating the *N*-dimensional hyperplane which optimally splits the data into categories. Support vector machine models are closely connected to neural networks. The Support vector machine model, in which the sigmoid kernel function is used resembles the two-layer (PNN) perceptron neural network (Rosenblatt, 1961; Dutra da Silva et al., 2011).

In the language of support vector machine literature, the *attribute* is a predictor variable, and an altered attribute which defines the (HP) hyperplane is known as a *feature*. The process of selecting the most appropriate representation is called the feature *selection*. Set of features which describes one of the cases is known as a *vector*. The goal of SVM (support vector machine) modeling is to discover the optimum hyperplane which splits the groups of vector in a way that cases with one category of the target variable are on one side of the plane and cases with the other category are on the other side of the plane (Block et al., 1962; Novikoff, 1963; Freund & Schapire, 1999). The vectors closest to the hyperplane are known as the *support vectors*.

7.7.2 K-Means Clustering

This technique comprises of the uncomplicated steps. In the beginning K (number of the cluster) is determined and the center of the clusters is assumed. Any random objects are taken as the primary center or the first K objects in the structure can also function as the primary center (Teather, 2006; Yusupov, 2007). Then three steps mentioned below are performed by the K means algorithm until convergence. Iterate until stable.

i. Determining the distance of every object from the center

ii. Determining the center coordinate

iii. Grouping the objects based on the minimum distance

K-means flowchart is shown in Figure 7.16.

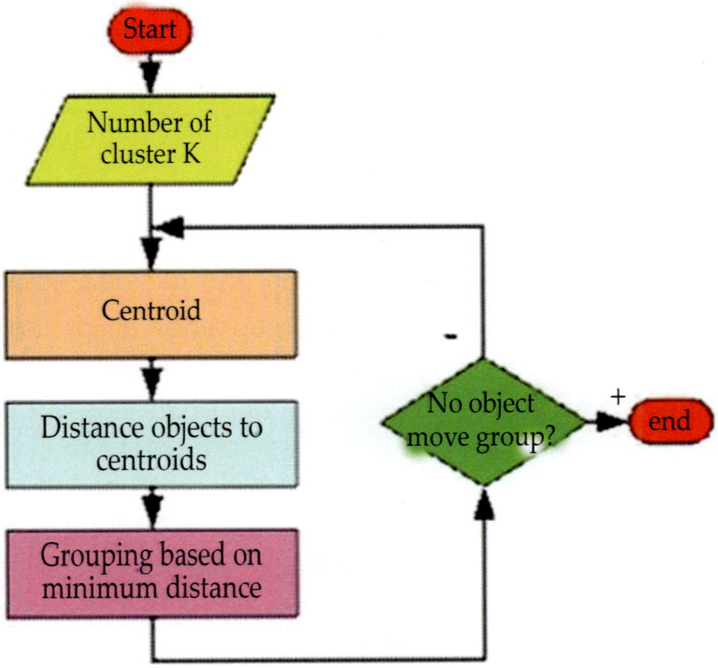

Figure 7.16. Schematic illustration of K-means iteration (Source: Taiwo Oladipupo Ayodele, Creative Commons License).

K-means clustering is an easiest unsupervised learning algorithm which provides the solution of the well-known clustering problem. The process adopts a simple way to categorize the given data set amongst the definite number of clusters. For each cluster, K centroid is to be defined. These centroids must be positioned in a scheming way because different results can be obtained from a different location (Franc & Hlaváč, 2005; González et al., 2006). The more appropriate choice is to position the centroids as far as possible from each other. The next step involves taking each point from the given data and associating the point to the adjacent centroid. When there is no point left, it indicates the completion of the first step and an early grouping is done (Oltean & Dumiterscu, 2004; Fukunaga, 2008; Chali, 2009). Now here re-calculation of 'k' new centroids is to be done. After obtaining the new centroids, a fresh binding amongst the same points and the adjacent new centroid is to be done. A loop is produced. Due to this loop, the k centroids adjust their position gradually until there are no more changes. Thus the centroids don't move anymore (Oltean & Groşan, 2003; Oltean, 2007). This algorithm goal at diminishing an *objective function*, a squared error function in this particular case. The objective function:

$$J = \sum_{j-1}^{k} \sum_{i-1}^{x} \left\| x_i^{(j)} - c_j \right\|^2 ,$$

$\left\| x_i^{(j)} - c_j \right\|^2$ is a selected distance measure between $x_i^{(j)}$ (data point) and c_j (cluster center). It is a sign of distance of *n* data points with respect to their particular cluster centers.

The algorithm for this technique consists of the steps defined below:

i. K points are placed into the space denoted by objects which are being clustered. These points denote primary group centroids.
ii. Each object is assigned to the group which has the nearest centroid.
iii. The positions of K centroids are recalculated after all of the objects have been allocated.
iv. Steps ii and iii are repeated as long as the centroids are moving. This creates a partition of objects into the groups from where the minimized metric can be calculated.

Though it can be ascertained that the process will always terminate, this k-means clustering algorithm does not essentially find the most optimum configuration equivalent to the minimum global objective function (Burke et al., 2006; Bader-El-Den & Poli, 2007). The K-means algorithm is also considerably delicate to the primary arbitrarily selected cluster centers. This algorithm is run numerous times to diminish this effect. K-means algorithm has been modified to many problem fields. This algorithm is a worthy contender for modification to work with the fuzzy feature vectors (Tavares et al., 2004; Keller & Poli, 2007).

Assume that n-sample feature vectors (**x** 1, **x**2, $\mathbf{x}_3$ ..., **x** n) are available, all of the similar class and they plunge into the k dense clusters where k < n. Assume $\mathbf{m}_i$ to be the mean in the cluster **i**. We can implement the minimum distance classifier to split the clusters if they are well separated. It can be said that the **x** is present in the cluster **I** only if || **x** – $\mathbf{m}_i$ || represents the minimum of all k distances. This recommends the following process in order to find the k means:

i. Supposing the values for means (**m**1, **m**2,$\mathbf{m}_3$ ..., **m**k) unless no modifications in any of the mean occur
ii. Classifying the samples into the clusters using the estimated means
iii. For the cluster **i** from the range 1 to k
iv. Swap **m**i by, mean of all the samples for the cluster **i**
v. end_for
vi. end_until

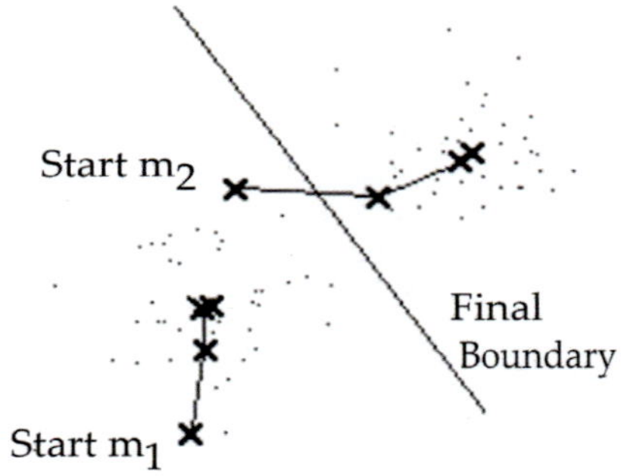

Figure 7.17. Demonstration of the motion for m1 and m2 means at the midpoint of two clusters (Source: Taiwo Oladipupo Ayodele, Creative Commons License).

This is an easy form of the k-means process. It can be observed as the greedy algorithm for separating the n models into k clusters to reduce the totality of squared distances to cluster centers. Some weaknesses of this algorithm do exist:

i. The method to set the means wasn't stated. One famous way to start the mean is to arbitrarily choose k of the models.
ii. It is possible that a set of models nearby to **mi** is vacant so that the **mi** can't be upgraded. This is an irritation which must be looked after in an implementation.
iii. The outcomes yielded are dependent on the primary values for the mean, and it commonly happens that the suboptimum partitions are originated. The standard solution for this is to go for a number of dissimilar starting points.
iv. The outcomes are dependent on the metric which is used to quantify || **x** – **mi** ||. The standard way out is to standardize every variable by its typical deviation, although this is not desirable every time.

7.7.3 Neural Network

Neural networks can, in fact, execute a number of reversion and classification jobs at once, though normally each network executes only one (Forsyth, 1990; Bishop C. M., 1995; Poli et al., 2007). In the majority of cases, there is only one particular output variable for the network. For many state classification problems, this may relate to the number of outcome units. If you outline a network with numerous output variables, then it might suffer from cross-talk. The concealed neurons have difficulty in learning as they are trying to model as a minimum two functions. The best possible solution is that for each output, train the separate network and then combine them into one so that they can perform as a unit. Neural network methodologies are listed below:

1. Multilayer Perceptron
2. Training Multilayer Perceptron
3. Back Propagation Algorithm
4. Over-learning and Generalization
5. Selection of Data

7.7.4 Self-Organized Map

SOFM (Self-Organizing Feature Map) networks are utilized in a different way as compared to other networks. Other networks are planned for the supervised learning tasks whereas the Self-Organizing Feature Map networks are designed mainly for the unsupervised learning tasks (Haykin, 1994; Patterson, 1996; Fausett, 1994). Training data set in supervised learning comprises of the cases containing input variables organized with the related outputs whereas the training set in unsupervised learning consists of input variables only. This may appear weird at the first glance. What can a network learn without the outputs? The answer to this question is the Self-Organizing Feature Map network tries to absorb the configuration of the data.

Kohonen (Kohonen, 1997) explained that one possible use of SOFM is in the exploratory data examination. The Self-Organizing Feature Map (SOFM) network can pick up to identify the data clusters and can relate classes which are alike. The consumer of the network can figure out the understanding of data, which is then utilized to improve the network. As the classes of the data are acknowledged, they can then be labeled in order to make the network capable of the classification tasks. The Self-Organizing Feature Map networks can be used for classification when the output classes are available instantaneously. The benefit in this situation is their capability to highlight the resemblances between the classes.

A second potential use of this network is in the novelty detection. The Self-Organizing Feature Map networks can acquire to identify the clusters in training data and then respond. If the new data come upon, the network is unsuccessful to identify it and this specifies novelty.

The Self-Organizing Feature Map network consists of the following two layers:

i. An output layer with radial units (topological map layer). In topological map layer, the units are positioned in space i.e. in the two dimensions.
ii. The input layer.

With the help, an iterative algorithm the Self-Organizing Feature Map networks are skilled (Patterson, 1996). Beginning with the random set of the radial centers, the algorithm adjusts them progressively to reveal the clustering of the data. This algorithm, at one stage, relates with sub-sampling and the *K*-Means algorithms which are used to allocate centers in the SOM (Self-Organize Map) network. The Self-Organizing Feature Map algorithm can be utilized to allocate centers for these kinds of networks.

The basic iterative SOFM algorithm goes through a number of periods, on every single epoch implementing the training case and employing the following algorithm:

i. Selection of the winning neuron. The neuron whose center is closest to the input situation is known as the winning neuron.
ii. Adjusting the winning neuron so that it can resemble the input case.

The iterative training technique also organizes the network in a way that the units demonstrating centers close to each other in input layer are also located close to each other on the topological layer. The topological layer of the network can be thought of as a crude 2-dimensional lattice, which must be crumpled and slanted into N-dimensional input layer to preserve the original structure in the best possible way. Any effort to characterize the N-dimensional space into the two dimensions will outcome in the loss of detail. This method can be useful in letting the user think about the data which otherwise might be difficult to understand.

The iterative algorithm utilizes the time decaying learning rate, implemented to accomplish the weighted sum. It also confirms that the modifications become more delicate as the period's pass. This guarantees that the centers snuggle down to a cooperative demonstration of the cases that helps the particular neuron to win. By adding the thought of neighborhood to the iterative algorithm the topological assembling property is accomplished. The set of neurons adjacent to the winning neuron is called a neighborhood. The neighborhood similar to the learning rate deteriorates over time. Initially, a big number of neurons are located in the neighborhood whereas with the passage of time the neighborhood will be empty. In the Kohonen or SOFM algorithm, the modification of neurons is practiced on all the fellows of the current neighborhood.

The consequence of this neighborhood apprises is that primarily big areas of a network are pulled towards the training cases and are dragged considerably. The network cultivates a crude topological arrangement with the similar cases triggering the clusters of neurons inside the topological map. Both the learning rate and the neighborhood decreases with the passage of time so that the better differences within the areas of the map can be made, eventually resulting in the fine-tuning of an individual neuron. Very often the training is intentionally organized in two separate phases:

i. A comparatively short phase with usually the high learning rates and neighborhood.

ii. A long phase having the low learning rates and zero neighborhoods.

Self-Organizing Feature Map networks, when executing classification also utilizes the accept threshold. The triggering extent of the neuron in the Self-Organizing Feature Map network is its distance from the input, the accept threshold plays the role of the maximum documented distance. If the initiation of winning neuron is much larger as compared to this distance then the Self-Organizing Feature Map network is considered as undecided. By tagging all the neurons and allocating the accept threshold suitably, a Self-Organizing Feature Map network can perform as the novelty detector.

Self-Organizing Feature Map network as articulated by Kohonen (Kohonen, 1997) are motivated by some of the known characteristics of the brain. The cerebral cortex is really a large smooth sheet with identified topological properties.

Once the network is able to identify configuration in the data, the network can be utilized as a visualization device to inspect the data. With the help of this network Win, Frequencies Datasheet can be observed to see if the discrete clusters have been made on the map. The Individual cases are implemented and topological map examined, to observe if some significance can be allotted to clusters. Once the clusters are recognized, the neurons present in the topological chart are labeled to specify their meaning. When the topological chart has been plotted in this way, then new circumstances can be given to network. The network can execute arrangement on the condition that winning neuron must be tagged with the class name. If not, then the network is considered as undecided.

7.8 PROGRAMMING LANGUAGES

For the employment in machine learning procedures, you may want to contemplate libraries available in multiple languages coupled with the abilities listed on present job advertisements when selecting a language to master in with machine learning.

Python is the most asked-for computer language in the machine learning professional discipline inferred from information taken from job advertisements on indeed.com in December 2016. Java, then R, then C++ comes behind Python.

The maximized development of deep learning structures available for this language presently, including TensorFlow, PyTorch, and Keras may be linked to Python's acclaim. Python confirms to be mighty and direct both for preprocessing information and working with data precisely as a language that has legible syntax and the quality to be utilized as a scripting language. NumPy, SciPy, and Matplotlib are various existing Python items that Python developers may already be accustomed to and the scikit-learn machine learning library is made on top of it. You can read our workshop series on "How To Build a Machine Learning Classifier in Python with scikit-learn" or "How To Perform Neural Style Transfer with Python 3 and PyTorch" or "How To Code in Python 3" to begin with Python.

Apex desktop application designers who are also grappling with machine learning at the campaign level commonly use Java which is extensively used in enterprise programming. It is preferred by those with experience in Java advancement to pertain to machine learning and generally, it is not the initial choice for those fresh to programming who want to study machine learning. Alongside cyber-attack and fraud recognition use tasks, Java tends to be employed more than Python for system security in terms of machine education applications in the industry.

MALLET (MAchine Learning for LanguagE Toolkit) permits machine learning applications on text, in addition to native language processing, topic designing, document categorization, and clustering; and Weka, a set of machine learning systems to use for information mining cases and Deeplearning4j, an open-source and divided deep-learning assemblage written for both Scala and Java are amid machine learning libraries for Java.

For statistical processing, an open-source coding language used chiefly for it is R. It is preferred by many in academic circles and in recent times, has grown in fame. Due to an elevated interest in information science, it has soared in industrial applications but it is not commonly used in industrial manufacturing environments. e1071 which comprises tasks for statistics and probability philosophy, caret (which is the abbreviation of Classification And REgression Training) for making predictive designs and general Forest for categorization and regression are contained in renowned packages for machine learning in R.

For artificial intelligence and machine learning, C++ is the language of desire in-game or robot software (inclusive of robot locomotion). Because of their expertise and amount of command in the language, installed computing hardware designers and electronics engineers are more inclined to prefer C++ or C in machine learning programs. The open-source and modular Shark, scalable ml pack, and Dlib offering far-reaching machine learning algorithms are a few machine learning libraries you can utilize with C++.

7.9 HUMAN BIASES

Being based on the information does not mean that machine learning products are neutral, that is certainly not the case; even if data and computational examination may make us think that we are getting objective information. How machine learning will work with that data heavily depends upon human prejudice and the role it plays in how information is collected, arranged, and ultimately in the algorithms that decide the interaction among data and machine learning (Char et al., 2018).

A computer may not categorize a shark as a fish in the instance when individuals are supplying pictures for "fish" as information to teach an algorithm, and these individuals overwhelmingly choose images of goldfish. Sharks would not be considered as fish as this would develop a bias against sharks as fish.

A computer may not appropriately categorize scientists who are also humans of color or women when using historical images of scientists as training information. AI and machine learning software display human-like biases that consist of race and gender intolerance according to the indication of fresh peer-reviewed research.

Systematic problems prolonged by uncaught biases may stop people from getting same-day delivery options, from being authorized for loans, or from being presented ads for high-paying job possibilities as machine learning is growingly leveraged in business (Caliskan et al., 2017).

It is very important to be mindful of human bias and to work towards removing it as much as imaginable as it can negatively affect others. Making sure that diverse individuals are testing and critiquing a project and diverse individuals working on a scheme is one way to work towards obtaining this. To perform ethics analysis as part of information science project preparation, building substitute systems that can recognize biases, and to observe and audit algorithms, regulatory third parties have been reached out for by others. To fight bias in this field, it is essential to be conscious of our own unconscious biases, organizing equity in our machine learning programs and pipelines, and boosting awareness about biases.

ACTIVITY 7.1

A local health clinic wants to implement a machine learning model to predict the likelihood of patients developing diabetes based on their medical history and lifestyle factors. As a computer science student, you are assigned to develop this predictive model.

1. What type of machine learning algorithm (supervised, unsupervised, or reinforcement) would be best suited for this task, and why?
2. Identify the relevant features or variables (such as age, BMI, blood pressure, etc.) that you would consider using to train the model.
3. How would you evaluate the performance of the model and ensure its predictions are accurate and reliable for the health clinic to use in making informed decisions about patient care?

SUMMARY

This chapter focuses on the fundamentals of machine learning. It starts with an introduction to machine learning, its history, and terminology used in this field. The chapter then discusses the machine learning process, background theory, and various approaches used in machine learning such as k-nearest neighbor, decision tree learning, and deep learning. The chapter also covers different machine learning methods including supervised learning, unsupervised learning, semi-supervised learning, and reinforcement learning. It highlights various machine learning algorithms such as linear classifiers, K-means clustering, neural network, and self-organized map. Furthermore, the chapter explores programming languages used in machine learning such as Python, R, and MATLAB, and their importance in this field. Lastly, it discusses the concept of human biases and their impact on machine learning.

REVIEW QUESTIONS

1. What is machine learning and how does it differ from traditional programming?
2. What is the history of machine learning and how has it evolved over the years?
3. What are the different types of machine learning approaches and how do they differ from each other?
4. What are the different methods used in machine learning and what are their applications?
5. What are the different machine learning algorithms and how do they work?
6. What are the different programming languages used in machine learning and what are their advantages and disadvantages?
7. What is the impact of human biases in machine learning and how can they be mitigated?
8. What are the different steps involved in the machine learning process and what is their importance?

MULTIPLE CHOICE QUESTIONS

1. What is the main focus of this chapter in the book?

a. Artificial Intelligence
b. Fundamentals of Machine Learning
c. Human Biases
d. Programming Languages

2. Which of the following is not a machine learning approach?

a. K-nearest neighbor

b. Decision Tree Learning
c. Probability Theory
d. Deep Learning

3. **Which machine learning method is used when both labeled and unlabeled data are available?**
    a. Supervised Learning
    b. Unsupervised Learning
    c. Semi-supervised Learning
    d. Reinforcement Learning
4. **Which machine learning algorithm is used for unsupervised learning?**
    a. Linear Classifiers
    b. K-Means Clustering
    c. Neural Network
    d. Self-Organized Map
5. **Which programming language is not used in machine learning?**
    a. Python
    b. R
    c. MATLAB
    d. C++
6. **Which of the following is not a component of the machine learning process?**
    a. Data preprocessing
    b. Model selection
    c. Model deployment
    d. Linear regression
7. **What is the primary goal of supervised learning?**
    a. To predict output values based on input features
    b. To cluster data into groups
    c. To learn from feedback
    d. To discover patterns in data
8. **What is the impact of human biases in machine learning?**
    a. It can lead to inaccurate predictions and decisions
    b. It can improve the performance of machine learning algorithms
    c. It can make the algorithms more robust
    d. It has no impact on machine learning

Answers to Multiple Choice Questions

1. (b) 2. (c) 3. (c) 4. (b) 5. (d) 6. (d) 7. (a) 8. (a)

REFERENCES

1. Akbulut, A., Ertugrul, E., & Topcu, V., (2018). Fetal health status prediction based on maternal clinical history using machine learning techniques. *Computer Methods and Programs in Biomedicine, 163*, 87–100.
2. Bader-El-Den, M., & Poli, R., (2007). Generating SAT local-search heuristics using a GP hyper-heuristic framework. In: *International Conference on Artificial Evolution (Evolution Artificielle)* (pp. 37–49). Springer, Berlin, Heidelberg.
3. Balasubramanian, V., Ho, S. S., & Vovk, V., (2014). *Conformal Prediction for Reliable Machine Learning: Theory, Adaptations, and Applications* (Vol. 1, pp. 1–24).
4. Biamonte, J., Wittek, P., Pancotti, N., Rebentrost, P., Wiebe, N., & Lloyd, S., (2017). Quantum machine learning. *Nature, 549*(7671), 195–202.
5. Bishop, C. M., (1995). *Neural Networks for Pattern Recognition.* Oxford, England: Oxford University Press.
6. Block, H. D., Knight, Jr. B. W., & Rosenblatt, F., (1962). Analysis of a four-layer series-coupled perceptron. II. *Reviews of Modern Physics, 34*(1), 135.
7. Bowers, A. F., Giraud-Carrier, C., Kennedy, C., Lloyd, J. W., & MacKinney-Romero, R., (1997). A framework for higher-order inductive machine learning. In: *Proceedings of the COMPULOGNet Area Meeting on Representation Issues in Reasoning and Learning* (Vol. 1, pp. 19–25).
8. Briggs, F. B. S., Ramsay, P. P., Madden, E., Norris, J. M., Holers, V. M., Mikuls, T. R., & Barcellos, L. F., (2010). Supervised machine learning and logistic regression identify novel epistatic risk factors with PTPN22 for rheumatoid arthritis. *Genes & Immunity, 11*(3), 199–208.
9. Buczak, A. L., & Guven, E., (2015). A survey of data mining and machine learning methods for cyber security intrusion detection. *IEEE Communications Surveys & Tutorials, 18*(2), 1153–1176.
10. Buduma, N., & Locascio, N., (2017). *Fundamentals of Deep Learning: Designing Next-Generation Machine Intelligence Algorithms* (Vol. 1, pp. 1–33). "O'Reilly Media, Inc."
11. Burke, E. K., Hyde, M. R., & Kendall, G., (2006). Evolving bin packing heuristics with genetic programming. In: *Parallel Problem Solving from Nature-PPSN IX* (pp. 860–869). Springer, Berlin, Heidelberg.
12. Caliskan, A., Bryson, J. J., & Narayanan, A., (2017). Semantics derived automatically from language corpora contain human-like biases. *Science, 356*(6334), 183–186.
13. Camastra, F., & Vinciarelli, A., (2015). *Machine Learning for Audio, Image and Video Analysis: Theory and Applications* (Vol. 1, pp. 1–22). Springer.

14. Caron, M., Bojanowski, P., Joulin, A., & Douze, M., (2018). Deep clustering for unsupervised learning of visual features. In: *Proceedings of the European Conference on Computer Vision (ECCV)* (Vol. 1, pp. 132–149).
15. Caruana, R., & Niculescu-Mizil, A., (2006). An empirical comparison of supervised learning algorithms. In: *Proceedings of the 23rd International Conference on Machine Learning* (Vol. 23, pp. 161–168).
16. Chali, S. R., (2009). Complex question answering: Unsupervised learning approaches and experiments. *Journal of Artificial Intelligent Research*, 1–47.
17. Char, D. S., Shah, N. H., & Magnus, D., (2018). Implementing machine learning in health care—Addressing ethical challenges. *The New England Journal of Medicine, 378*(11), 981.
18. Chen, Y., Wang, J. Z., & Krovetz, R., (2005). CLUE: Cluster-based retrieval of images by unsupervised learning. *IEEE Transactions on Image Processing, 14*(8), 1187–1201.
19. Chetlur, S., Woolley, C., Vandermersch, P., Cohen, J., Tran, J., Catanzaro, B., & Shelhamer, E., (2014). *cuDNN: Efficient Primitives for Deep Learning* (Vol. 1, pp. 1–22). arXiv preprint arXiv:1410.0759.
20. Cho, S., Asfour, S., Onar, A., & Kaundinya, N., (2005). Tool breakage detection using support vector machine learning in a milling process. *International Journal of Machine Tools and Manufacture, 45*(3), 241–249.
21. Cios, K. J., Swiniarski, R. W., Pedrycz, W., & Kurgan, L. A., (2007). Unsupervised learning: Association rules. In: *Data Mining* (Vol. 1, pp. 289–306). Springer, Boston, MA.
22. Claveau, V., & L'Homme, M. C., (2005). Structuring terminology using analogy-based machine learning. In: *Proceedings of the 7th International Conference on Terminology and Knowledge Engineering, TKE* (Vol. 1, pp. 17–18).
23. Criminisi, A., Shotton, J., & Konukoglu, E., (2012). Decision forests: A unified framework for classification, regression, density estimation, manifold learning and semi-supervised learning. *Foundations and Trends® in Computer Graphics and Vision, 7*(2, 3), 81–227.
24. DasGupta, A., (2011). *Probability for Statistics and Machine Learning: Fundamentals and Advanced Topics* (Vol. 1, pp. 1–12). Springer Science & Business Media.
25. Dasgupta, A., Sun, Y. V., König, I. R., Bailey-Wilson, J. E., & Malley, J. D., (2011). Brief review of regression-based and machine learning methods in genetic epidemiology: The genetic analysis workshop 17 experience. *Genetic Epidemiology, 35*(S1), S5–S11.
26. Dempster, A. P., Laird, N. M., & Rubin, D. B., (1977). Maximum likelihood from incomplete data via the EM algorithm. *Journal of the Royal Statistical Society: Series B (Methodological)*, 1–38.
27. Deng, L., & Yu, D., (2014). Deep learning: Methods and applications. *Foundations and Trends in Signal Processing, 7*(3, 4), 197–387.
28. Denoeux, T., (2008). A k-nearest neighbor classification rule based on Dempster-

Shafer theory. In: *Classic Works of the Dempster-Shafer Theory of Belief Functions* (Vol. 1, pp. 737–760). Springer, Berlin, Heidelberg.

29. Dietterich, T. G., (2000). Ensemble methods in machine learning. In: *International Workshop on Multiple Classifier Systems* (Vol. 1, pp. 1–15). Springer, Berlin, Heidelberg.
30. Doan, A., Madhavan, J., Domingos, P., & Halevy, A., (2004). Ontology matching: A machine learning approach. In: *Handbook on Ontologies* (Vol. 1, pp. 385–403). Springer, Berlin, Heidelberg.
31. Du, K. L., & Swamy, M. N. S., (2014). Fundamentals of machine learning. In: *Neural Networks and Statistical Learning* (Vol. 1, pp. 15–65). Springer, London.
32. Dudani, S. A., (1976). The distance-weighted k-nearest-neighbor rule. *IEEE Transactions on Systems, Man, and Cybernetics*, (4), 325–327.
33. Dutra Da, S. R., Robson, W., & Pedrini, S. H., (2011). Image segmentation based on wavelet feature descriptor and dimensionality reduction applied to remote sensing. *Chilean J. Stat., 2.*
34. Fausett, L., (1994). *Fundamentals of Neural Networks.* New York: Prentice Hall.
35. Figueiredo, M. A. T., & Jain, A. K., (2002). Unsupervised learning of finite mixture models. *IEEE Transactions on Pattern Analysis and Machine Intelligence, 24*(3), 381–396.
36. Forsyth, R. S., (1990). The strange story of the perceptron. *Artificial Intelligence Review, 4*(2), 147–155.
37. Franc, V., & Hlaváč, V., (2005). Simple solvers for large quadratic programming tasks. In: *Joint Pattern Recognition Symposium* (pp. 75–84). Springer, Berlin, Heidelberg.
38. Freund, Y., & Mason, L., (1999). The alternating decision tree learning algorithm. In: *ICML* (Vol. 99, pp. 124–133).
39. Freund, Y., & Schapire, R. E., (1999). Large margin classification using the perceptron algorithm. *Machine Learning, 37*(3), 277–296.
40. Fukunaga, A. S., (2008). Automated discovery of local search heuristics for satisfiability testing. *Evolutionary Computation, 16*(1), 31–61.
41. Gaddam, S. R., Phoha, V. V., & Balagani, K. S., (2007). K-Means+ ID3: A novel method for supervised anomaly detection by cascading K-means clustering and ID3 decision tree learning methods. *IEEE Transactions on Knowledge and Data Engineering, 19*(3), 345–354.
42. Garcia, V., Debreuve, E., & Barlaud, M., (2008). Fast k nearest neighbor search using GPU. In: *2008 IEEE Computer Society Conference on Computer Vision and Pattern Recognition Workshops* (Vol. 1, pp. 1–6). IEEE.
43. Ge, Z., Song, Z., Ding, S. X., & Huang, B., (2017). Data mining and analytics in the process industry: The role of machine learning. *IEEE Access, 5*, 20590–20616.
44. González, L., Angulo, C., Velasco, F., & Catala, A., (2006). Dual unification of bi-class support vector machine formulations. *Pattern Recognition, 39*(7), 1325–1332.

45. Goswami, R., Dufort, P., Tartaglia, M. C., Green, R. E., Crawley, A., Tator, C. H., & Davis, K. D., (2016). Frontotemporal correlates of impulsivity and machine learning in retired professional athletes with a history of multiple concussions. *Brain Structure and Function, 221*(4), 1911–1925.
46. Gross, G. N., Lømo, T., & Sveen, O., (1969). *Participation of Inhibitory and Excitatory Interneurones in the Control of Hippocampal Cortical Output*. Per Anderson, The Interneuron.
47. Grzymala-Busse, J. W., & Hu, M., (2000). A comparison of several approaches to missing attribute values in data mining. In: *International Conference on Rough Sets and Current Trends in Computing* (pp. 378–385). Springer, Berlin, Heidelberg.
48. Grzymala-Busse, J. W., Goodwin, L. K., Grzymala-Busse, W. J., & Zheng, X., (2005). Handling missing attribute values in preterm birth data sets. In: *International Workshop on Rough Sets, Fuzzy Sets, Data Mining, and Granular-Soft Computing* (pp. 342–351). Springer, Berlin, Heidelberg.
49. Guzella, T. S., & Caminhas, W. M., (2009). A review of machine learning approaches to spam filtering. *Expert Systems with Applications, 36*(7), 10206–10222.
50. Haykin, S., & Network, N., (2004). A comprehensive foundation. *Neural Networks, 2*(2004), 41.
51. Haykin, S., (1994). *Neural Networks: A Comprehensive Foundation.* New York: Macmillan Publishing.
52. Herbrich, R., (2017). Machine learning at Amazon. In: *WSDM* (Vol. 1, pp. 520–535).
53. Hofmann, T., (2001). Unsupervised learning by probabilistic latent semantic analysis. *Machine Learning, 42*(1, 2), 177–196.
54. Holmes, G., Donkin, A., & Witten, I. H., (1994). Weka: A machine learning workbench. In: *Proceedings of ANZIIS'94-Australian New Zealand Intelligent Information Systems Conference* (Vol. 1, pp. 357–361). IEEE.
55. Honghai, F., Guoshun, C., Cheng, Y., Bingru, Y., & Yumei, C., (2005). A SVM regression based approach to filling in missing values. In: *International Conference on Knowledge-Based and Intelligent Information and Engineering Systems* (pp. 581–587). Springer, Berlin, Heidelberg.
56. Hornik, K., Stinchcombe, M., & White, H., (1989). Multilayer feedforward networks are universal approximators. *Neural Networks, 2*(5), 359–366.
57. Jain, P., Garibaldi, J. M., & Hirst, J. D., (2009). Supervised machine learning algorithms for protein structure classification. *Computational Biology and Chemistry, 33*(3), 216–223.
58. Jordan, M. I., & Mitchell, T. M., (2015). Machine learning: Trends, perspectives, and prospects. *Science, 349*(6245), 255–260.
59. Kaelbling, L. P., Littman, M. L., & Moore, A. W., (1996). Reinforcement learning: A survey. *Journal of Artificial Intelligence Research, 4*, 237–285.
60. Kamiran, F., Calders, T., & Pechenizkiy, M., (2010). Discrimination aware decision

tree learning. In: *2010 IEEE International Conference on Data Mining* (Vol. 1, pp. 869–874). IEEE.

61. Kearns, M., & Mansour, Y., (1999). On the boosting ability of top–down decision tree learning algorithms. *Journal of Computer and System Sciences, 58*(1), 109–128.
62. Kelleher, J. D., (2016). Fundamentals of machine learning for neural machine translation. In: *Proceedings of the Translating European Forum* (Vol. 1, pp. 1–42).
63. Kelleher, J. D., Mac Namee, B., & D'arcy, A., (2015). *Fundamentals of Machine Learning for Predictive Data Analytics: Algorithms, Worked Examples, and Case Studies* (Vol. 1, pp. 1–32). MIT press.
64. Keller, J. M., Gray, M. R., & Givens, J. A., (1985). A fuzzy k-nearest neighbor algorithm. *IEEE Transactions on Systems, Man, and Cybernetics*, (4), 580–585.
65. Keller, R. E., & Poli, R., (2007). Linear genetic programming of parsimonious metaheuristics. In: *Evolutionary Computation, 2007: CEC 2007; IEEE Congress on* (pp. 4508–4515). IEEE.
66. Kenett, R. S., & Shmueli, G., (2015). Clarifying the terminology that describes scientific reproducibility. *Nature Methods, 12*(8), 699.
67. King, D. E., (2009). Dlib-ml: A machine learning toolkit. *The Journal of Machine Learning Research, 10*, 1755–1758.
68. Kingma, D. P., Mohamed, S., Rezende, D. J., & Welling, M., (2014). Semi-supervised learning with deep generative models. In: *Advances in Neural Information Processing Systems* (Vol. 1, pp. 3581–3589).
69. Kohonen, T. (1997, June). Exploration of very large databases by self-organizing maps. In Proceedings of international conference on neural networks (icnn'97) (Vol. 1, pp. 1-6). IEEE.
70. Kononenko, I., (2001). Machine learning for medical diagnosis: History, state of the art and perspective. *Artificial Intelligence in Medicine, 23*(1), 89–109.
71. Kotsiantis, S. B., Zaharakis, I., & Pintelas, P., (2007). Supervised machine learning: A review of classification techniques. *Emerging Artificial Intelligence Applications in Computer Engineering, 160*(1), 3–24.
72. Kumar, V., Kalitin, D., & Tiwari, P., (2017). Unsupervised learning dimensionality reduction algorithm PCA for face recognition. In: *2017 International Conference on Computing, Communication and Automation (ICCCA)* (Vol. 1, pp. 32–37). IEEE.
73. Kumar, V., Verma, A., Mittal, N., & Gromov, S. V., (2019). Anatomy of preprocessing of big data for monolingual corpora paraphrase extraction: Source language sentence selection. In: *Emerging Technologies in Data Mining and Information Security* (Vol. 1, pp. 495–505). Springer, Singapore.
74. Lavecchia, A., (2015). Machine-learning approaches in drug discovery: Methods and applications. *Drug Discovery Today, 20*(3), 318–331.
75. LeCun, Y., Bengio, Y., & Hinton, G., (2015). Deep learning. *Nature, 521*(7553), 436–444.

76. Li, D., Deogun, J., Spaulding, W., & Shuart, B., (2004). Towards missing data imputation: A study of fuzzy k-means clustering method. In: *International Conference on Rough Sets and Current Trends in Computing* (pp. 573–579). Springer, Berlin, Heidelberg.
77. Li, M., Zhu, X., & Gong, S., (2018). Unsupervised person re-identification by deep learning tracklet association. In: *Proceedings of the European Conference on Computer Vision (ECCV)* (Vol. 1, pp. 737–753).
78. Liu, Y., Zhang, D., & Lu, G., (2008). Region-based image retrieval with high-level semantics using decision tree learning. *Pattern Recognition, 41*(8), 2554–2570.
79. Luengo, J., García, S., & Herrera, F., (2012). On the choice of the best imputation methods for missing values considering three groups of classification methods. *Knowledge and Information Systems, 32*(1), 77–108.
80. Gonzalez, L., Angulo, C., Velasco, F., & Catala, A. (2005). Unified dual for bi-class SVM approaches. Pattern Recognition, 38(10), 1772-1774.
81. Michie, D., Spiegelhalter, D. J., & Taylor, C. C., (1994). Machine learning. *Neural and Statistical Classification, 13*(1994), 1–298.
82. Mnih, V., Kavukcuoglu, K., Silver, D., Rusu, A. A., Veness, J., Bellemare, M. G., & Petersen, S., (2015). Human-level control through deep reinforcement learning. *Nature, 518*(7540), 529–533.
83. Monostori, L., Márkus, A., Van, B. H., & Westkämpfer, E., (1996). Machine learning approaches to manufacturing. *CIRP Annals, 45*(2), 675–712.
84. Mooney, S. J., & Pejaver, V., (2018). Big data in public health: Terminology, machine learning, and privacy. *Annual Review of Public Health, 39*, 95–112.
85. Muggleton, S., & De Raedt, L., (1994). Inductive logic programming: Theory and methods. *The Journal of Logic Programming, 19*, 629–679.
86. Navigli, R., Velardi, P., & Gangemi, A., (2003). Ontology learning and its application to automated terminology translation. *IEEE Intelligent Systems, 18*(1), 22–31.
87. Ng, V., & Cardie, C., (2002). Improving machine learning approaches to coreference resolution. In: *Proceedings of the 40th Annual Meeting of the Association for Computational Linguistics* (pp. 104–111).
88. Nielsen, H., Brunak, S., & Von, H. G., (1999). Machine learning approaches for the prediction of signal peptides and other protein sorting signals. *Protein Engineering, 12*(1), 3–9.
89. Novikoff, A. B., (1963). *On Convergence Proofs for Perceptrons*. Stanford research Inst Menlo Park Ca.
90. Olden, J. D., Lawler, J. J., & Poff, N. L., (2008). Machine learning methods without tears: A primer for ecologists. *The Quarterly Review of Biology, 83*(2), 171–193.
91. Olga, R., Deng, J., Su, H., Krause, J., Satheesh, S., Ma, S., & Berg, A. C., (2015). *Large Scale Visual Recognition Challenge.* ImageNet http://arxiv. org/abs/1409.0575.
92. Oltean, M., & Dumitrescu, D., (2004). Evolving TSP heuristics using multi expression

programming. In: *International Conference on Computational Science* (pp. 670–673). Springer, Berlin, Heidelberg.

93. Oltean, M., & Groşan, C., (2003). Evolving evolutionary algorithms using multi expression programming. In: *European Conference on Artificial Life* (pp. 651–658). Springer, Berlin, Heidelberg.
94. Oltean, M., (2007). Evolving evolutionary algorithms with patterns. *Soft Computing, 11*(6), 503–518.
95. Parmar, C., Grossmann, P., Bussink, J., Lambin, P., & Aerts, H. J., (2015). Machine learning methods for quantitative radiomic biomarkers. *Scientific Reports, 5*, 13087.
96. Patterson, D., (1996). *Artificial Neural Networks.* Singapore: Prentice Hall.
97. Pedregosa, F., Varoquaux, G., Gramfort, A., Michel, V., Thirion, B., Grisel, O., & Vanderplas, J., (2011). Scikit-learn: Machine learning in python. *The Journal of Machine Learning Research, 12*, 2825–2830.
98. Poli, R., Woodward, J., & Burke, E. K., (2007). A histogram-matching approach to the evolution of bin-packing strategies. In: *Evolutionary Computation, 2007: CEC 2007; IEEE Congress on* (pp. 3500–3507). IEEE.
99. Price, J., Buckles, K., Van, L. J., & Riley, I., (2019). *Combining Family History and Machine Learning to Link Historical Records* (No. w26227, pp. 1–33). National Bureau of Economic Research.
100. Rasmussen, C. E., (2003). Gaussian processes in machine learning. In: *Summer School on Machine Learning* (Vol. 1, pp. 63–71). Springer, Berlin, Heidelberg.
101. Rosenblatt, F., (1961). *Principles of Neurodynamics Unclassifie—Armed Services Technical Informatm Agency*. Spartan, Washington, DC.
102. Rouet-Leduc, B., Hulbert, C., Lubbers, N., Barros, K., Humphreys, C. J., & Johnson, P. A., (2017). Machine learning predicts laboratory earthquakes. *Geophysical Research Letters, 44*(18), 9276–9282.
103. Sammut, C., & Webb, G. I., (2017). *Encyclopedia of Machine Learning and Data Mining* (Vol. 1, pp. 1–34). Springer.
104. Schaffalitzky, F., & Zisserman, A., (2004). Automated scene matching in movies. *CIVR 2004: Proceedings of the Challenge of Image and Video Retrieval,* London, LNCS, 2383.
105. Schlegl, T., Seeböck, P., Waldstein, S. M., Schmidt-Erfurth, U., & Langs, G., (2017). Unsupervised anomaly detection with generative adversarial networks to guide marker discovery. In: *International Conference on Information Processing in Medical Imaging* (Vol. 1, pp. 146–157). Springer, Cham.
106. Schmid, S. R., Hamrock, B. J., & Jacobson, B. O., (2014). *Fundamentals of Machine Elements: SI Version* (Vol. 1, pp. 1–22). CRC Press.
107. Schmidhuber, J., (2015). Deep learning in neural networks: An overview. *Neural Networks, 61*, 85–117.
108. Sclano, F., & Velardi, P., (2007). Termextractor: A web application to learn the shared

terminology of emergent web communities. In: *Enterprise Interoperability II* (Vol. 2, pp. 287–290). Springer, London.

109. Sebastiani, F., (2002). Machine learning in automated text categorization. *ACM Computing Surveys (CSUR), 34*(1), 1–47.
110. Shami, M., & Verhelst, W., (2007). An evaluation of the robustness of existing supervised machine learning approaches to the classification of emotions in speech. *Speech Communication, 49*(3), 201–212.
111. Shrestha, D. L., & Solomatine, D. P., (2006). Machine learning approaches for estimation of prediction interval for the model output. *Neural Networks, 19*(2), 225–235.
112. Snelson, E. L., (2007). *Flexible and Efficient Gaussian Process Models for Machine Learning* (Vol. 1, pp. 1–22). Doctoral dissertation, UCL (University College London).
113. Song, S. K., Choi, Y. S., Chun, H. W., Jeong, C. H., Choi, S. P., & Sung, W. K., (2011). Multi-words terminology recognition using web search. In: *International Conference on U-and E-Service, Science and Technology* (Vol. 1, pp. 233–238). Springer, Berlin, Heidelberg.
114. Srinivasan, K., & Fisher, D., (1995). Machine learning approaches to estimating software development effort. *IEEE Transactions on Software Engineering, 21*(2), 126–137.
115. Tan, S., (2005). Neighbor-weighted k-nearest neighbor for unbalanced text corpus. *Expert Systems with Applications, 28*(4), 667–671.
116. Tavares, J., Machado, P., Cardoso, A., Pereira, F. B., & Costa, E., (2004). On the evolution of evolutionary algorithms. In: *European Conference on Genetic Programming* (pp. 389–398). Springer, Berlin, Heidelberg.
117. Teather, L. A., (2006). Pathophysiological effects of inflammatory mediators and stress on distinct memory systems. In: *Nutrients, Stress, and Medical Disorders* (pp. 377–386). Humana Press.
118. Timothy, J. S. P. J., (1998). Decision fusion using a multi-linear classifier. In: *Proceedings of the International Conference on Multisource-Multisensor Information Fusion.*
119. Vartak, M., Subramanyam, H., Lee, W. E., Viswanathan, S., Husnoo, S., Madden, S., & Zaharia, M., (2016). ModelDB: A system for machine learning model management. In: *Proceedings of the Workshop on Human-In-the-Loop Data Analytics* (Vol. 1, pp. 1–3).
120. Vellido, A., Martín-Guerrero, J. D., & Lisboa, P. J., (2012). Making machine learning models interpretable. In: *ESANN* (Vol. 12, pp. 163–172).
121. Voyant, C., Notton, G., Kalogirou, S., Nivet, M. L., Paoli, C., Motte, F., & Fouilloy, A., (2017). Machine learning methods for solar radiation forecasting: A review. *Renewable Energy, 105*, 569–582.
122. Wilson, A. C., Roelofs, R., Stern, M., Srebro, N., & Recht, B., (2017). The marginal value of adaptive gradient methods in machine learning. In: *Advances in Neural*

Information Processing Systems (Vol. 1, pp. 4148–4158).

123. Witschel, H. F., (2005). Terminology extraction and automatic indexing. *Terminology and Content Development, 1*, 350–363.
124. Ye, Q., Zhang, Z., & Law, R., (2009). Sentiment classification of online reviews to travel destinations by supervised machine learning approaches. *Expert Systems with Applications, 36*(3), 6527–6535.
125. Yoganarasimhan, H., (2020). Search personalization using machine learning. *Management Science, 66*(3), 1045–1070.
126. Yu, X., Pu, K. Q., & Koudas, N., (2005). Monitoring k-nearest neighbor queries over moving objects. In: *21st International Conference on Data Engineering (ICDE'05)* (Vol. 1, pp. 631–642). IEEE.
127. Yusupov, T., (2007). *The Efficient Market Hypothesis Through the Eyes of an Artificial Technical Analyst.* Doctoral dissertation, Christian-Albrechts Universität Kiel.
128. Zhang, H., Goodfellow, I., Metaxas, D., & Odena, A., (2019). Self-attention generative adversarial networks. In: *International Conference on Machine Learning* (Vol. 1, pp. 7354–7363).
129. Zhang, L., Tan, J., Han, D., & Zhu, H., (2017). From machine learning to deep learning: Progress in machine intelligence for rational drug discovery. *Drug Discovery Today, 22*(11), 1680–1685.
130. Zhu, X. J., (2005). *Semi-Supervised Learning Literature Survey*. University of Wisconsin-Madison Department of Computer Sciences.
131. Zhu, X., & Goldberg, A. B., (2009). Introduction to semi-supervised learning. *Synthesis Lectures on Artificial Intelligence and Machine Learning, 3*(1), 1–130.
132. Zhu, X., Ghahramani, Z., & Lafferty, J. D., (2003). Semi-supervised learning using gaussian fields and harmonic functions. In: *Proceedings of the 20th International Conference on Machine Learning (ICML-03)* (pp. 912–919).
133. Zoltan-Csaba, M., Pangercic, D., Blodow, N., & Beetz, M., (2011). Combined 2D-3D categorization and classification for multimodal perception systems. *Int. J. Robotics Res. Arch, 30*(11).
134. Zuccala, A., Van, S. M., & Van, B. M., (2014). A machine-learning approach to coding book reviews as quality indicators: Toward a theory of megacitation. *Journal of the Association for Information Science and Technology, 65*(11), 2248–2260.

CHAPTER 8

COMPUTER SECURITY AND ETHICS

UNIT INTRODUCTION

Today's modern digital age has significantly benefited individuals and organizations through the growing usage of information technology, which has enhanced efficiency, communication, and decision-making. Yet, to guarantee that using information security does not result in harm or exploitation, these advantages come with ethical and security concerns that need to be addressed (Dhillon & Backhouse, 2000).

Computer science' ethical ramifications for confidentiality, reliability, accessibility and copyrighted material are covered here. When computer science are created to prevent specific demographics, such as people with impairments, from accessing the information, accessibility concerns can occur. Intellectual property issues occur when material protected by copyright or a trademark is used without authorization (Bansal et al., 2021).

Phishing, botnets, malware, and denial-of-service attacks are a few security challenges affecting computer science. These dangers have the potential to jeopardize the confidentiality, integrity, and accessibility of data and systems, resulting in monetary loss, damage to one's reputation, as well as legal and regulatory repercussions. Addressing these ethical and security challenges becomes more critical as our reliance on information technology increases (Siponen & Oinas-Kukkonen, 2007). This chapter will delve deeper into the ethical and security concerns pertaining to computer science in this chapter. The author will talk about how these problems affect people and organizations (Figure 8.1).

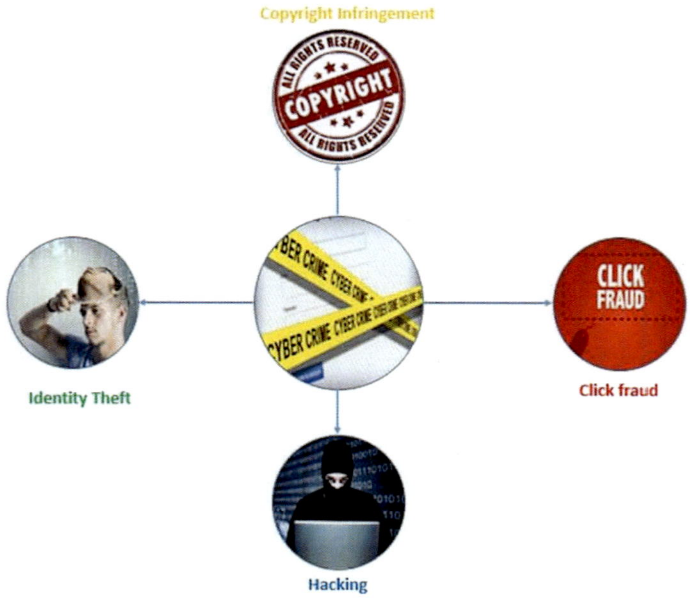

Figure 8.1. Illustration of ethical and security issue of informative system (Source: Guru99, Creative Commons License).

Learning Objectives

At the end of this chapter, the reader will be able to understand

- The ethical and security issues of the informative system
- The importance and issues about the privacy of information system
- The concept of intellectual property
- The issues of viruses and malicious programs
- The concept of phishing

Key Terms

- Denial of Service
- Phishing
- Botnets
- Drive-by Download Attacks
- Malicious Programs
- Zero-Day Exploits
- Malvertising
- Ransomware

8.1 ETHICAL ISSUES OF COMPUTER SCIENCE

Computer science are now essential for enabling efficient leadership, data analysis, and decision-making in the digital age. However, several ethical issues that have emerged due to the increasing use of computer systems must be addressed to assure their ethical and responsible usage (Rogerson et al., 2019).

Computer science' primary ethical problems about privacy, accuracy, accessibility and intellectual property. When personal data is collected and utilized without the subject's consent, privacy issues arise. Inaccurate or altered information might cause accuracy problems. When computer science are created in a way that prevents particular groups of individuals from accessing the information, accessibility issues may occur. Intellectual property issues occur when material protected by copyright or a trademark is used without authorization. To prevent harm or exploitation from occurring due to the usage of computer science, businesses, and organizations must be knowledgeable of these ethical challenges and take action to solve them (Paradice et al., 2018).

Remember

Accuracy problems can develop when data is falsified or altered, while privacy concerns can arise when personal data is gathered and utilized without the individual's agreement.

8.2 PRIVACY IN COMPUTER SCIENCE

Several novel approaches to data processing seemed unthinkable just a few years ago. Nowadays, few people are shocked by technology like profiling, banner advertisements, or personalized services. When creating client data-based online services and information technology solutions, merely adhering to legal requirements and privacy rules is no longer acceptable. The security of personal data could be threatened by these technologies. Consider national healthcare applications as an illustration. Computer systems gather much personal information about inherited disorders, age, race, health information, and lifestyle (such as bad habits and mobility) (Bélanger & Crossler, 2011).

Another illustration would be financial software and services like internet banking, tax preparation, or digital wallets. The consequences of a confidentiality breach can be severe and frequently permanent.

First employed by casinos to identify cheaters, it now helps law enforcement. Yet, it also compromises people's right to privacy (Kalloniatis & Mouratidis, 2014) (Figure 8.2).

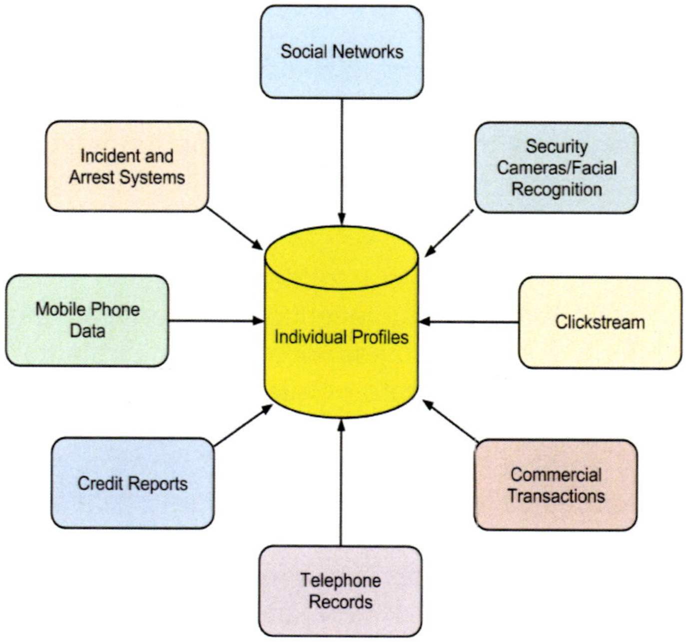

Figure 8.2. Flow diagram of NORA (Non-Obvious Relationship Awareness) (Soure: opentext books, Creative Commons License).

Tech corporations are eager to offer any product or service they provide for free to collect personal data continuously. In turn, this causes "privacy inflation." The user must give access to an ever-increasing variety of identifiable data to receive any new or enhanced service. These dishonest actions come in many forms and get more complex every time. Deloitte defines conduct risk as a collection of unethical tactics businesses use to get more personal information about their clients, such as fine print, unclear contract terms, the imposition of unneeded services, or customer misinformation (Smith et al., 2011).

Due to concerns with confidentiality in IT, the Privacy by Design framework was developed and put into practice. This framework is based on the usage of information through seven core principles:

1. Respect for user privacy—keep it user-centric.
2. Privacy as the default setting;
3. Whole lifecycle protection and end-to-end security;
4. Embedded into the design;
5. Full functionality—positive-sum, not zero-sum;
6. Proactive rather than reactive; preventative rather than corrective;
7. Visibility and transparency—keep it open;

A site was developed by the NCSA (National Cyber Security

Alliance) to track privacy preferences and data security. It contains links to well-known social media platforms, email and phone services, google searches, and e-commerce websites. The NCSA advises updating its privacy controls on well-known online services and gadgets by clicking these links (Onsrud et al., 1994) (Figure 8.3).

Figure 8.3. Image of NCSA (National Cyber Security Alliance) (Source: Stat Safe Online, Creative Commons License).

8.3 INTELLECTUAL PROPERTY

Intellectual property protection is the next touchy subject concerning ethical dilemmas in information technologies. The collective phrase “intellectual property” denotes the sole ownership of the outcomes of creative effort and means of individualization (Stock & Stock, 2006).

a) It’s simple to get unauthorized access to content. Few people consider the ethical implications and factors.

b) Free streaming, downloading, and sharing practices on the Internet have an impact on how people comprehend the idea of intellectual property. Piracy of software and content is frequently accepted as the standard.

c) In the context of digital media, people frequently lack empathy for those who are impacted by their decisions.

d) Confusion increases with easy access to a lot of content.

Proprietary information, franchises, patents, and copyrights safeguard intellectual property. Businesses employ trade secrets to safeguard sensitive information that is strategically valuable but that they are unwilling to share. When non-tangible landowners disclose information that needs to be protected, legal professionals utilize the other three terms (Lavenue, 1997).

8.4 ACCESSIBILITY

The term “accessibility” describes how computer science are created and put into use so that people with disabilities may use and access them. To prevent disability prejudice and exclusion, companies must face this ethical dilemma (Culnan, 1985) (Figure 8.4).

Figure 8.4. Picture of Web Accessibility (Source: Search Engine Journal, Creative Commons License).

8.4.1 Lack of Accessibility in Computer science

When businesses fail to give accessibility top priority throughout the development and creation of their systems, the ethical problem of accessibility in computer science may arise. As a result, people with disabilities may be unable to use certain technologies because they are inaccessible.

8.4.2 Failure to Ensure Accessibility

When businesses do not take the necessary steps to make sure that their computer networks are usable by people with impairments, the ethical problem of accessibility might also come up. Even if availability is a top priority for the company, this could lead to technology that is not entirely accessible (Culnan, 1984).

8.4.3 Consequences of Inaccessibility

The negative effects of having inaccessible computer science are severe because they can prevent people with disabilities from participating fully in society, limit their prospects, and have legal and regulatory repercussions. Furthermore, it may prevent organizations from realizing their full potential while excluding a sizable population segment (Kovach & Cathcart, 1999).

8.5 ACCURACY

Ensuring that the information and data are accurate and error-free is a crucial ethical concern in computer science. Inaccurate information can influence decisions that are harmful to people and society.

8.5.1 Causes of Inaccurate Information

Human mistake is one of the main reasons why information is wrong. Any phase of the computer network, from data entry through analysis and reporting, is susceptible to this. Nevertheless, misinformation might be supplied due to falsified or biased data. This might happen either on purpose or accidentally (Thapa & Bossler, 1992).

TIPS

NORA (Non-Obvious Relationship Awareness) technology should be used by private and public institutions to gather massive amounts of data and integrate it into profiles.

8.5.2 Consequences of Inaccurate Information

Inaccurate data can have serious repercussions on people as well as society at large. For instance, inaccurate medical information may lead to the patient receiving the wrong diagnosis and treatment, which is harmful. Financial losses and poor investment choices can be caused by inaccurate financial knowledge. The dissemination of false information that causes public alarm or harm is one example of how inaccurate information can have negative effects on society (Peabody et al., 2004).

8.6 SECURITY ISSUES OF INFORMATION SYSTEM

Computer science are susceptible to security risks that could endanger data availability, confidentiality, and integrity. Since the scale and variety of security risks continue to rise in the modern digital era, security has elevated to the top priority list for businesses and organizations.

Attacks on computer science using malware, phishing scams, denial-of-service assaults, and malicious advertising are among the top security concerns. Malicious software can degrade information system security or compromise it through malware assaults. Social control methods like phishing trick people into disclosing sensitive information. Malvertising is disseminating harmful software through internet advertising, whereas denial-of-service assaults target the disruption of computer science' regular operations. To safeguard their computer science from these dangers, businesses, and organizations must implement strong security measures, such as routers, cryptography, systems for detecting and preventing intrusions, and staff training on best security practices (Bosch-Capblanch et al., 2009) (Figure 8.5).

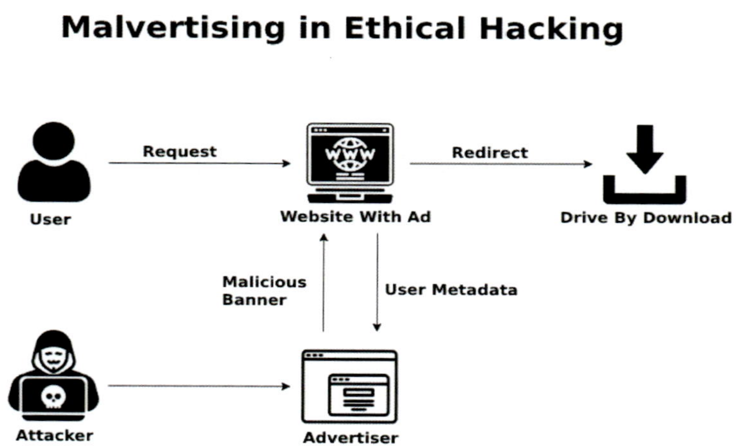

Figure 8.5. Illustration of malvertising (Source: Vaibhav Rawal, Creative Commons License).

8.7 VIRUSES AND MALICIOUS PROGRAMS

As Internet usage develops, the likelihood of malicious software, such as viruses, entering a firm's computer network increases. Malware is an aspect of software material that is inserted to another application and remains dormant until it is activated by an unknowing user. This could be as easy as downloading a file from a webpage or opening an attachment. Viruses can be comical, displaying an amusing image on the user's computer, or extreme, deleting data files permanently. Even the most modern anti-virus technologies can not keep up with an international surge in viruses and malicious programs. Viruses can be created for a variety of purposes, including financial gain, the aim to express a political agenda, personal entertainment, to demonstrate the existence of a software vulnerability, deceit, and service rejection, or just because hackers are interested in cyber-security concerns. These viruses and malicious software can have disastrous repercussions, destroying a company's network and electronic data (McGraw & Morrisett, 2000).

8.8 PHISHING

A phishing scam is one of the most common cyberattacks. Hacking is when a con artist sends them phony emails, texts, or websites to trick them into divulging sensitive personal data, including bank details, numbers for Social Security, or login credentials.

Fraudsters utilize the information they provide to steal their cash, identity, or both. Scammers also utilize phishing emails to access their network or computer and install malicious software that can prevent them from accessing critical data on their computer (Wright & Marett, 2010).

Scammers use phishing to trick their victims into thinking they are safe to do this by creating fake versions of well-known and reliable company logos that belong to established and respected companies. Alternatively, they can pretend to be a friend or member of the family. Phishing is a sort of online fraud in which the perpetrators make it appear as though the victim or another person's personal information is required immediately or else terrible things will occur. They can say that their bank account will be closed, that they won't get a tax refund, that their manager will become angry, that a member of their family might get wounded, or that they might even get arrested. They intentionally mislead individuals in order to elicit information from those individuals (Sharma et al., 2022).

8.9 DENIAL OF SERVICE

When a hostile cyber threat actor prevents authorized users from accessing data management, gadgets, or other network resources, it is said to be a denial-of-service (DoS) attack. Services that rely on the impacted computer or network, such as email, internet, online accounts, or other services, may also be impacted. By overwhelming the targeted host or system with traffic until it becomes unresponsive or fails, a denial-of-service attack blocks access for authorized users. DoS attacks can cost companies money and time while their services and resources are unavailable. Not one, but two, but a staggering six U.S. institutions were the targets of a series of denial-of-service attacks in 2012. The victims comprised Bank of America, JP Morgan Chase, U.S. Bancorp, Citigroup, and PNC Bank, none of which were small-town banks (Paulson & Weber, 2006). These are but a handful of security concerns related to computer science. In the interest of safeguarding computer systems from theft, damage to their hardware, software, or electronic data,

Did you Know?

According to a report by Radware, the number of DDoS attacks increased by 20% in the first quarter of 2020 compared to the same period in 2019.

and interruption or diversions of the services they offer, these dangers highlight the need for increased cybersecurity. Due to the expanding use of computer systems, the Internet, wireless networks like Bluetooth and Wi-Fi, and the proliferation of "smart" gadgets like smartphones, televisions, and the numerous items that make up the Internet of Things, the field is becoming more and more important (Zlomislić ET AL., 2017) (Figure 8.6).

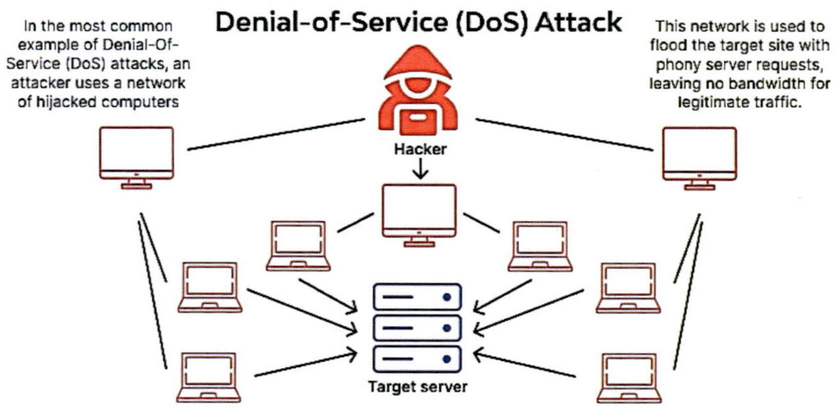

Figure 8.6. Schematic of Denial of Service attack (Source: Wallarm, Creative Commons License).

8.10 BOTNETS

A group of Internet-connected devices, such as PCs, smartphones, servers, and IoT devices that have been infected and are being controlled remotely by a common form of malware is known as a botnet. The botnet software typically scours the internet for susceptible devices. The threat actor who builds a botnet wants to infiltrate as many smart devices as possible, taking advantage of their computational power and resources for automated actions that are typically hidden from the owners of the devices. These botnets are controlled by threat actors, who are frequently cybercriminals. They are used to send spam emails, run click-fraud operations, and produce malicious traffic for widespread denial-of-service assaults (Frank et al., 2018).

8.10.1 Drive-by Download Attacks

Drive-by download attacks are a security problem when a person visits a website infiltrated by hackers and unintentionally installs malicious software onto their desktop or smartphone. Unlike classic malware attacks, drive-by download attacks can occur just by visiting a hacked website, where another user must click on a phishing email or install an infected file (Akiyama et al., 2010). Here are some crucial specifics regarding drive-by download attacks.

8.10.2 Working on Drive-by Download Attacks

Hackers frequently compromise by taking advantage of software flaws or inserting malicious code into legitimate websites. When a user accesses the infected website, the infected code is executed and secretly downloads ransomware onto the user's device. After that, the virus may perform several tasks, including stealing confidential information, installing other malware, or taking control of the user's device (Sood & Zeadally, 2016).

8.10.3 Types of Drive-by Download Attacks

Drive-by download assaults come in a variety of forms.

8.10.3.1 Malvertising

By inserting harmful code into trustworthy ad networks or by making false advertising that links visitors to malicious websites, hackers exploit adverts to spread malware.

8.10.3.2 Watering Hole Attacks

Hackers compromise webpages that the target audience will likely visit to target particular user groups. For instance, hackers may compromise websites associated with a certain sector or government organization (Krithika, 2017).

8.10.3.3 Zero-Day Exploits

These assaults infected a user's device using previously undiscovered software flaws.

8.10.4 Consequences of Drive-by Download Attacks

For people and businesses, drive-by installation attacks can have major repercussions, including:

a) Theft of private data, including financial and personal information.

b) Installing further malware may cause the device to run slowly or introduce new security holes.

c) If the gadget is hijacked, the attacker may be able to operate it remotely.

d) A decrease in productivity since users might have to devote resources to cleaning malware or recovering their devices.

8.11 RANSOMWARE

The malicious program known as ransomware encrypts a victim's files, rendering them unavailable, and then requests money in exchange for the decryption. It is one of the most important security risks that people and companies face today because it may seriously harm one's finances and reputation (Gaurav et al., 2022).

These details relate to ransomware.

Figure 8.7. Picture of Exploit kit (Source: Trendmicro, Creative Commons License).

8.11.1 Working of Ransomware

Phishing emails, malicious advertising, or taking advantage of flaws in technology or systems are the most common ways ransomware is propagated. It encrypts files after infecting a machine, rendering them unavailable. The victim is then shown a message alerting them that their data have been encrypted and requesting payment in return for the decryption key, typically in a pop-up window or text file (Ali, 2017).

8.11.2 Impact of Ransomware

Attacks with ransomware can potentially seriously harm people's finances and reputations. Critical data and systems may become inaccessible to victims, causing downtime and lost production. The organization's reputation could suffer due to the ransomware assault and the high expense of both repaying the ransom and rehabilitating from it.

8.11.3 Prevention of Ransomware Attacks

The strongest defense against ransomware attacks is prevention. Companies can adopt robust security measures like firewalls, anti-virus, and detection systems for intrusions to lower the chance of infection. Frequent data backups are also crucial since they enable victims to recover their files without ransom. It's also essential to teach staff members how to spot phishing emails and the dangers of ransomware.

8.12 EXPLOIT KITS

A programming tool called an exploit kit lets someone without experience programming software code create, alter, and spread malware. Other names for exploit kits are infection kits, crimeware kits, DIY attack kits, and malware toolkits. Cybercriminals use these toolkits (Figure 8.7).

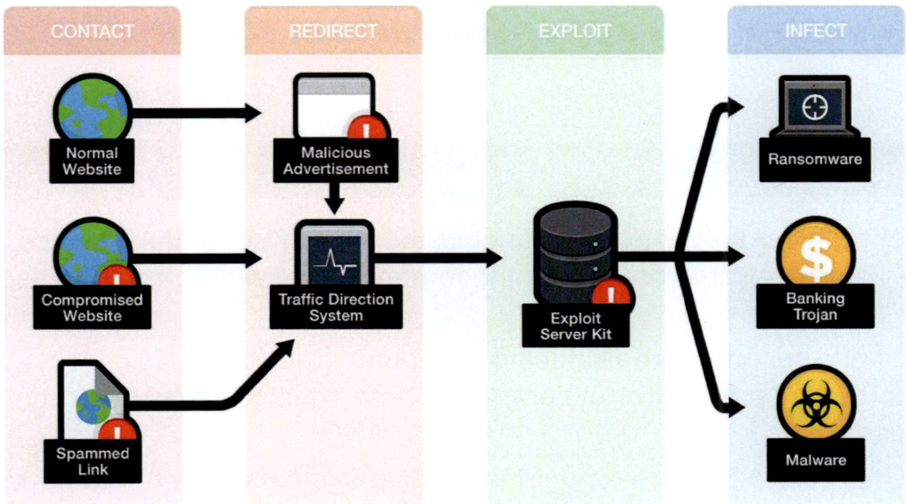

8.13 ADVANCED PERSISTENT THREAT ATTACKS

A targeted cyberattack known as an advanced persistent threat (APT) occurs when an unauthorized intruder breaches a network and does so while going unnoticed for a considerable amount of time. An APT attack aims to observe network activity and steal data to acquire access, using exploit kits and malware rather than harming a system or network. Cybercriminals generally use APT attacks to steal data from high-value targets like large businesses and nation-states over an extended period (Alshamrani et al., 2019).

ACTIVITY 8.1.

You are an employee at a large corporation, and you receive an email from what appears to be your company's IT department asking you to click on a link to update your password due to a recent security breach. The email looks legitimate, and you are worried about the security of your account, so you click on the link and enter your login credentials. A few days later, you notice some unauthorized transactions on your company credit card. Was this a case of phishing? How could you have avoided falling for this scam?

SUMMARY

This chapter focuses on the importance of ethical and security considerations in the development and implementation of computer science. The chapter highlights the ethical concerns related to privacy, accuracy, property, and accessibility. It also discusses various security issues such as unauthorized access, hacking, and malware attacks, and the measures to mitigate them. Overall, the chapter stresses the significance of addressing ethical and security issues in computer science to protect individuals' rights and maintain the integrity of the system. It encourages organizations to adopt ethical principles and implement robust security measures to prevent any breaches that can harm individuals or organizations.

REVIEW QUESTIONS

1. What are the main ethical concerns surrounding the use of computer science in modern society? Provide examples of how these concerns have been addressed in practice.
2. What are the primary security threats facing computer science today? Describe some of the most common forms of cyberattacks and explain how organizations can protect themselves
3. How do businesses ensure that the use of informative systems adheres to ethical standards and legal regulations?
4. What measures can organizations take to protect sensitive data and prevent cyber attacks on their informative systems?
5. How can the use of informative systems impact individual privacy and data protection?
6. What are some of the challenges associated with balancing the benefits

MULTIPLE CHOICE QUESTIONS

1. Which of the following is an ethical issue that can arise in computer science when individuals or organizations claim ownership of creative works or ideas that are not their own?

a. Accessibility
b. Accuracy
c. Intellectual Property
d. Phishing

2. **What is the term used to describe the principle that computer science should be designed to be usable by all individuals, regardless of their abilities or disabilities?**
   a. Accessibility
   b. Accuracy
   c. Intellectual Property
   d. Phishing
3. **Which of the following is a security issue that can arise in computer science when the information contained within them is not correct or up to date?**
   a. Accessibility
   b. Accuracy
   c. Intellectual Property
   d. Phishing
4. **What is the term used to describe a type of cyber-attack where an attacker attempts to trick individuals into divulging sensitive information through fraudulent emails or websites?**
   a. Phishing
   b. Denial of Service
   c. Botnets
   d. Intellectual Property
5. **Which of the following is a security issue that can arise in computer science when an attacker attempts to overwhelm a computer system or network with traffic, preventing legitimate users from accessing it?**
   a. Phishing
   b. Denial of Service
   c. Botnets
   d. Accessibility
6. **What is the term used to describe a collection of compromised computers or devices that are controlled by an attacker and used to carry out various cyber-attacks?**
   a. Phishing
   b. Denial of Service
   c. Botnets
   d. Intellectual Property

Answers to Multiple Choice Questions

1. (c) 2. (a) 3. (b) 4. (a) 5. (b) 6 (c)

REFERENCES

1. Akiyama, M., Iwamura, M., Kawakoya, Y., Aoki, K., & Itoh, M., (2010). Design and implementation of high interaction client honeypot for drive-by-download attacks. *IEICE Transactions on Communications, 93*(5), 1131–1139.
2. Ali, A., (2017). Ransomware: A research and a personal case study of dealing with this nasty malware. *Issues in Informing Science and Information Technology, 14*, 087–099.
3. Alshamrani, A., Myneni, S., Chowdhary, A., & Huang, D., (2019). A survey on advanced persistent threats: Techniques, solutions, challenges, and research opportunities. *IEEE Communications Surveys & Tutorials, 21*(2), 1851–1877.
4. Bansal, G., Muzatko, S., & Shin, S. I., (2021). Information system security policy noncompliance: The role of situation-specific ethical orientation. *Information Technology & People, 34*(1), 250–296.
5. Bélanger, F., & Crossler, R. E., (2011). Privacy in the digital age: A review of information privacy research in computer science. *MIS Quarterly,* 1017–1041.
6. Bosch-Capblanch, X., Ronveaux, O., Doyle, V., Remedios, V., & Bchir, A., (2009). Accuracy and quality of immunization computer science in forty-one low income countries. *Tropical Medicine & International Health, 14*(1), 2–10.
7. Culnan, M. J., (1984). The dimensions of accessibility to online information: Implications for implementing office computer science. *ACM Transactions on Computer Science (TOIS), 2*(2), 141–150.
8. Culnan, M. J., (1985). The dimensions of perceived accessibility to information: Implications for the delivery of computer science and services. *Journal of the American Society for Information Science, 36*(5), 302–308.
9. Dhillon, G., & Backhouse, J., (2000). Technical opinion: Information system security management in the new millennium. *Communications of the ACM, 43*(7), 125–128.
10. Frank, C., Nance, C., Jarocki, S., & Pauli, W. E., (2018). Protecting IoT from Mirai botnets; IoT device hardening. *Journal of Computer Science Applied Research, 11*(2), 33.
11. Gaurav, A., Gupta, B. B., & Panigrahi, P. K., (2022). A comprehensive survey on machine learning approaches for malware detection in IoT-based enterprise information system. *Enterprise Computer Science, 1*, 1–25.
12. Joloudari, J. H., Haderbadi, M., Mashmool, A., GhasemiGol, M., Band, S. S., & Mosavi, A., (2020). Early detection of the advanced persistent threat attack using performance analysis of deep learning. *IEEE Access, 8*, 186125–186137.

13. Kalloniatis, C., Mouratidis, H., Vassilis, M., Islam, S., Gritzalis, S., & Kavakli, E., (2014). Towards the design of secure and privacy-oriented computer science in the cloud: Identifying the major concepts. *Computer Standards & Interfaces, 36*(4), 759–775.
14. Kovach, K. A., & Cathcart, Jr. C. E., (1999). Human resource computer science (HRIS): Providing business with rapid data access, information exchange and strategic advantage. *Public Personnel Management, 28*(2), 275–282.
15. Krithika, N., (2017). A study on WHA (watering hole attack)–the most dangerous threat to the organization. *Int. J. Innov. Sci. Eng. Res. (IJISER), 4*, 196–198.
16. Lavenue, L. M., (1997). Technical data rights in government procurement: Intellectual property rights in computer software and the indicia of computer science and information technology. *USFL Rev., 32*, 1.
17. McGraw, G., & Morrisett, G., (2000). Attacking malicious code: A report to the infosec research council. *IEEE Software, 17*(5), 33–41.
18. Onsrud, H. J., Johnson, J. P., & Lopez, X., (1994). Protecting personal privacy in using geographic computer science. *Photogrammetric Engineering and Remote Sensing, 60*(9), 1083–1095.
19. Paradice, D., Freeman, D., Hao, J., Lee, J., & Hall, D., (2018). A review of ethical issue considerations in the computer science research literature. *Foundations and Trends® in Computer Science, 2*(2), 117–236.
20. Paulson, R. A., & Weber, J. E., (2006). Cyberextortion: An overview of distributed denial of service attacks against online gaming companies. *Issues in Computer Science, 7*(2), 52–56.
21. Peabody, J. W., Luck, J., Jain, S., Bertenthal, D., & Glassman, P., (2004). Assessing the accuracy of administrative data in health computer science. *Medical Care, 1*, 1066–1072.
22. Rogerson, S., Miller, K. W., Winter, J. S., & Larson, D., (2019). Computer science ethics–challenges and opportunities. *Journal of Information, Communication and Ethics in Society, 17*(1), 87–97.
23. Sharma, P., Dash, B., & Ansari, M. F., (2022). Anti-phishing techniques: A review of cyber defense mechanisms. *IJARCCE, 11*(7), 153–160.
24. Siponen, M. T., & Oinas-Kukkonen, H., (2007). A review of information security issues and respective research contributions. *ACM SIGMIS Database: The DATABASE for Advances in Computer Science, 38*(1), 60–80.
25. Smith, H. J., Dinev, T., & Xu, H., (2011). Information privacy research: An interdisciplinary review. *MIS Quarterly*, 989–1015.
26. Sood, A. K., & Zeadally, S., (2016). Drive-by download attacks: A comparative study. *It Professional, 18*(5), 18–25.
27. Stock, M., & Stock, W. G., (2006). Intellectual property information: A comparative analysis of main information providers. *Journal of the American Society for Information Science and Technology, 57*(13), 1794–1803.

28. Thapa, K., & Bossler, J., (1992). Accuracy of spatial data used computer science. *Photogrammetric Engineering & Remote Sensing, 58*(6), 835–841.

29. Wright, R. T., & Marett, K., (2010). The influence of experiential and dispositional factors in phishing: An empirical investigation of the deceived. *Journal of Management Computer Science, 27*(1), 273–303.

30. Zimba, A., Chen, H., Wang, Z., & Chishimba, M., (2020). Modeling and detection of the multi-stages of advanced persistent threats attacks based on semi-supervised learning and complex networks characteristics. *Future Generation Computer Systems, 106*, 501–517.

31. Zlomislić, V., Fertalj, K., & Sruk, V., (2017). Denial of service attacks, defenses and research challenges. *Cluster Computing, 20*, 661–671.

INDEX

D

E

F

G

H

I

J

K

L

M

N

O

P

Q

R

S

FSC
www.fsc.org
MIX
Papier | Fördert gute Waldnutzung
FSC® C083411

Kolibri 360 GmbH
Ferdinand-Jühlke-Straße 7
99095 Erfurt, Deutschland
produktsicherheit@kolibri360.de